MW00905723

Hearing God in the Battle:

"The War is On!"

Dr. Paris D. Davis

Copyright © 2007 by Dr. Paris D. Davis

Hearing God in the Battle:
"The War is On!"
by Dr. Paris D. Davis

Printed in the United States of America

ISBN 978-1-60266-814-0

All rights reserved solely by the author. The author guarantees all contents are original and do not infringe upon the legal rights of any other person or work. No part of this book may be reproduced in any form without the permission of the author. The views expressed in this book are not necessarily those of the publisher.

Unless otherwise indicated, Bible quotations are taken from the King James Version Bible. Copyright © 1975, 1981, 1983, 1988 by Thomas Nelson, Inc., Publishers.

www.xulonpress.com

Dedication

I dedicate this book, "Hearing God in The Battle: The War is On!", back to my Lord and Savior, Jesus Christ, who is and always will be the Head of my life. Thank YOU for saving me, for giving me Your precious Spirit, and for entrusting and empowering me with the knowledge of YOU!

I dedicate this book to my ancestors in the previous generations of Johnsons, Reasbys, Simpsons, Walkers and Kimballs who prayed for us to pick up the mantel, especially you Aunt Shirley Johnson! Also, to those in this present generation building a legacy and praying NOW for the generations to come, you know who you are, especially you, Dannielle Owens! Stay encouraged in the Lord and know that your earnest prayers will certainly come to pass!

And to all that dare to pursue their dreams:

"Desire generates Determination, Determination generates Persistence; Persistence generates Results; and Results are what help transition our Dreams into Reality. Press on, Warrior, for the Battle is already won!" PDD 5/07

Acknowledgments

To my husband and partner for life, *Jeffrey Davis.* I will love you always!

To our sons, **Christopher and Cameron**, always remember that you are our daily inspiration to do well and continue to live strong for Christ!

To my mother, ***Fredericka Simpson,*** who made me the woman I am today!

In loving memory of my father, ***H. Marvin Simpson***, who I miss greatly, and can't wait to see dancing in Heaven!

Shelley E. Brown II, a.k.a. "Little Beans", continue to LIVE strong, represent Jesus, and always remember how proud I am of you!

With love, to all my ***Davis Family*** members, Arthur Sr., Audrey, Denise, Craig, Jason, Joy, Arthur Jr., Audra, Norvell, Shelley, Dwight, Phil, Marsha, Brad, Austin and Zack, thank you for all your love and support.

Bishop Simon Gordon, my Pastor and spiritual father, thank you for stability and always helping me get through the process, without looking like I was going through!

Pastor Ronald Nelson, Alias, my friend and sounding board, I thank you for having the holy boldest of God, Jesus' broad shoulders of compassion, and the Spirit of Truth in the Holy Ghost!

Dr. Mildred C. Harris, to an excellent educator, exhorter, and edifier! I thank you for continuously pushing me to learn beyond the "books". Mother Harris, know that my life will never be the same since I have met you!

Bishop William Murphy, thank you for challenging me to press on and be the Spiritual Warrior that God called me to be.

Pastors Sylvester and Renee Johnson, thank you for taking the time to teach, train and impart Prophetic Intercession to all the up and coming Warriors willing to fight the good fight of faith! The impact that you made on my life will never be forgotten.

Especially to my prayer partners, ***Elder Lynn Munson*** and ***Elder Lorece White***, it's been an interesting journey, with awesome experiences in the Lord! Thank you for standing with me and "being" who God called you to be in the Kingdom. To ***Vita Kay,*** thank you for accountability. I am so glad that God divinely partnered us all together. And of course to my church family, ***Triedstone FG Baptist Church*** in Chicago, IL, where "It's Goin' on at the 'Stone!"

Table of Contents

Foreword

Foreword for
Hearing God in Battle: "The War is On!"

Congratulations to Dr. Paris Davis on an exciting opportunity for readers to enjoy a victorious life of communication with God! This book embraces what you hear, how you hear it, and what you should do with what you hear.

Dr. Davis demonstrates that there is an art of listening and that it must be a part of the believer's arsenal and strategy when under attack!

This book is full of insights woven together by scripture and you cannot read it without learning more about yourself as you grow in your knowledge of God!

Woven within Dr. Davis words are clear, true, and formidable practices that will assist a new or mature believer in being a keen discerning Christian.

Read it once, twice, or more and you will gather new insights each time. Congratulations Dr. Paris Davis! Your work certainly supports the movement of God in this kingdom age.

Bishop Simon Gordon
Senior Pastor, Triedstone Full Gospel Baptist Church
Midwest Regional Bishop, International Full Gospel Baptist
Church Fellowship

INTRODUCTION

Hearing God in The Battle: "The War is On!"

To build a solid foundation of understanding of this book, you will be given quite a few key scriptures and definitions as we go. I want you to be clear on what you are being taught and to continue to use this material as reference for the rest of your walk with the Lord. If you do not have a journal to write in about your Christian walk and what God is saying to you, get one. I strongly recommend that you write down and keep an account of God's awesome workings in your life. Doing this will build your faith as you look back on what He has already said and done for you. Additionally, it will encourage you during the tough times while you wait for His next move. In fact, this is important enough that I will talk more about keeping journals later. Amen. Ok, so enough of the administrative stuff. Let's get started!

HEARING GOD! Hearing directly from God is still something that many spirit filled Christians are uncertain about. Some have difficulty accepting this truth and recognizing rather or not it is actually possible. In fact, this is probably true for some reading this book right now. Or, if they do believe it is possible, they don't believe it is possible for them personally. So, to get an idea of where you stand, I have a couple of questions for you to consider before you go further into this area.

For those who do not think that God will talk directly to you in a way that you are able to hear and understand Him, take a minute to write down some of the reasons why you **think** God will not talk to you directly, clearly and in an audible, understandable voice.

For those of you who think that God will talk directly to you, take a minute to write down your responses to the following questions:

- How do you currently hear from God?
- How do you know if it is really God?
- How do you deal with the counterfeits?
- How do you desire to hear from God? In what areas of your life do you want God to "turn up the volume"?

I want you to keep track of your responses. Prayerfully, by the end of this book, we will have resolved many of your questions and hindrances. By faith, you will be hearing God speaking to you at new levels, directly, clearly and understandably.

Before we go any further, let's begin this journey with a prayer of salvation. But, before we do a prayer of faith for your spirit hearing, we need to make sure that the basics are in order. For this book to help you grow closer to God, there is a critical prerequisite to hearing from God. It is a relational issue. You must be in relationship with the Lord to hear from Him. You must believe in Him and belong to Him to hear from Him. Because you are your reading this book, you are already searching for the Lord at another level and looking to draw nearer. If you are not in a relationship with the Lord, this information will be of no use to you. Again, in order for this to make any sense to you, you must be in relationship with our Lord and Savior Jesus Christ. As the Lord states in **John 14:6**:

"I am the way, the truth, and the life: no man cometh unto the Father, but by me."

So if you are not in relationship with Jesus or are unsure of whether or not you are saved and will spend eternity in Heaven with Him, let's take a few minutes to set things in order. You can do this by inviting the Lord into your life by confessing with your mouth and believing in your heart this simple Prayer of Salvation:

"Lord Jesus, I admit that I have messed up. I admit that I have sinned. I acknowledge that I need You in my life. I believe in my heart that You are the Son of God. I believe that You died for my sins and were raised from the dead. I confess You Jesus as Lord in and over my life. I denounce Satan's authority in and over my life. And now I exalt You as Lord. Thank You Lord Jesus for my salvation! Amen."

Yes, it is that simple to obtain the eternal gift of salvation! Now we are ready to press further!

A Prayer of Faith

Let's stand in agreement on that God's purpose for this book be fulfilled in your life by speaking this prayer from your mouth directly to the heart and ear of God. Please repeat this:

By faith, I expect to be Hearing God.
By faith, I am prepared for Hearing God.
By faith, I believe I can hear God.
By faith, I know that I am able to hear God.
By faith, I can hear God's audible voice.
By faith, I can understand what God is saying to me.
By faith, and the Word of God, I can discern the difference in God's voice and the voice of others.
By faith, I know how and when to respond to what God has spoken to me.
By faith, I speak these things which are not as though they were and believe and decree them as done in Jesus' name. Amen.

Now, celebrate your victory and applaud God's awesome works in your life because by the expression of your faith, God's promises shall manifest! Now that you are open and ready to receive what God has in store for you in this book, your life will never be the same again. The development of a lifestyle of hearing God is ongoing and ever-changing for each level of growth and achievement you reach in Him.

There are times when hearing God will be a matter of life or death, but He will also speak to you on the day to day matters that you face. Hearing God is a serious area and it's a privilege given by Him to His sons and daughters. It is not to be taken lightly. It's an awesome skill and weapon to have against the enemy in your daily walk.

Finally, as we get started let me give you a couple of helpful points of advice: "*Continuously referencing the Word of God builds and establishes your ability for Hearing God clearly. So whenever you get the chance, seal what you have received from God by going to the Word of God.*"

The other point is that there is no peace like the peace of knowing that you are walking in God's divine will because you got your instructions directly from the Source for yourself. God's peace must be present in all that you do, especially **what** you hear from Him. **Colossians 3:15** confirms this.

> "*And let the peace of God rule in your hearts, to which also ye are called in one body; and be ye thankful.*"

You must also remember to be thankful for this precious gift because it is a privilege that He has given us. Therefore, you need to study this area of God closer for your own personal revelation and growth, even after you are finished reading this book, because this is really just the beginning.

We must recognize that there are many ways that the Lord communicates with us. He does this through impressions made in your heart, time spent in prayer, strong impressions or intuitions to do or say something at a particular time, confirmation from others, dreams, and visions. The list can go on and on. Yes, we know there are many ways that God communicates with us, and now its time to go deeper in Him. It's time to develop another level of understanding of Him. As we take this spiritual walk through the Battle, we will study and discover keys to hearing God directly, audibly and in an understandable voice during, and throughout this journey with Him.

Part 1:

"Getting Into the Battle!"

CHAPTER 1

Getting God's Strategy for Battle: The Hearing Process & His Love

I would like to lay a foundation of understanding that will allow us to be of one accord as we go forward so that you can receive all that God has in store for you in this book. So, let's get started by examining the components for Hearing God. Let us build this foundation by starting with a better understanding of the Battle and the Hearing Process, both natural and spiritual.

The Battle

This lifestyle that we have chosen to accept and walk in, as disciples of Jesus, is a battle. It is one to be strategically fought and won on a daily basis. Whoever thinks, or was told, that once you become saved everything would be like a "stroll through the park on a bright, sunny day" is, and has been, misinformed. A needed point of clarity is this: The battle for your very life and everyone dear and near to you will rage on, with or without your consent and whether or not you choose to participate! So why not choose willingly to take up your cross and strategically fight this battle with the Most High God as your strength, support and Counselor?

To be as victorious as you can possibly be, the first thing to remember and use in your daily walk is that the LOVE of the Lord has to be the key principle to everything that you will ever know, do, see and hear in your relationship with Him and others. Love is critical to fighting this battle strategically God's way. Why? Because the battle is not yours but God's as stated in **2 Chronicles 20:15:**

1 *"And he said, Hearken ye, all Judah, and inhabitants of Jehoshaphat, Thus saith the LORD unto you, Be not afraid nor dismayed by reason of this great multitude; for the battle is not your, but God's."*

Again, whether you accept it or not, this lifestyle is a battle to be fought and won to the glory of our Lord. The only way this can be done successfully is to have a heart that is turned towards Him. A heart that is sensitive to the flow of His Spirit and the sound of His voice. This is a heart infiltrated with His love. This is the same love that is to govern your life and to be shared with others.

Even though there will be difficult times, the good news is that we have already been predestined to be victorious. Additionally, this battle is not to be fought alone, but together with the other saints of God! Together we are to take possession of the promises of God for each of our lives, and for one another. Therefore, it is critical to hear, respond and react with a spirit of love. This should be the same spirit of love that our Lord has already given each of us. Let's look at **I Thessalonians 4:9:**

"But as touching brotherly love ye need not that I write unto you: for ye yourselves are taught of God to love another."

Here Apostle Paul addresses Christian living and states clearly that we are taught **by** God to love one another. The blessings of this great commandment that are given by our Father is further emphasized in **Psalm 133:1-3:**

"¹Behold, how good and how pleasant it is for brethren to dwell together in unity! ²It is like the precious ointment upon the head, that ran down upon the beard, even Aaron's beard: that went down to the skirts of his garments; ³As the dew of Hermon, and as the dew that descended upon the mountains

of Zion: for there the LORD commanded the blessing, even life forevermore."

There are great blessings in dwelling in unity and love with the family that we gain when we become a part of God's Kingdom. As one of His, you are officially a "Kingdom Kid" blessed with all that the Father has available to Him, including the gift of hearing and knowing His voice! With that said, let's get about the Father's business and gain further clarity in this area. Let's look at the Hearing Process.

The Hearing Process

So, what does it mean to "hear" something? What's involved in hearing? What's the process? Well, according to Webster's Dictionary, **"To Hear"** means to perceive or understand by the ear; it is to gain knowledge by listening with attention; and it means to receive communications. **Hear(ing)** is the process of perceiving sound. It is the special sense by which external noises and tones are received as stimuli to the brain, which in turn, then makes a decision based on what has been heard.

There are 2 distinct parts for physical and spiritual hearing. Within the first part of each one, there are 3 components. Let's look at the Natural Hearing process first. Physically, or in the natural, to detect a sound requires two parts. The first part is an organ of hearing, which is usually the ear. I say "usually" because there are some of us that may require hearing aides. But we're not babies in this pursuit to draw nearer to the Lord, so we are expecting to hear for ourselves, without prompts or assistance.

The second part for physical hearing is called equilibrium. Equilibrium is a balance and filter for what's coming into the hearing device. The next thing to note is that the natural ear has three distinct and separate components. First there is a sound collecting outer ear. Next there's the sound transmitting middle ear, which sorts out the sound taken in by the outer ear into patterns. Last, there is the sensory inner ear that makes the final decision about what has been heard and in turn, what is forwarded to the brain for a response.

The sense, or act of hearing in the natural is very complicated, thus all three components of the ear are needed for proper hearing. The impairment, or loss of any one component impacts and can hinder the other two components from functioning properly.

Now, let's look at the similarities in the Spiritual Hearing process. Spiritually hearing God requires similar parts and components just like hearing physically. Where the ear is the first part and key organ to hearing physically; for hearing spiritually the first part and key organ is the Heart. Just as the physical ear is supported and protected by the outer, middle and inner components of the ear; the spiritual ear, which is the heart, is supported and protected by 3 components too. They are:

1. Focus;
2. Obedience; and
3. Faith.

Focus is taking the time to prepare and expecting to hear from God. Obedience deals with your immediate reaction to what the Lord has spoken to you. Faith is, both knowing that He will speak to you and you will hear and understand Him. Each of these 3 components can vary in levels that can directly affect, and in some cases, infect your spiritual ear. The stronger your level in each of these 3 components, the stronger and clearer your spiritual hearing will be. Just as with your natural hearing, if any one component is off or not functioning properly, your spiritual hearing will be affected negatively. Additionally, the longer it takes to correct or adjust any impairment, the more contaminated, or unreliable your spiritual hearing will become. The deeper the roots of contamination, the longer it will take to regain and purify the source of hearing. Each of these three components will be covered in more detail in later chapters. But briefly:

1. Your level of Focus helps you to determine what you will accept or take into your spirit at any given time based on what's going on around you. Focus is the first point of contact that causes you to take notice of whatever is being

presented to you. It involves the drawing of your attention, both naturally and spiritually, even if only for a moment. Focus also includes having the ability to recognize what is of God and what is not and being able to discern the difference. The sharper your level of discernment, the more heightened your level of focus will be in being able to filter out those things that you will accept initially.

2. Your level of Obedience helps you to sort out what you have taken in into useable, applicable information needed for your Spiritual Walk. Note here what is acceptable, or what is a conviction for one by God, may not be the same for you, or me. But with this second component of spiritual hearing, you know what God has told **you** personally about your life and your lifestyle. Once you clearly know what that is, at that point, you keep what you own and throw away the rest.

3. Your level of Faith is the innermost sensitive and critical component for spiritual hearing. Without faith, you can not hear God. You must strive to build a solid foundation of faith based on the Word of God and your personal relationship with Him. Doing this will make you better equipped to focus, hear and make decisions about what has been taken in. The stronger your level of faith in God and the things of God, the more powerful you will be in this walk and in the Battle.

Staying Spiritually Balanced

Remember, earlier I stated that the second part for hearing physically is equilibrium, which is a balance and filter for what you have heard. The equilibrium component for hearing spiritually consists of the Word of God and the Spirit of God. The two together function as your balance and filter for what you hear spiritually. These two important elements give you spiritual equilibrium. The Word of God brings a state of intellectual and emotional balance. It is your foundation, your Battle Winner, Enemy Defeater, and Lifestyle Operating Manual. The Spirit of God helps you to maintain balance between your day to day life and your Spiritual Walk. He serves as your spiritual discernment for what's going on around you, in you and through you.

The more Word of God that you have in you, the stronger, more reliable and more sensitive your filter will be for responding to the Spirit of God. Things that are not of God, will hit a brick wall because of your spiritual discernment. They won't even be able to move your focus. Foolishness and circumstances going on around you won't even break your stride. You must study the **Word of God** and be yielded to the **Spirit of God** in **all** areas of your life in order to keep your **equilibrium** working properly for your spiritual hearing. Your spiritual equilibrium is also critical in helping you to know who and what you are hearing spiritually. Is it God, is it you, or is it someone else? Later, we will cover some discernment tools to help you tell and confirm the difference. Another important distinction you need to know and understand is this:

Your natural, or physical hearing, is external, which means that who or what you are hearing is coming from outside of you;

VERSUS

Your spiritual hearing is internal, which means that who or what you are hearing is coming from inside of you.

How do we know this for sure? Let's back it up with the Word of God. In doing this, here's a question for your consideration: "Are you a born again, spirit-filled Christian?". This is not a trick question. If you have accepted Christ as your Lord and Savior, then your answer should be, "Yes"! Given that your answer is "Yes". Do you realize what that means? This means that the Holy Spirit, the Spirit of the Living God, lives inside of you. Not really sure about that concept? Let's go to the Word and look at **I Corinthians 3:16** which says:

"Know ye not that ye are the temple of God, and that the Spirit of God dwelleth in you?"

Yes, child of God, you are the temple of God. "Dwelleth" means to continuously live in a place, which in this case is YOU. Who is doing this? The Spirit of God! Need more proof? Let us look at **John 14:22-23**:

> *"Judas (not Iscariot), said to Him, "Lord, how is it that You will manifest Yourself to us, and not to the world?" Jesus answered and said to him, "If a man love me, he will keep my words; and my Father will love him, and we will come unto him, and make our abode with him."*

Judas, the brother of James, is asking the Lord to help him and the others understand how they will know that Jesus is still going to be with them. Judas is asking the Lord what will be the tangible proof that they can easily accept in their minds, and confirm it by what they are able to see. What will convince them that He is forever accessible to them as His followers? The Lord Jesus answers him by giving some tangible directions that also apply to you today.

First, the condition is given: You must love Him. As stated earlier, His love is critical to everything that pertains to Him. It is the very fiber that flows from Him, through us and unites us with Him. So, how do you demonstrate your love for Him? The answer is in the very next set of words: "Keep My words". In other words, your obedience to His Word demonstrates your love towards Him. From this, the promise follows: Based on your actions, He promises an everlasting relationship with the Father, Himself and the Holy Spirit.

This relationship is referred to as the divine indwelling. Divine is relating to, or coming directly from God. We already know that indwelling, in this instance, is living continuously in you! Therefore, in this promise to you, the Lord is with you always and will never leave you uncovered. *Allow His love to quiet you so that you can hear His voice.* By His very Spirit He will give you guidance in all things that you seek Him for and in some cases, even when you don't seek Him first. These tangible results that you can understand, see, feel and touch, will show up in your life as you live obediently to His Word and Spirit.

So based on this, would it not stand to reason and make sense that when God speaks, you would hear His Voice from the inside or internally? Ponder this for a moment: "Listening <u>internally</u> for the voice of God". Interesting isn't it? Strategic, isn't it? So like God to give us internally what we need to grow in Him and be victorious in this life! So now that you know this, how do you develop and sharpen this skill? Well, I'm going to tell you. Read on.......

CHAPTER 2

Getting God's Anointing for the Battle: The Key for Hearing God & His Presence

Going in search of God to hear what He has to say pertaining to your life and about you specifically! What does that mean? I'm glad you asked! It means you have been given the privilege of spending time with the Lord in order to prepare and equip you for life's challenges. In order to hear the Lord, you must first seek Him out. When I say "Seeking Him", I mean taking the time to get in His presence. Why? Because getting anointed for the Battle requires that you spend time in His Presence. What's the battle? Anything that you may have to face, resolve or go through during this journey called Life. And the first step to doing that involves having a heart that is surrendered to Him. This brings us to the key for Hearing God - your Heart.

The Key for Hearing God

I want to share something very interesting with you that I found out as I was preparing for this book a while back. Write down the word heart: H-E-A-R-T. Now, draw a line through the "T". What word do you get? You should see the word: H-E-A-R. Now, drop the "H" from the word H-E-A-R. Now, what do you see? E-A-R. Right? Now, notice right in the middle of the word **HEART** is the word EAR. Is this a coincidence? I don't think so! If it is, it is a very simple, yet powerful illustration of the next point. Which is: would it not make sense that the main thing needed for receiving from God would have the key concepts wrapped in it? Your EAR to HEAR God is right in the center of your HEART!

Your spiritual ear is your heart and this is the key to hearing God. The resource is already within you. However, for it to be activated and function properly, an ongoing relationship must be developed and nurtured with the Source. The pruning and purification of your heart to becoming sensitive to His voice can only be achieved in His presence. Just as God's people in **2 Chronicles 30** prepared their hearts for seeking God to hear from Him, so should we. Keeping a heart that is sensitive to the voice of God is an ongoing process and you will find, just as Hezekiah did, that keeping your heart right before God will cause Him to pay close attention and respond when you call!

So keep in mind, hearing God begins in and with your Heart. Once your heart is prepared for Him, you are able to hear God with your spiritual ear. So, I offer to you this: 'To hear in the natural, you perceive and understand with your head, mind, intellect and physical ear. To hear spiritually, you must perceive and understand God with your heart first, which is your spiritual ear.'

Pressing Into His Presence

To further gain a better understanding of this, let's look at our key scripture, which is **Psalm 27:8:**

"When thou saidst, ¹Seek ye my face; my heart said unto thee, Thy face, LORD, will I seek."

Stated another way, when He calls you, you will know by the tugging on your very being. As you grow stronger in this area, His voice will be unquestionable to your spirit man, and depending on the situation, your natural man also. Your response to His summons to come into His presence will manifest as a desire in your heart to go in search of an encounter with the Lord!

Before we go further, since this verse is the foundation for where we are going, let's take it apart to gain a better understanding of what God is saying to us here. There are a few key words and phrases that we need to grasp to do this. The words are Seek, Face, Heart, Will and When.

☐ **Seek:** means to go to; to go in search of; to try to discover and to ask for.

☐ **Face:** is a little more complicated. According to Webster's Dictionary, "Face is a means of identification; it is the countenance or demeanor of one's character." Also, it means to be in one's presence and at the same time, being fully aware of what is going on around you. According to Vine's Expository Dictionary, "face" is the Old Testament word: panim (pay-nim). Which is one's countenance, or visible side; it is used anthropomorphically of God, which means in a way we can relate to or better comprehend what is being said to us. In the New Testament, "face" is prosopon (pro-soo-pon), which means countenance, or outward appearance.

☐ **Heart:** According to Webster's Dictionary, means personality, disposition, the emotional or moral part of a person as opposed to the intellectual part. According to Vine's Expository Dictionary, "heart" is the Old Testament word: kardia. It occupies the most important place in the human system. It's man's entire mental and moral activity, both the rational and the emotional elements. The heart is used figuratively for the hidden springs of one's personal life. It is also the sphere of Divine influence.

The heart is also the organ that by its rhythmic contraction acts as a force pump maintaining the circulation of blood throughout the body. As we are studying hearing God, disregard this definition for the heart! It does not apply in this case. I want to identify and remove as many hindrances as possible, as we go along. Don't get hung up on the physical, natural definition of a heart. Stay focused on the spiritual definition, which is that the heart is one's inner most character and feelings. It is the very center, essential, and most vital part of you. Your heart is the real YOU that God knows fully.

Will: According to Webster's Dictionary is used to express desire, choice, willingness, determination, or the power of control over one's own actions or emotions.

When: Means that at any or every time or just at that moment something happens.

Next, there are three key phrases we need to look at before we put this verse, **Psalm 27:8,** back together. First, you have to believe that the Lord desires to have a conversation with you. Let's talk about **"thou saidst"** and having a conversation with God. Having a conversation is communication between two or more people. Speaking and hearing are the two main parts of communicating. When you read in the Word, "the Lord said" or "thus saith the Lord", God spoke it and someone had to hear it! Put the equation together. If He said it, then He spoke it. If He spoke, someone heard it. There was communication going on. There are numerous examples in the Word where God spoke directly to or had a conversation with one or more of His children. If God spoke to them (which He did) then He will speak directly to you. "Said" means to have vocalized or communicated. However, God speaks to us in many ways! So, pay attention to what is going on around you. In this case, we are investigating the spoken way. **Believe that God desires to have a conversation with you.**

Next, know that the Lord has not stopped talking! In the Word we see that God likes to talk to, and with us. Some Old Testament examples for your reference include our Father and Jeremiah in **Jeremiah 1:4-7,** and to the numerous conversations between God and Moses in **Exodus.** Also, wherever you see "red" in the New Testament, the Lord was speaking to someone. That someone heard it, understood it, and wrote it down. In our key scripture, note that "saidst" implies that it has not stopped, His talking is still continuing. **Know that**

God is always talking. The questions are: Are you listening? Are you really receiving what He is saying?

Be prepared to receive from Him. Don't go seeking His presence without expectation. Don't go to Him not knowing why you are there or what you want to say or do! Prepare beforehand, just as you should prepare in advance if you were going to a meeting. Know what your issues are; what you need His help and guidance with; and what questions you want answered. Not doing this is just like receiving that phone call from that friend that likes to just sit on the phone and talk about a lot of nothing. They will call and say, "Hey, whatcha' doing?" You say, "Nothing. Whatcha' you doing?" They say, "Nothing." That's the exact purpose and outcome of that conversation. NOTHING! Try not to be caught off guard by His presence! Live a lifestyle that is always expecting and preparing to receive from Him! **Know that God wants to talk to you about the matters that concern you.**

Now notice in our key scripture, **Psalm 27:8,** that there is a conversation taking place. Let us pull it all back together to see what's happening. God has initiated the conversation and here is what He is saying:

> *"Every time He calls you or requests your attention, you are to answer by searching Him out and coming into His presence. But not just any way, not just with any old disposition, but with the same manner and with the same character as His. In other words, your heart, your inner most being, and your spirit has to be just like His before and while you are in His presence. You must be transparent and open to Him with nothing hidden. Your heart must be focused on Him, you must be obedient when He calls, and you must have the faith to know that He has and is calling you."*

Seeking God's face is seeking His very presence, His very being. The important thing here is that you do it by choice. You have decided and are determined to do whatever is required to be with Him, in His presence. You do it willingly and with desire, and this is your passion for Him. Coming into God's presence this way also means that you are fully aware of what is going on around you. Do you know why you are going to Him? You are going to Him because you desire to have a conversation with Him. In addition, you are going into His presence to hear God speak His word and His will into your life! Doing this consistently is hard work! The things of God are not always easy to achieve and maintain. You have to choose and make up in your mind and will, that this is what you are going to do. Also, know that each time you get to a place where you are almost comfortable, God moves the bar up a notch or two, or sometimes, even more. He says, "Come closer, My Child. Come UP some more, come on, come closer." As we are told in **Philippians 3:12-14***:*

> *"Not as though I had already attained, either were already perfect: but I follow after, if that I may apprehend that for which also I am apprehended of Christ Jesus. Brethren, I count not myself to have apprehended: but this one thing I do, forgetting those things which are behind, and reaching forth unto those things which are before, I press toward the mark for the prize of the high calling of God in Christ Jesus."*

Paul is saying here: Look at this. I am all caught up in and 110% sold on Jesus. The Lord had Paul's heart, lock, stock and barrel. I am totally sold. I don't already have it, and I'm certainly not perfect. But I am not letting that stop me from pursuing Jesus and to know Him even better. And because of this, I will become better! Paul wanted more of Him. With those things that happened in the past, they are just that: the past. He knew he needed to continue looking ahead to the future. Paul knew to do that, he had to hear from God. He had to get in His very presence. He had to have more of Him. How did he do that? Paul tells us in the previously mentioned passage. He pressed towards Christ Jesus and what he had been assigned to do.

Many of us have experienced His power and His presence. Thus we are drawn to know and do more in Him. Right? Do you remember what that first "experience" was like with Him? The first time you felt His presence? Its like, "Please do it again, Lord!" Right? God knows what He has in store for you.

Now, I need you to get on the same page with me here. How do you get more of **anything** you really want and need? You go after it! You pursue it. You press on until you get it. Right? You know that neither a substitution nor an impostor will do. Especially once you have experienced the REAL deal. Right? Yes, of course, you know I am right!

That's what God is saying in the two passages of **Psalm 28:7** and **Philippians 3:12-14**: Come after Me, pursue Me, and you will find Me! To receive the fullness of His promises, you must pursue Him with a passion that will lead you directly into His very presence. We will look at this aspect of passion in more detail in **Chapter 13.** But, for now, know that passion for the Lord is a critical weapon in our arsenal. Passion is one of the main ingredients for assessing the presence of the Lord and receiving **all** that He has for you. When I say "All", I mean experiencing everything that comes from being in the Lord's very presence. Don't leave anything on the table that our King has prepared for you. With a spirit of thanksgiving, receive it all!

CHAPTER 3

Getting God's Instructions for the Battle: The Key to Hearing God & His Purpose

Hmmmm: in search of the heart of God. You must know how to listen for His voice and openly receive what He is saying to you. The ability to effectively use this gift is a progression. Now, you may say, "I understand and I hear clearly, but how do I receive what I have heard? What type of receiver am I? The goal here is to be open and, thus, learn to do better, in order to get all that the Lord has for you to lead you through the Battle. So let's move on.

So What Kind of Listener Are You?

Here is another important area I wanted to include to help you progress in your walk. It addresses what type of Listener you are and how effective you are in receiving His directions. So, let's get started. There are basically three types of Listeners: Empathetic, Passive, and Sympathetic. Each one identifies how you receive, process and act on what you have heard. The strongest type, and ultimate position of a listener to be in, is the one of the Empathetic Listener. If you are not currently there, this is the level of receiving from the Lord that you should strive towards obtaining. We will look closer at this type of listener later in the chapter. But for now know that, yes, in this Battle, you should desire and strive towards becoming an Empathetic Listener ready to receive the fullness of God at all times.

Soldier of the Most High God, it's a tough charge, I know. But the secret to accomplishing this is simple. You must be, **or begin,** living a disciplined lifestyle. This is a lifestyle that is directed and ordered on a daily basis by the Word of the Lord.

So, now that we know where we want to go, let's look at the transitional components of becoming an effective Empathetic Listener by looking at each one of the three types in more detail. So, are you an Empathetic, Passive, or Sympathetic? Just what kind of listener are you? Identifying what your type is will help you see where you are. And, if you have struggles in hearing the Lord clearly, this will also help you develop a more rounded, balanced approach to **listening for** the voice of the Lord.

After you finish reading the following sections on the three types, take the time to identify where you currently are and write down a few things that you can begin doing to move you to the next level. If you are already an Empathetic Listener, take the time to write down a few things you can do to maintain this position and go to a deeper dimension in it with the Lord. All of our weapons and skills must be sharpened on a regular basis. Once you know where you are, commit to progressing to the position of listening empathetically for the voice and heart of God.

Let's start by understanding a few key definitions. Let's look at Listener. A Listener is: one that pays attention with thoughtful observation in order to hear something for their consideration. How well you listen to what is being spoken does directly tie in to how well you are able to stand in the Battle. However, a "listener" does not necessarily go into action or keep what they heard for further or future use. That is what a "Receiver" does, and we will discuss that position in detail later in the chapter. For now, let's get a deeper understanding of the more specific types of Listener, starting with the Empathetic Listener.

Empathetic Listener

The Empathetic Listener operates in the realm of clearly demonstrating the will of God based on four things:

1. Hearing the voice of the Lord.
2. Comprehending what He said.
3. Receiving it fully in their heart.
4. Responding in a focused, obedient and faithful manner that will glorify our Father.

In other words, operating in a lifestyle that consists of doing what the Lord has instructed you to do, how He instructed you to do it, when He told you to get it done, and within the boundaries that He set forth.

Empathetic means involving and calling forth or bringing out something that has been existing in a temporary inactive, hidden and unexpressed state. It is characterized by or based on the projection of a subjective state, which is your perception, into an object so that the object appears to be infused or joined with its surroundings. According to Webster's Dictionary, empathetic is 'the action of understanding, being aware of, being sensitive to and vicariously experiencing the feelings, thoughts and experiences of another in order to fully communicate in an objectively explicit manner". OK, Paris translate that please. I'm glad you asked - try this: Caring enough to pay attention, wise enough to discern what is important, firm enough to disregard and discard what is not, skillful enough to take a stance and take action, and strong enough to move forward.

The Greek word is "empatheia", which literally means passion. It comes from "empathes", which is emotional and is derived from em + pathos (feelings) or put into, onto or covered with feelings. In other words, this type of Listener hears, receives and responds with their heart. An Empathetic Listener can generally see the glory of God, be it in a person or in a situation. At times, this can also manifest itself into the very presence of God. This is similar to His Shekinah Glory, which is the brightness of His presence that transcends the heavens and appears visible to the natural eye.

Empathic listening is done with passion and purpose in order to experience the fullness of God in your life or a particular situation. The key here is looking for God's glory in whatever you are hearing from God! That's an Empathetic Listener, one that listens with his/her heart! Look at **Deuteronomy 5:24**:

> *"And ye said, Behold, the LORD our God hath showed us his glory and his greatness, and we have <u>heard</u> his voice out of the midst of the fire: we have <u>seen</u> this day that God doth talk with man, and he liveth."*

Just like then, yes God is still very much alive and is still talking to His people. Just as the Lord Jesus tells us in **Matthew 5:8**:

> *"Blessed are the pure in heart: for they shall see God."*

Let's look at one more passage to help us transition and obtain this dimension of seeing and hearing the voice of the Lord, **Hebrews 10:22**:

> *"Let us draw near with a true heart in full assurance of faith, having our hearts sprinkled from an evil conscience, and our bodies washed with pure water."*

To become an Empathic Listener, your faith is a definite requirement! Your faith is what connects you to the spiritual attributes of God. A purified heart allows us to draw closer to God. It is a prerequisite to entering into His presence, into the Holy of Holies. This also taps into the realms of intimacy in your relationship with God. It is the actual manifestation of His love, because you are listening and yielding to His love! Would it not make sense that the Church that emulates this type of listening is closest to the Church of Philadelphia, the Church of Brotherly Love, which is known as the most faithful church in all ages? Let's look at **Revelation 3:7-13**:

> *"7And to the angel of the church in Philadelphia write; These things saith he that is holy, he that is true, he that hath the*

key of David, he that openeth, and no man shutteth; and shutteth, and no man openeth; ⁸ I know thy works: behold, I have set before thee an open door, and no man can shut it: for thou hast a little strength, and hast kept my word, and hast not denied my name. ⁹ Behold, I will make them of the synagogue of Satan, which say they are Jews, and are not, but do lie; behold, I will make them to come and worship before thy feet, and to know that I have loved thee. ¹⁰ Because thou hast kept the word of my patience, I also will keep thee from the hour of temptation, which shall come upon all the world, to try them that dwell upon the earth. ¹¹ Behold, I come quickly: hold that fast which thou hast, that no man take thy crown. ¹² Him that overcometh will I make a pillar in the temple of my God, and he shall go no more out: and I will write upon him the name of my God, and the name of the city of my God, which is new Jerusalem, which cometh down out of heaven from my God: and I will write upon him my new name. ¹³ He that hath an ear, let him hear what the Spirit saith unto the churches."

The love of Christ strengthens us to do all things in His name, including standing steadfast on His commandments and as His representative, on the earth before man. Because of this, there is no good thing that He will withhold from you, including opening doors and positioning us in ways that no man, including ourselves, can do. But we must continuously strive, as a lifestyle, the ability to hear, recognize and acknowledge His voice. The promise of the Lord to keep us during our most trying times as we keep His Word is prevalent in this passage. Our perseverance through our trials in His name gains us the promise of a place with Him in the Kingdom. This is achievable through relentlessly receiving and abiding in the love of Christ.

Additionally, we are able to give testimony freely to the love of God and serve one another without fear or apprehension. A comprehensive unveiling of who we are to Him and His promises move us into further alignment with His mission. Why? Because of our love for Him, we desire to be obedient to His will and, therefore, become servants to the fulfilling of our Kingdom purposes. In doing this, we come into an even deeper relationship with Him. You cannot continuously come into the presence of God and NOT be transformed! It's not possible. Yes, it takes discipline to retain and progress in the change, but know that if you continue to pursue Him at this level, He will allow you to see as He sees, in love!

In the Book of Revelation as the Lord speaks to the seven Churches, each one of the passages end with encouragement and the declaration: *"He that hath an ear, let him hear what the Spirit saith unto the churches."* An ear, meaning a listening, purified heart inclined to discern and comprehend what is being said by the Lord.

Now let's look at the other two types of Listeners to see where we need to mature and grow to the dimension of listening empathetically as God desires us to. Let's look at the Passive Listener next.

Passive Listener

The Passive Listener walks with an attitude of indifference. According to Webster's Dictionary, "to be passive means easily receptive to outside impressions or influences; to lack in energy or will; non resistant to the point of being; or simply a follower that is not active or operating. This type of behavior is usually the result of disinterest or ignorance. Disinterest meaning lack of self interest; to take away from or withhold appropriate authority, property, title or position".

Actions of disinterest disregard the proper acknowledgment of someone or something for what they really are and is the same as denying their true identity or value. Ignorance, on the other hand, means to refuse to take notice of; to reject or to lack the knowledge or education about a particular situation, person or thing. Passiveness is the same as being indifferent, and responding to situations, people and things in a halfhearted manner.

The Passive Listener is a rather dangerous position for listening because it is really considered to be a lukewarm approach to what is being heard, understood, and received by the individual. As the Lord said in **Revelation 3:14-19** to the Church of Laodicea:

"¹⁴And unto the angel of the church of the Laodiceans write; These things saith the Amen, the faithful and true witness, the beginning of the creation of God; ¹⁵ I know thy works, that thou art neither cold nor hot: I would thou wert cold or hot. ¹⁶ So then because thou art lukewarm, and neither cold nor hot, I will spue thee out of my mouth. ¹⁷ Because thou sayest, I am rich, and increased with goods, and have need of nothing; and knowest not that thou art wretched, and miserable, and poor, and blind, and naked: ¹⁸ I counsel thee to buy of me gold tried in the fire, that thou mayest be rich; and white raiment, that thou mayest be clothed, and that the shame of thy nakedness do not appear; and anoint thine eyes with eyesalve, that thou mayest see. ¹⁹ As many as I love, I rebuke and chasten: be zealous therefore, and repent."

The Lord is speaking to the group of His people that are riding the fence and/or standing right in the middle of the road, not heading one way or the other. Jesus is commanding us to choose: either stand with Him or not, be for something or be against it. But don't be two-faced until you can see or figure out how you can best gain and benefit from it.

Additionally, the Lord tells us that those that function in this realm are spiritually poor, blind and naked. Even though the people of Laodicea were extremely prosperous as a society, and individually, in the natural they lacked tremendously in the spirit. They were ignorant to the things of God. Therefore, they were exceptionally vulnerable and exposed to the tricks and wiles of the enemy.

When you live as the people of Laodicea in this passage, even though outward appearances make it seem as though you have it all together because the world and most people can't tell what's in your heart, you are actually deceiving and cheating yourself. Why and how? Because you don't even realize what you are actually missing or the true state you are in! You not only have a nasty disposition and outlook on things, you are also only getting mediocre results from your efforts and don't even realize it. Though you believe you are living among the most elite, you are really considered common *to them*. And yes, it gets worse because you have also become confused by your perception of people and the world versus what is really going on: therefore exposing yourself at an even greater level to the deception of the enemy and everything else that desires to challenge and destroy you.

Continuing to live this way will most certainly end with us being without a place or position in either place! The Lord is telling us in this passage that He will force us away from His very presence, if we continue to choose to walk in this manner! For living in this way, He is saying that He will move us away from Him as our source. Why? While being in this position of passiveness, we are really worthless and ineffective. Worthless to ourselves, those around us, and especially to the Kingdom! This position is really symptomatic of someone who is living their life oblivious to the fact that they really do need help and can do better, or believing that it doesn't get any better than what it is right now! And worse yet (yes there is a worse yet scenario) this person does not have enough common sense to recognize the state they are in. He or she has become accepting of living in a state of indifference.

Actually, if we call a spade a spade, another side to the Passive Listener is that they are lazy and unattached because, for whatever reason, they really feel in their heart and mind that they do not need the Lord. Or worse yet, having Him would make no difference. They either think or feel that they are doing well by them selves, be it financially, physically, relationship wise, etc., or that things are so terribly unbearable that all is lost. They are just lukewarm, running right down the middle of the road and everything else in their lives. In addition, they think that they are staying under the radar, undetected by God and non-threatening to the enemy. So they think. Wow. They are really just lukewarm, nothing sparking energy or excitement; nothing causing enough pain to send them into action. Indifferent, hmm. Yes, both Indifferent and passive. Hmmm, yes, just lukewarm.

If this mindset takes hold of you, it will make you very lazy in your pursuit of God and indifferent to what He is saying for your life on the earth. Be careful because this position is just like blinking. This "away" time will cost you something, up to and including exclusion from the very things that you have come to treasure. The Lord tells us **He is** the direction and source.

Of course, neither of these cases are you. But if by chance it is, SNAP out of it! Pay attention! Take a stance for righteousness! The Lord says He is the source and the way! Jesus is instructing us to allow Him to process us in order to remove our character flaws and strengthen our hearts and minds so that we can become **sure** assets within the Kingdom.

Stop letting yourself, people and things sway you and say things that cause you to miss the directions of God. Stop getting in your own way by being fickle. Stop outside influences from speaking any old thing into your spirit as though they have the authority and right to do so. If you have been living this way, tell the Lord that you are sorry and submit to His process of helping you mature in this area. You belong to the King, therefore, all that you have to do is realize it and walk decisively in it!

So, how do you recover and move to the next level in your hearing? The answer is in **Revelation 3:19.** First, recognize that this is where you are. Next, receive the correction of the Lord, and then repent with all your heart. Now that you know better, you are responsible for doing better, and the Lord will be holding you accountable. Take a firm stance and the authority that God has given you. Use this position to access and receive His power that awaits you!

Now let's look at the final type of Listener, the Sympathetic Listener.

Sympathetic Listener

I call this one the Drama Ministry. To be sympathetic means to have an inclination to think or feel alike. It is the act of entering into or sharing the feelings or mental state of another, brought on by sensitivity and emotion. This type of listening will get you into trouble, if you cannot separate the drama of life around you from the real emergencies, issues, and circumstances. As a Sympathetic Listener, it is difficult to remove yourself from the immediate situation in order to ask your self, or the ones involved in the particular issue, the hard questions such as:

- Will you tell me the truth I need to hear to grow?
- Will you only tell me what you think I want to hear or feel I can handle?
- Do you cry with me even when you should really be telling me to get a grip?
- Is our relationship with one another, or to that particular person, place or thing, purely emotional?

Additionally, you need to settle down long enough to invite God into these situations. You need to ask:

- What is the real draw or pull for me to listen to what is being said, on a personal level, when the Lord is speaking?
- Do you only turn and submit to God when you are in a crisis mode and, therefore, out of control emotionally?
- Do you become so hyped up emotionally, because of what is going on around you that you can't hear a word He is saying?

You need to be able to identify, resolve and take control of the emotional and intellectual aspects of the situation in order to hear the Lord clearly and accurately. This is necessary because some of the worse decisions of many of our lives have been made when we have been out of control of our feelings, thoughts and emotions. This is a lot like what the Lord said to the Church of Thyatira in **Revelation 2:18 - 28**:

> *"[18] And unto the angel of the church in Thyatira write; These things saith the Son of God, who hath his eyes like unto a flame of fire, and his feet are like fine brass; [19] I know thy works, and charity, and service, and faith, and thy patience, and thy works; and the last to be more than the first. [20] Notwithstanding I have a few things against thee, because thou sufferest that woman Jezebel, which calleth herself a prophetess, to teach and to seduce my servants to commit fornication, and to eat things sacrificed unto idols. [21] And I gave her space to repent of her fornication; and she repented*

not. [22] *Behold, I will cast her into a bed, and them that commit adultery with her into great tribulation, except they repent of their deeds.* [23] *And I will kill her children with death; and all the churches shall know that I am he which searcheth the reins and hearts: and I will give unto every one of you according to your works.* [24] *But unto you I say, and unto the rest in Thyatira, as many as have not this doctrine, and which have not known the depths of Satan, as they speak; I will put upon you none other burden.* [25] *But that which ye have already hold fast till I come.* [26] *And he that overcometh, and keepeth my works unto the end, to him will I give power over the nations:* [27] *And he shall rule them with a rod of iron; as the vessels of a potter shall they be broken to shivers: even as I received of my Father.* [28] *And I will give him the morning star.*"

Thyatira means continual sacrifice. Be careful not to be lead astray by self proclaiming prophets. Discern! "Morning star" here means day light. Be steady fast in the faith! Do not be moved by what you hear and feel from others. There are those leading the church and others into areas of false doctrine, idolatry and immorality. However, you cannot be pulled into the drama of all the "current" events and new way teachings. You must strive to flow in alignment with the Word of God. Do not be deceived, especially in what you are hearing. Do not be persuaded by others and even yourself to allow anything to come between you and God. As we are enabled to persevere, the Lord promises to give us His eternal, everlasting presence! Glory to God!

Now you may be thinking OK, so we have proven by the Word that God has given us the capability to listen for, hear and receive His voice internally. We have proven by the Word that God is speaking and calling us to Him with a desire to have a conversation with Him about the things He has for you. Let's now gain a better understanding of the importance for openly receiving all that He has to say to you.

Receiving in Battle

Let us look at the position of the receiver. The receiver is weightier and more responsive to instruction and guidance than a listener. The receiver is one who comes into possession of something; takes hold of it; absorbs it into their mind and spirit; and thoroughly comprehends it. It is as though they take what they have heard, and consume it like nourishment for their mind, senses, and spirit. From here, the receiver considers the weight of what they have consumed, be it instructions, directions, or words of encouragement, **before** giving a response or going into action. Hmmmm, exactly like we should do Jesus, the Bread of Life, on a daily basis! The key here is that the receiver takes action based on what they have "digested".

In our lives as God's warriors, a "receiver" is one who believes what they have taken in and acts according to their belief system. The differences in the levels of power and strength of the receiver are based on where their heart is and what their perceptions are pertaining to the world around them. Simply put, how they think and feel based on their previous experiences determine how they respond to what they have taken in, both naturally and spiritually. The closer they walk according to the Word of God, the higher and more proficient their degree of accuracy will be on the Battlefield when responding to the Lord during the Battle.

One of the ultimate goals as a Soldier in God's Army and in the Battle, is to become a Spiritual Receiver. Please **do not** confuse this "title" of Spiritual Receiver with anything else other than what I have defined here for preparing yourself for Battle. The discipline described here is for accessing God's instructions in the life of the Spiritual Receiver and can be seen in the way they live their daily lives. This is where their skills are truly developed, nurtured and sharpened for Wartime! As we are told in **Isaiah 28:10,** day to day, precept upon precept, experience upon experience. This is how their foundation becomes solid in the Lord!

Now that you are better equipped in understanding the differences between the Listener and the Spiritual Receiver (and how we take in, retain and use information in each of these modes) it's time to discuss connecting all of the instructions to obtain a clear, distinct plan.

How can I be sure that I am saying what He wants me to say?

How do you really know the Lord has given you the capabilities to understand and respond accurately to what He is saying? Well, let us back this up with the Word, too! Let's look at **Acts 2:17-18**.

"And it shall come to pass in the last days, saith God, I will pour out of My Spirit upon all flesh: And your sons and your daughters shall prophesy, and your young men shall see visions, and your old men shall dream dreams: And on My servants and on my handmaidens I will pour out in those days of My Spirit; and They shall prophesy:"

This passage contains a two part promise. One, that God promises to communicate with you. Two, that He will enable you to communicate with Him, and others on His behalf. The purpose for this empowerment is for you, and His church, to manifest His glory and purpose throughout the earth.

Also, notice that these two parts come with a condition of operation. They can only be accomplished after His Spirit resides in you and you are in relationship with Him. How so? He says that He will give you a part of Him. Most of us miss the "out of" and have repeated for a long time, "I will pour out My Spirit on...". That is not what the scripture says! In this passage, God says that He will pour out of His Spirit upon all flesh. To "pour out" or "outpourings" means "spiritual awakenings". His Spirit is alive and He promises to let us, as sons and daughters, to be partakers of the things that are of Him. Allowing us to receive, see, hear and speak direct impartations from His Spirit places us in the position of joint heirs to the things that God wants to accomplish on the earth. These outpourings are the divine revelation of His plan, His purpose, your destiny, your assignments and the same for those around us that He deems appropriate for you to know. So WAKE UP, sons and daughters!

"Wait", you may be saying. So exactly why is God doing this? Why is He waking us up spiritually? To draw us closer to Him, to commune with Him, to hear what He is saying and to speak what He has said. God does this in order to enable, equip and empower you with the knowledge and wisdom you need to accomplish your purpose and assignments on the earth for His glory. God says we will prophesy. This is not complicated for those whose hearts are truly turned towards Him, who have a passion for Him, and whose heart's desire is to do His divine will. To prophesy is merely speaking the will of God into your life, the life of others, and on the earth.

In order to speak it out, you must understand what He is saying. To understand what He is saying, you must have His Spirit dwelling within you. The outpouring from His Spirit allows your spiritual ear, which is your heart, to perceive and hear the revelation of God's word. In order for you to have received God's written, or Logos Word, in your heart, God must have given His Rhema, or spoken Word, to His sons and daughters first! Prophecy is receiving directly from God and saying what He has said about things to come. Why? For His manifested glory to come to pass on the earth! Oh, it's going to come to pass! This part of speaking it out also helps build and establish your faith and testimonies, as His promises do come to pass. So speak it out. That is the only way this gift of hearing will be developed and sharpened.

Here is one more thing to pay attention to when looking at "come to pass". Come to pass doesn't necessarily mean decades from now. It could mean within the next hour, minute, or even by the time you turn this page. It could literally mean right now! Right now, we have the capabilities to know the divine will of God. The divine will of God is what we, as Christians, are to strive to achieve. So, when we, as Christians say "divine", we are referring to anything of, relating to, or coming directly from God, and not from psychics, tarot card readers, soothsayers, horoscopes, fortune tellers, or folks speaking to dead relatives! Saints, please turn the television channels or find another section of the paper to read! These things are not a part of God's divine will for our lives. These things are abominations before our Father. Therefore, why are you still peeking at them, flirting with them or even playing with them? If you have a question about any of these methods used to get answers for your life and whether or not they are acceptable to God, check out **Deuteronomy 18:9-14:**

"When you come into the land which the LORD your God is giving you, you shall not learn to follow the abominations of those nations. There shall not be found among you anyone who makes his son or his daughter pass through the fire, or one who practices witchcraft, or a soothsayer, or one who interprets omens, or a sorcerer, or one who conjures spells, or a medium, or a spiritist, or one who calls up the dead. For all who do these things are an abomination to the LORD, and because of these abominations the LORD your God drives them out from before you. You shall be blameless before the LORD your God. For these nations which you will dispossess listened to soothsayers and diviners; but as for you, the LORD your God has not appointed such for you."

God makes it pretty clear what things He is **not** pleased with! How can you accurately and clearly hear and speak the word of God, when your spirit is cluttered with all kinds of perpetrators and imitators of the truth? We will look closer at the issues in this passage in **Chapter 6**. But, note that our Father clearly says in the above scripture that even though we are in the same land, we are not to be participants in their ways and the things that they have declared acceptable. Stop haphazardly walking into the enemy's territory! Our Lord has given us the privilege of being able to go directly to Him as our source of guidance and comfort. As an awesome woman of God, Kathryn Kulhman, said, "If you really want to know what's going to happen in the future, turn to the Word of God, because what's to come is no secret!" Don't take the privilege that God has given you lightly.

Another key point to note in **Acts 2:17**, is that this passage of scripture says "all flesh" will be affected. All flesh does not mean just the Bishops, just the Pastors, just the Elders, or Ministers. All means All and you are included in that ALL. Yes, as a spirit-filled Christian, we are able to prophesy according to the divine Will of God. Since this is true, as His sons and daughters, we are all capable of hearing God, understanding, and speaking what He has spoken.

There is yet one more thing to grasp before we move on. Those that God spoke to in the Old Testament (and they heard and responded to Him), did not have the indwelling of His Spirit. Remember, His Spirit is a major part of your equilibrium for hearing spiritually. Now looking at **Acts 2:17**, we are told that He has given us the gift of His Spirit to understand and speak His will on the earth. **Acts 2:18** tells us one of the main purposes of His Spirit is for us to speak forth His Will in the earth. So how much more capable has He made us to hear, understand and speak His will than the people in the Old Testament? How much more effective has He equipped us to be as Spirit-filled Christians endued with the power of His Spirit? The possibilities and our potential are endless.

So far, we have established five key principles to hearing God and the tools for developing a greater ability to hear. So, you may be thinking, OK, so we have proven by the Word of God that our Father has (1) given us the capability to listen for and (2) hear His voice internally. We have proven, by the Word of God, that (3) our Father is speaking with a desire to have a conversation with us. We, also, have proven by the Word of God, that (4) we are able to understand and (5) speak what He has spoken. In addition, now, we can tell the type of Listener we are and the position of receiving we must strive towards. Right? Amen. So, now, you may be asking, "Why does He want to talk to directly me?"

So, why does He want to talk to me directly?

Well, let's look it up in His Word! A critical connection to make is that we have His Spirit to lead and direct us according to the will of God, not by our whims, wills and desires. Take a look at **I Corinthians 2:10-12**:

> *"But God hath revealed them unto us by his Spirit: for the Spirit searcheth all things, yea, the deep things of God. For what man knoweth the things of a man, save the spirit of man which is in him? even so the things of God knoweth no man, but the Spirit of God. Now we received, not the spirit of the world, but the spirit which is of God; that we might know the things that are freely given to us of God."*

In looking at the verse, the "them" refers to the things you want to know, the mysteries of God and the plans that He has for you! The next part is "even so the things of God knoweth no man, but the Spirit of God". This is all about discernment. Remember we confirmed earlier that we have received the Spirit of God and He dwells within us. Therefore, it is important to strengthen your spirit man with the Word of God! This also takes you back to your spiritual balance and equilibrium, the Word and Spirit of God. Why? We need to know the things that are freely given to us by God. Discernment is free. It is another gift and it doesn't cost you anything but time and obedience. The total cost is the time it takes to hear God's direction and the obedience it takes to do it!

The Lord wants to continuously reveal issues, situations, events, and revelations directly to you through His Spirit all of the time. God does not want His children to be ignorant of what's going on around them, or of what's coming. Remember, from our key scripture **Psalm 27:8**, when we are in His presence, we are aware of what's going on around us. There is nothing happening on this earth, or anywhere else, that God does not know about past, present, or future. This passage in **I Corinthians**, further confirms the need for receiving the gift of hearing in your heart that God so freely gives to us. We know that everything God does has a purpose. We may not understand it, but if God did it, it has a purpose! This scripture tells us the purpose for why God wants to talk to us directly - so that we are aware of what's going on around us on the earth!

Why would He do all of this for you? It is done all for His Glory, of course. Don't you know you are His Glory? In **John 17:1-10,** Jesus tells us all about our relationship to Him and the Father, and how our relationship links to God our Father's Glory on the earth. As one of God's children, you are His glory on the earth. Because of this relationship, the Lord wants to talk directly to you. Why? Specifically because:

- You are His Child;
- You belong to Him;
- He wants what's best for you in your life; and
- He loves you.

51

Remember communication flows two ways! How do you give wise counsel and advice to someone you love and care about? You have a conversation with them. The two of you talk to each other, one on one. One listens, while the other talks. Then the other listens, while the other one responds to what has been said. As stated in **Isaiah 1:18**, you can go into God's presence and the two of you can reason together. When you are reasoning together, remember that the key to hearing God begins and is established in your heart, which is your spiritual ear. This connection is made when:

- You go after God prepared and expecting to hear Him speak;
- You believe that you are able to hear and understand what He has spoken; and
- You know that God, our Father, desires to speak directly to you, and into your life.

Now, let's look at the "Links" that give us this key access to the Lord. Take a look at a key. Each key has a set of teeth. Each tooth is a link that connects with the tumbler in the lock. As the teeth line up with the correct links in the tumbler, the lock is loosened a little with each direct connection. As the links come into full alignment, the lock is opened and whatever it is you are trying to gain access to is made available. You are given full access with the right hook up! As we continue our journey of hearing God, we will learn that the key that opens our heart for hearing God works when the components or links of **Focus, Obedience,** and **Faith** are all in sync with the will of God. There is nothing more frustrating than thinking that you have the right key - only to find that what you have doesn't work.

Your key starts in your heart. Your heart for hearing God consists of these three Links. What are they? Focus is the outer component. Obedience is the middle link, or component. Finally, Faith is the last or innermost link or component. Let's begin by looking at each of these gifts froim the outside first, then the middle and finally, the critical innermost link. Therefore, let's begin with the link of Focus.

Part 2:

"Focus and Discern!"

CHAPTER 4

Developing Concentration During the Battle: Focus

We are living in a steadily progressing age of high speed technology and entertainment as we enter into this new millennium. This is both good and bad. Good because our outreach and evangelistic efforts have a further reach into the world. Bad because our attention spans are extremely short and our imaginations are being short circuited by an overwhelming influx of outside influences. If we are not entertained or mesmerized by what we are involved in at any given moment, we quickly loss interest and look for the next "entertaining" thing or suggestive answer.

Concentrating on the things of God to allow Him to lead us is crucial, especially now. To concentrate means that we are devoted and focused on one particular task at a specific time. Developing concentration is skill and discipline, that many of us have never learn, let alone master. Warrior, just imagine the number of ideals and directions we have missed because we were unable to stay focused long enough to capture the whole thought or impression that the Lord placed in our hearts and/or minds. Not to mention, actually taking the time to document it somewhere for future use. Additionally, our prayers really need to go up for the educators of our time who must keep up with the developing minds of our current and upcoming generations. They have to keep the attention of our children long enough to teach them. Wow! Yes, there is a need to be able to concentrate, or better stated, focus on a given assignment long enough to complete it well.

This brings us to the point of examining the area of focus, and how to not only develop it, but master it. Do you know one of the major reasons we as the children of God lose ground in the Battle? How we sometimes even suffer major set backs and forfeit promised opportunities? One of the major factors in how the Battle is fought and won, and the number of hits and fatalities we incur can be directly linked to a shift or loss of focus on our part!

The Necessary Link of Focus for Hearing God

Focus is the link of spiritual hearing that is most like the outer ear for hearing naturally. Remember, the outer ear collects and sorts all of the things going on around you. As you decipher what to disregard and what to keep your focus begins to zero in on the things you have decided to "let in for a closer look". Your level of focus helps you to determine what you will accept or take into your spirit at any given time based on what's going on around you. It directly affects your ability to hear clearly from the Father.

How many times have you wanted to be obedient to the will of God, but just were not sure that it was the Lord you were hearing? More often than not, a key reason that we are not immediately obedient to what God is saying to us is that we want to be sure that it is God who is saying it! This certainty and confidence requires a highly developed, disciplined level of focus. This comes over time and is developed as you walk a disciplined lifestyle to and with the Word of our Father. This level of focus is tunnel vision that continuously looks head-on with spiritual concentration towards the things of God. It is the fine-tuning between the Spirit of the Lord and your spirit that clears and removes the barriers and distractions that can block your ability to hear with spiritual accuracy.

Lord, I can see You clearly now!

Take a few minutes to do this very simple, yet effective example of how your level of focus can directly and immediately impact and change your ability to hear God clearly. First, a couple of key instructions to prepare you:

1. Using your hands as a shield, cup them together and hold them away from your face.
2. Your cupped hands represent the Lord.
3. Beyond your hands are the world, people, and situations around you.
4. Slowly begin to move your cupped hands upwards, towards your face, keeping your eyes focused on the center of your hands.
5. Stop once your hands are touching your face.
6. Now move your hands away again.
7. Finally, begin to slowly move your hands back to your face. Each time you move your hands, remember to keep your eyes focused on the center of your hands.

What did you see when your hands, which represent the Lord, were the furthest away from your face? What did you see when your hands were closest to your face?

There are a couple of helpful points about focus that comes from this exercise. First, notice that even though you can see your cupped hands as the center of your focus, the further your hands move away from your face, the more visible the outside world, people, and things in the area around become to you. If something moves, I guarantee you that your eyes, or focus, will shift away from your hands and towards that object, even if it is just for a moment. Just as your hands are right there in front of you, so is our Lord. Notice that you move He doesn't! You shift into or out of position, God does not! Also, notice that your hands become smaller and appear to take up less space in your range of view the further you move them away from your face. Interesting! This gives you something else to ponder here: the further away you hold God, the smaller the impact He will be able to have in your life.

Now consider this. Even though your eyes are focused on your hands, you can see the other things around you. Notice that neither your hands, nor the other things, are totally clear. Why? Because your focus was "divided" and until you chose to focus on one particular thing, this division only leads to confusion and double mindedness.

On the other side of this is a narrower view. The closer you move your hands towards your face, the more God will become the center of your focus once you do decide that He is who and what you are going to focus on. As you draw your hands nearer to touch your face and actually cover your eyes, you will sense a closeness that represents a more "up close and personal" encounter with Him. Notice that God becomes bigger in your focus and the outside influences become smaller. As your level of focus becomes more God-ward, you will know that He must become the center of your focus. No matter what is going on around you, you learn to become focused on Him. Therefore, you are not led by the world, people and your situations. You must grow and live at a level in this Spiritual Walk where you are focused on God and, therefore, led by His Spirit, according to His will, in truth, in all situations. The choice is yours.

Lord, Is that You?

Focus is the hearing connection between God, you and the world. Many times, we place the world between us and the Lord. The Lord never intended for us to do that. Let nothing come between you and God! Though we are in the world, we are not of the world. So how do you tell the difference? Or the questions could be: How do you know it's God you are really hearing? Are you sure that what you heard was what God actually said? Who is talking and how can you know and discern the difference between God, you or someone else?

First and foremost, anything said that is contradictory to the Bible is not God. God's Word proves itself again and again and will not be at odds with itself. Anything or anyone that does not confess or exalt Jesus as Lord is not God! As stated in God's Word in **John 14:6**, the only way to the Father is through the son. God is our Father. Jesus is the Son. This means that you must have a personal relationship with the Son in order to have an eternal relationship with the Father, and the Son's name is Jesus. There is **no** other way. If you are going to believe and follow the truth of God, then follow the whole truth.

Otherwise, you are following a partial truth that is simply and directly put, a lie and you are being deceived! Lastly, anything said that does not give you peace in your spirit is not God. I don't mean peace to your flesh! I mean peace in your spirit. You'll know the difference between the two! To further help us, God has given instructions on how to tell the difference. Let's look at **I Corinthians 12:1-3**:

> *"Now concerning spiritual gifts, brethren, I would not have you ignorant. Ye know that ye were Gentiles, carried away unto these [silent]dumb idols, even as ye were led. Wherefore I give you to understand, that no man speaking by the Spirit of God calleth Jesus accursed: and that no man can say that Jesus is the Lord, but by the Holy Ghost."*

Remember, your spiritual hearing is a gift. God does not want you ignorant, which means uninformed or naive concerning what He has blessed you with. This also includes being unaware of what to do with what God has given you. God wants you to be an informed recipient and user of His gifts. He gives us, by His Spirit, the secret to knowing when what you are hearing is of Him and when it is not.

In these verses, God has given you two simple, yet powerful filtering techniques for testing what you are hearing. I say "are hearing", not heard. I say this because if you realize early enough, by using these techniques, that it is not God speaking, then you need to stop the speaker or noise immediately in its tracks! How? You can handle this by binding up that distracting spirit in the name of Jesus and then immediately loose understanding and clarity to hear the Lord's voice in the name of Jesus. If the distractions are so ridiculous that you can't regain focus right away, in faith, plead the Blood of Jesus, or simply call His name until you have peace and quiet. As **Philippians 2:10** says:

> *"That at the name of Jesus, every knee should bow, of the things in heaven, and things in earth, and things under the earth;"*

Don't let the obstacles and distractions that you will face keep you from progressing in this gift of hearing. That's exactly what the enemy wants. He wants you to give up and feel as though it is too difficult or unattainable. We already know that this is something that God desires for you so that He can draw you even closer to Him. Therefore, once things are under control again, try again because the only way your spiritual hearing will become sharper is if you continually use it.

Each of us hears God differently and you know your flesh, your friends and the enemy can be pretty convincing at times. So if you are still unsure who's talking, God's Word says "try the spirit". Which means test it, check it out, and confirm the source for your self. The wonderful thing about hearing God is you can ask immediately, "God, is that you?" He will answer. One way or another, He will answer. So don't limit or restrict the ways He will respond.

Sometimes there is still interference, or static, that you will need to clear up. **I John 4:1-6**, tells us what we need to do to gain and keep our focus. Take a look at it.

"¹Beloved, believe not every spirit, but try^(ltest) the spirits whether they are of God: because many false prophets are gone out into the world. ²Hereby know ye the Spirit of God: Every spirit that confesseth that Jesus Christ is come in the flesh is of God. ³And every spirit that confesseth not that Jesus Christ is come in the flesh is not of God: and this is that spirit of antichrist, whereof ye have heard that it should come; and even now already is it in the world. ⁴Ye are of God, little children, and have overcome them: because greater is he that is in you, than he that is in the world. ⁵They are of the world: therefore speak they of the world, and the world heareth them. ⁶We are of God: he that knoweth God heareth us; he that is not of God heareth not us. Hereby know we the spirit of truth, and the spirit of error."

Note that whenever you see ":" (colons) it means two things. The first part of the statement is true because of, or as a result of what follows. The second part of the statement or proclamation is the life-giving instructions that you need. In this case, it is to sharpen your focus. To sharpen your focus, you must develop keen, spiritual discernment.

In this passage, God is giving you many proclamations of truth concerning focus and discernment. We will go into more details about discernment later in this chapter. But for now, as you study this passage, read each statement of truth. At each ":" you encounter in the passage, ask, "How?" "How can I tell?" "Who?" or "Why?". See how God gives you the answer to each situation pertaining to how you can bring and maintain clarity in your focus. Ready? Good.

So, let's go deeper into this passage. God is talking about conversations here. How do we know? He describes hearing and speaking. He's telling us about conversations between Himself and us, people in the world and us, and us with one another. There's a lot of talking going on here. God is giving us spiritual "etiquette" for how to carry on conversations depending on who you are listening and talking to, or who is listening and talking to you.

Starting with **I John 4:1,** God is telling us first and foremost don't have **faith** or place your trust in everything and everyone that you encounter that expresses the desire to speak to you, or that has something to say to you, or even is determined to impart something they feel is important into your life. If you do that, your **focus** will become blurred. What we are to do is to investigate and determine what the source of that spirit is. Is it God? If it's not, you don't want to be bothered with it! Tell them to move on and don't receive any of their conversation in your mind, spirit or heart.

You can tell if it's of God by its conversation. How? By who and what they are talking about. You can ask questions to determine its source and be mindful that the "it" can be another person and yes, even another Christian. Remember the conversation in **Matthew 16:23** between Jesus and Peter, where Jesus had to put him in check about some of the things that Peter was saying. If the Lord had listened to Peter, His focus could have been shifted from His purpose!

Keep in mind too, that you can do this without being offensive or indignant to the other person. Keep the door open for any opportunities for witnessing the truth to this person at another time. Always know that you must take the proper authority over what is spoken to you. To be more comfortable and secure in getting to what you need, just remind yourself that you ask questions in a conversation anyway! Right? I am sure you do!

I John 4:2 tells us that here is how you know it is of God. How? You will know by any conversation that claims and embraces Jesus as Lord. **I John 4:3** tells that us you know it is not of God if its conversation does not acknowledge Jesus as Lord. In addition, this passage goes on to identify this spirit as the antichrist. The spirit of the antichrist is basically anything that is in opposition to God, God's plan and His people. Look closely! **I Thessalonians 2:3** further supports this by telling us to let no man draw you away from God, His ways, and His teachings no matter what the enemy says or does because this will cause a separation between God and you. That's not a place you want to be in because you **really cannot** hear God then! So be very careful of who you let speak into and over your life!

I John 4:4 gives us the Good News though! God tells us we belong to Him. And we have triumphed over all of the things of and under the world. How? You are already victorious because you are a vessel of the Holy Spirit. Remember, in **Chapter 2**, we talked about and confirmed your ability to hear from God, because of the indwelling of the Holy Spirit. **I John 4:3-4** is where our equilibrium, the Word of God and the Spirit of God, is further strengthened. Here we are given further guidance and wisdom pertaining to how to use our God-given discernment to stay focused.

In **I John 4:5,** God tells us to leave those of the world to their conversations. As they speak to one another, you will be able to tell who they are by what they are talking about. They will understand among themselves their dialogue and mannerisms.

In **I John 4:6**, God confirms again we are His, and that we know we belong to Him because in our conversations, we speak and understand one another as though we are speaking a common foreign language. If someone is not in His family, they can not comprehend or effectively participate in our conversations, not to mention their inability to receive or hear directly from God for themselves. Additionally, God describes another powerful weapon that we have available to help us. It is discernment. Discernment is the ability to know the truth from deception.

So, how can we tell easily and effortlessly? Well, let me first say that it won't always be easy. However, the answer leads us right back to our Spiritual Equilibrium for hearing spiritually. We are able to do so by the gift of discernment that God has given us to know the difference by His Spirit. Reality from make believe, and truth from fiction. God has given us the gift of spiritual hearing and specific instructions for how to use it properly. Interference, distractions, and people will come from all directions. You have been given the power to withstand all of these situations because the Spirit that is IN you is greater than anything and anyone that is in the world. You must remember in order to clearly hear God's voice through your circumstances your focus must be totally and completely stayed on Him.

When things start to get heavy and are attacking your faith and focus in your ability to hear God clearly, confound the enemy and his distracting spirits by breaking out in praises to God. In song, in scriptures, even sing a simple love song to Jesus! Do like King David did through the majority of the Book of Psalms, praise God in all situations and circumstances for what He's doing, what He's already done, and what He's about to do in your life. When you do it with focused effort from your heart, this really messes the enemy up big time! He and his imps want to get as far away from you as possible and as fast as they can!

Keep in mind, your spiritual focus is so critical that the enemy will send everything he possibly can to knock you off your foundation. Many things will occur and you must be able to tell the who, what, why and how of an attack. This battle can only be fought and won effectively and deliberately by hearing God clearly and distinctly. In Chapter 5, we will cover in detail many of the tactics and strategies of the enemy. For now, know that the Lord has given us an important piece of weaponry, and this component has a name: Discernment. Remember, discernment is a crucial weapon. Therefore, the next section is devoted to better understanding it.

Lord, help me to see and know what's really going on!

We are in a time when discernment is critical! Discernment is a key component of your spiritual weaponry in hearing God. So, to better understand how to use it, first, let's understand what it is. What does discernment mean? To discern means to see or understand the difference in something, someone or a particular situation. To be discerning means having revealing insight and understanding. Therefore, discernment is the quality and ability to grasp **and** comprehend a specific issue, or circumstance. Quality means *to do it well or expertly.* The ability to grasp *means, "I got hold of it, it's in my hands!"* Comprehend means knowing what to do with what is in your hands. It is knowing whether to wait, prepare some more, proceed, complete, leave, or stay. Discernment is the added edge that God has given His people to know what to do every step of the way. It is a gift from our Father to His children. Let's look at **1 Corinthians 12:10**:

> *"To another the working of miracles; to another prophesy; to another discerning of spirits; to another divers kinds of tongues; to another the interpretation of tongues;".*

In this passage, discernment in the Greek language is *diakrisis*, which means a distinguishing, a clear discrimination, or judging by evidence whether they are evil or of God. Discernment is an intense level of focus on God, but does not require an intensity or flesh based sense of "spiritual deepness" to use it well. Discernment is the ability to HEAR, SEE, HEAR some more and KNOW what is NOT obvious! True discernment only develops into a sharpened weapon if you are focused, yielded and obedient to God's will.

I heard a Pastor on the radio one day say, "Accepting Jesus as Lord is the most important decision you will ever make in your life! After that, there is no other major decision you will have to make on your own because He will handle the rest. You only need to follow!" Discernment helps you to follow and do it effectively. It is the ability to identify the source of a spirit. Meaning whose side are they on: God's or the enemy's. Child of God, there is no in between. It is one or the other, and God has given you the power and authority to know the difference. It is also the ability to distinguish between true and false prophecy and prophets, which we will look at in Chapter 5.

Know that the church today needs people who are gifted with the authority and ability to discern the nature of messages spoken in God's name to them, and to His people. To do this effectively, you **must** not only sit in the presence of the Lord, but at His feet in order to truly sharpen your gift of discernment. What does that mean? It means you've got to PRAY, without ceasing and consistently!

As our Father tells us in **Isaiah 55:8**, His ways and thoughts are not our thoughts and ways. This means God does NOT view, perceive or handle people and matters the same way man generally would. From this, you also need to realize that the enemy will not always come from the same way we think either! In attacks, we look for the enemy to come a certain way, every time. The enemy is very cunning and we are not as smart as he is, even though we like to think so. Even the most skilled spiritual warrior of God has been disarmed and tripped up! Discernment is one of the key weapons for knowing the WAY to take and maintain what God says is yours and be steadfast in this battle!

Operating in the B.A.S.I.C.S.

Tying together hearing the Lord and the gift of discernment involves knowing and accepting the following **B.A.S.I.C.S.**. Discernment allows you to **B**oldly **A**ccess **S**piritual **I**nstructions **C**learly **S**tated by God! Boldly meaning showing, or requiring, a fearless, daring spirit! Access to spiritual instructions is the other side of your discernment where God answers you. God's instructions will always be clear. If you take the time to seek the Lord and submit yourself to His will, this allows Him to spiritually develop your discernment. Always keep in mind that the lack of understanding never comes from what He has spoken, but rather from what you believe you heard. Confusion and uncertainty can be avoided, if you continuously seek Him on a consistent basis for all the situations of your life. Our Father is a confirming God, so if you are unsure, ask for clarity! Once you have clarity, you must take Spirit-led action. You must move on the instructions that God has spoken!

As mentioned earlier, one of our biggest hindrances is that we are not confident in our ability to hear God clearly. Therefore, we are stalled at the gate. Doubt sets in and we become immobilized by our doubt. Doubt leads to fear. Fear paralyzes us, and causes us to procrastinate in doing what we need to do. From our indecisiveness and lack of mobility, we eventually become numb to what's going on around us. We are unable to focus, we don't feel, we don't hear, and therefore, we do not respond. From there, we become dumb to the things of God, our purpose, and even our very next step! In this case, "dumb" means lacking power and intelligence on what to do next. Stated another way, we become spiritually deaf and, therefore, spiritually and naturally ineffective. At this point, who is really winning the Battle and getting the glory from our actions?

So then what? How can you make sure that you are discerning accurately in order to hear clearly so that you can move by the will of God? I'm glad you asked! Clarity comes from our ability to consistently lean on and use our Spiritual Equilibrium, which consists of the Word **and** Spirit of God. Seeking the Lord in order to build and strengthen your Spiritual Equilibrium must become a habit. How do you develop this habit? By committing to do it, and then actually doing it one day at a time! In doing this, hearing the strategies of God, recognizing the enemy, and knowing when the attacks are on will become a natural reflex and an important part of your nature and lifestyle. Thereby further developing you into an even more effective, powerful spiritual warrior for God's Kingdom.

Remember the key is using God's **B.A.S.I.C.S.** to boldly go after your divine instructions. You must get to the point where you understand the authority and power God has given you to pursue and capture the promises that He has in store for your life. There are major results that can be accomplished by utilizing the gift of Discernment. Don't forget how to pull on this phenomenal power. So, now that the foundation has been set, let's see who our opponent really is.

CHAPTER 5

Discerning the Enemy, His Army & Attacks: Hold Your Position

Now you may be thinking, Paris, that's all wonderful stuff, but what does this have to do with me? Convince me that I need to know this, and explain to me what I need to do with all of this information. Wow! I am so glad we are flowing together and that you asked and have these questions! Let's go onto the Battlefield and gain a deeper understanding of what's really going on regarding who and what is around you. Why? Because God has given you the authority to know all that you need to be victorious in the Battle. This chapter is heavily laid out with Scriptures. This is one of those areas in God that you better know and have the Word firmly planted in your heart, and a cognitive understanding in your head in order to be an effective warrior for and in God's Kingdom.

At this point, I must give you words of caution. First, PLEASE do not go into spiritual territories in the Battle that first and foremost God has not released or sent you to go into. Know which fights you are to fight and recognize the ones you are to walk away from. Know that for the ones that you are to walk away from, God has your back and another spiritual warrior laying in wait for their release from Him to fight that Battle. They can't fight the battle if you are in the way! Remember, **God is** all knowing, we are not.

Secondly, once you are released, PLEASE do not go into the Battle if you have not taken the time to properly prepare yourself for the assignment. In other words, don't set yourself up to take any unnecessary whippings, both spiritually and in the natural! It would be the enemy's pleasure to accommodate you in either, or both of these areas! We, as warriors, need to recognize and take responsibility for our levels of preparedness. How do you know that you have prepared yourself? Easy! **You** know whether or not you have sought God for His instructions in a particular matter, whether or not you have been in the Word, and whether or not your heart is pure and your hands are clean before the Lord. No one can answer that for you, but YOU!

Finally, if you are feeling really uneasy about going this deep into Spiritual Warfare, please don't hesitate to skip Chapters 5 and 6 and come back to them when you do feel more ready or are lead by the Holy Spirit to read this information! Remember there is a time and season for everything.

Also, remember to keep hold of the gift of discernment, which is the ability to skillfully grasp **and** comprehend a specific issue or circumstance. You will need to have this working "24/7" to deal in this area of the Battle. Have you used it today? Well, after these 2 chapters, the next time you do go on the battlefield you will be even better equipped to recognize the enemy and his tactics.

I think it's only fair to start at **home** first when looking at all the tactics that can trip us up and harm us in the Battle. Uh huh, Saint of God, don't look at this book in that tone! You know we have issues in our House! So let's deal with one of the most prominent one, and as we do you need to be open, take what you need, and leave the rest until you need it later.

Ergo, let's get down to business by doing some housekeeping inside first before we cross over into deeper territories. Why do we need to do this? We need this because our guards have a tendency to be a little more relaxed around "family members" than neighbors and strangers. Even more importantly we are soldiers at all times who should rarely be surprised or tripped up by anything that people say or do, inside or outside the Church. So, let's continue to put our armor on by going a little further into the tactics that can be used against us. Let's deal with false prophets inside the Church.

False Prophets

Yes, False Prophets are in the House! Now, again, don't let this rattle you! God gives us some standards by which to judge this type of prophecy and situation; and surely you would not go to a fortune teller or a witch to speak to you about your life and destiny. Just in case you might, I promise you, you will think twice after reading these next few chapters. Why? Because you are becoming more accountable to God for what you are learning and now know.

To better understand exactly what a false prophet is, let's start with who a "prophet" is supposed to be. A prophet is one that speaks on behalf of God to His people. The contradiction in terms comes in when we add false to the word prophet. "False" here means intentionally untrue, attempting to mislead, and treacherous in nature. All aspects of this are done in a faithless manner.

These vessels are really not expecting their spoken words to come to pass. There is no unity in hope or agreement in the faith attached to what is being spoken. In fact, they too are either often mildly surprised when the things they have spoken do come to pass or obnoxiously arrogant about how they have impacted your life with their words. With that kind of spirit behind them, this makes you wonder who they really think is going to do these things that they are speaking of. Better yet, in who and what is their faith really in? Is it in them? Wow!

A closer look allows us to see that a false prophet speaks in diversions from the truth and its components. Let's look at **Matthew 7:15-20,**

> *"Beware of false prophets, which come to you in sheep's clothing, but inwardly they are ravening wolves. Ye shall know them by their fruits. Do men gather grapes of thorns, or figs of thistles? Even so every good tree bringeth forth good fruit; but a corrupt tree bringeth forth evil fruit. A good tree cannot bring forth evil fruit, neither can corrupt a tree bring forth good fruit. Every tree that bringeth not forth good fruit is hewn down, and cast into the fire. Wherefore by their fruits ye shall know them."*

In this passage, we are told to be fruit inspectors when it comes to being led by God's people and those that profess to be one of His. So, examine the fruit in the lives of the people who are prophesying or speaking directions to you for your life, supposedly on behalf of God. For clarity purposes, fruits include not only the actions they choose in their lives but more importantly the impact that these actions have on those they have encountered.

For example: what would the fruit look like as described by the spouse, siblings, children, parents, pastor, co-laborers, managers, coworkers, employees, etc. Would they all describe the same person especially when that person is away from the spot light? How does that prophet of God speak of the Lord, and how does what they say line up with the Word of God?

Again, what's in them will eventually come out. Yes it will definitely show up! Even when you can't easily discern what the true source is eventually the real source will tell on itself. Again, go back to the types of conversations we discussed in Chapter 4 from **I John 4:1-6**. What else is coming out of their mouths? What words are really being spoken forth at the times when they are not "prophesying in the spirit"? Why are they talking to you? Did God really send them? Is this confirmation to what you have already heard God say to you? Always ask the Lord what's really going on! Every time you receive a "word' from a representative of Christ, check it WITH Christ and His Word! Take what the Lord says is relevant to your journey and leave the rest. Don't get caught up in the mess, just leave it. Travel light and *only* take what you need as you travel through this life and on the Battlefield.

Finally, of course another true test is the Test of Time. Does it come to pass? If their fruit is rotten, then you will not have any problem determining their source of information and the degree of acceptance into your life's strategy. Discern, discern, discern!

So what else can a saint do to protect themselves in this area? First, know that when you apply God's standards to the situations and people in your life, you will not be fooled by any of them. But, you have to recognize them first! I didn't say broadcast it. I said recognize it. A major identifying trait is that these are the border line, low hanging fruit that can't wait to say, "Thus saith the Lord" directly in the House of God. Yes, these are the False Prophets. The ones that sit in church, and by all intents and purposes, appear to walk closely with God, but have issues that cloud even their own ability to hear from God clearly. They know this to a degree and still spew out their perverted version of what they think God is saying to the people. Again, discern, discern, discern!

God's response to them can be found in **Ezekiel 13:3-8.** Directly speaking, God says very bluntly, *"I am against you"*. This is definitely not a good place to be in! False prophets are just like Fruit Punch Kool Aid! What's the main fruit in it, anyway? It's all kinds of fruits mixed together until you can't tell what to pay attention to other than all the sugar or sweet stuff that's been added to make it more appealing. Hearing directly from God for yourself is extremely critical, especially if you are on the brink of God doing something miraculous in your life!

Many times, we hear the term, "False Prophets", and think this means the man or woman is not chosen or called by God. Sometimes that is the case, and they actually "went out" under their own guise versus being "sent out" in order by God. But hold on a minute, what about when they *are* called of God? You see, a false prophet can also refer to the chosen vessel that is not speaking what God has said for them to speak, or is mixing in their own comments with what God has spoken. So, how do you further discern the false prophets among us? Look at **Deuteronomy 13:1-5:**

> *"¹If there arise among you a prophet, or a dreamer of dreams, and giveth thee a sign or a wonder, ² And the sign or the wonder come to pass, whereof he spake unto thee, saying, Let us go after other gods, which thou hast not known and let us serve them; ³ Thou shalt not hearken unto the words of that prophet, or that dreamer of dreams: for the Lord your God proveth you, to know whether ye love the LORD your God with all your heart and with all your soul. ⁴ Ye shall walk after the LORD your God, and fear him, and keep his commandments, and obey his voice, and ye shall serve him, and cleave unto him. ⁵And that prophet, or that dreamer of dreams, shall be put to death; because he hath spoken to*

turn you away from the LORD your God, which brought you out of the land of Egypt, and redeemed you out of the house of bondage, to thrust thee out of the way which the LORD thy God commanded thee to walk in. So shalt thou put the evil away from the midst of thee. "

First and foremost, God is teaching us here that we are responsible for discerning the difference and that He will test us to make sure that **we know** that our hearts belong to Him. When I say "hearts" here I mean that our lifestyle as a whole is a direct, living witness that represents and immolates His Glory in the earth. As His people, we must know the FACT that God was always here. He is the same God spoken of in the first chapter of the Book of Genesis and in the last chapter of the Book of Revelation. He has not been hidden, and His people have come to know this FACT about Him over the generations. There were no others before Him, and there are and will be no others like Him. He **is** the great "I AM". Over time He continues to help us protect our hearts and the placement of our affections by allowing us to come to the realization that He is God and God all by Himself through all situations.

God is also letting us know that He will test us to see if He can trust us not to follow after those who we should be able to tell are misrepresenting Him. We are to be careful of who and what we are allowing to speak into our ears and impart into our spirits. These false prophets will be, and are, very beguiling in their approaches because they do have a blend of the Word in them and it is in what they are speaking.

So Warrior, consider this: how on earth is it that all of a sudden a "prophet" can say he or she had a dream or a seemingly unexplainable encounter or experience. As a result of this, then present this "event" to us, within our Father's House, with the conception of a "new god" for us follow in a whole "new way" contrary to or in alignment with *only some* of the Word. And based on their "word", we begin to buy into this "new" doctrine and follow without question? Wow, doesn't that sound like most of the major religions that exist today? Yes, God is the Giver of dreams. But to truly tell if the dream is from Him, we must test where the Glory is being **totally** directed.

Secondly, from this knowledge of who God is, we must not allow ourselves to begin following signs and wonders and then based on what we see, begin to follow them with our hearts like we are commanded to follow the Lord. Misguided affections get us in trouble every time! Our Father, the one and only Adonai, came first! He sent, and continues to send signs and wonders to encourage and strengthen us to endure our circumstances. It is not the other way around. Signs and wonders did not come before the Father.

This is another area where falsehoods of this type are spoken of by this person. They have it twisted and out of order. Isn't that just how the enemy operates? The spoken words of a false prophet are distorted angles on the truth, just like one of those crooked mirrors we see at fairs and amusement parks. The true image is there but it is out of focus and requires discernment to see the "real" picture and situation.

But the good news with our Father is that He always tells us how to persevere. The surviving and passing of the tests for us comes in us not allowing anyone or anything to lead us away the Lord. Especially based on what we have witnessed by foretelling, signs and wonders. Also we are told in **Deuteronomy 13:4** that we can stay free if we follow His instructions: *"..walk after the LORD your God, and fear him, and keep his commandments, and obey his voice, and ye shall serve him, and cleave unto him."* Our answer is right in front of our eyes!

So, how are the false prophets able to operate in this gifting? They are able to do this simply because our Father created them. He gave them these gifts of power, and these gifts are irrevocable as stated in **Romans 11:29**: *"For the gifts and calling of God are without repentance."*

However, just as Lucifer did, the false prophet has decided to use God's gift for their own benefits; be it pride, financial, or anything else that takes away from the glory of God. And over a span of time, the false prophets will eventually lead those that they have contact and influence with astray and away from God. In fact, many of these false prophets set up a dependency on themselves rather than directing God's people back to Him. They will give a "word" or sign to get the person to rely on them for "godly" wisdom and directions. Over time the person will continue to seek them out as their source for what God is saying and doing. It's almost like having a welfare mentality. "Feed me your interpretation of God's word, take care of me, but don't make me have to do it for myself. I'll even pay you for it. Don't let me have to develop the discipline myself to study, follow and hear directly from God for myself. It's just too hard!" Wow!

Yes, we have become accustomed to relying on only one aspect in the Word for identifying a true prophet of God. That is, if a man or woman of God is a true prophet of God, their spoken prophecies will come to pass, over time. Yes, the test of time is **one** of the indicators of authenticity. However, here in **Deuteronomy 13** of the Word, we are told we must look **deeper.** Look beyond just the test of time!

People of God, it is so important that you know God's Word for yourself. And that you desire, reach for, and perfect God's gift of hearing Him for yourself! If you cannot tell for yourself, you are at a high risk of being one of God's people that can, and will be easily influenced by the false prophets. As the Word says, these false prophets will lead the people after other gods and eventually cause them to rebel against the very will of God. Therefore it is critical that the Shepherds be watchful over their flocks and who they give access to the "ears" of the sheep.

It is, and can be difficult to tell the difference. However, you can tell. How? Through the gift of Discernment that God has given you. Discern! Discern! Discern! No matter who it is, you still must ask God to confirm it before you take it into your spirit. You are not only to ask God for confirmation, but also Godly wisdom and understanding for what has been spoken to you. Now the time is at hand where we as the people of God are being commanded to take the authority and responsibility for our own spiritual growth in Him and the things of God, especially in the area of the prophetic. **Warrior, grow up and come up in the Kingdom, the Battle is on!**

The next issue in this area is that we watch out for the individuals that have their hands out in the name of the Lord, asking to be paid for what doesn't belong to them in the first place. God's divine word is for His people! Now leaders in God, hear me out. I am in full agreement of God's leaders being blessed by the Most High and His people with the absolute best that God has to offer! My God, you have to deal with us, which can be absolutely amazing and draining at times, and we could never, ever pay you what you are truly worth to the Kingdom. But, for those that are misrepresenting God's word, their Kingdom position and authority and, therefore, misleading God's people, you know who you are. And you better repent and turn because God is going to deal directly with you!

In **Deuteronomy 13:5** it is pretty straight forward on the repercussion awaiting them and some others for such a betrayal of God and His people.

> *"And that prophet, or that dreamer of dreams, shall be put to death; because he hath spoken to turn you away from the LORD your God, which brought you out of the land of Egypt, and redeemed you out of the house of bondage, to thrust thee out of the way which the LORD thy God commanded thee to walk in. So shalt thou put the evil away from the midst of thee."*

People of God, let me take a station break here. One of the main reasons God's people have such a difficult time discerning the voice of the Lord is that they are not sitting still long enough. STOP church hopping! Who and what are you following anyway? If you go farther down in this passage in **Deuteronomy 13**, God asks who are we following, who can cause us to stray? So who are you following now? Are you following God, another man or woman, your mother, father, brother, sister, friend, today's personality of the week, or your flesh? You better know the difference, because God will be checking your heart for the true answer.

If this is you, ask the Lord where your church home and spiritual covering are. He is not a God of confusion or uncertainty. God has a purpose for you to fulfill within a given season in where ever He sets you. You just need to be still, seek God, get your directions, and be obedient to God's will. Yes, people are going to work your nerves and no one is excluded from the "getting on my last nerve" category on some days. Yes, you may even get bored or restless from time to time, especially if you haven't gotten up off your derriere and started working in the ministry. However, if it's time for you to move, God will tell you and CONFIRM for you that your season has shifted. Also, if your spiritual covering is listening to God pertaining to the flock that they have been given charge over, then it will be no surprise to them either. Whatever the case may be, be bold in the name of Jesus and get in your rightful place and stay there until He sends you elsewhere.

Do all things decent and in order. Remember, this is a test and God IS checking your heart and motives in order to prepare you for greater feats for His glory. Additionally, the enemy is watching your actions too. So you must know exactly who you are listening to. Who can lead you away from God's purpose and position for you and, therefore, render you ineffective and powerless for the Lord's Kingdom? And when this happens, who is really getting the glory from your actions? Hmmmm. There is nothing wrong with taking the time to check with God first, and waiting for Him to answer, BEFORE you make a move! When it is God, whatever it is will surely be there when you get there. Nothing is that urgent that you can't seek the Lord first, get an answer, and then move.

So now, here is where it gets interesting and a bit dangerous because remember the prophet *is* also a source of specific divine guidance. Well, here is where discernment comes in for you and them. Is it God or is it a "familiar" spirit, (which will be covered in detail in the next chapter), or is it the devil himself?! Pay attention to your spirit-man and the voice of God. You must stay focused to do this effectively. We don't want to get side tracked here with a teaching about prophets; but, what I do want us to focus on is that even the most elite have been misled, can be misled and are misleading God's people. Many times, these misleadings can send you right into a battle that God never intended for you or those following you to be in the vicinity of, let alone in the midst of it! Therefore, you must be able to discern the difference!

Finally, another key thing to know is that once God has forgiven your transgressions, they are forgotten. That means that no servant of the Lord should be bringing them up to you by stating that it is under the directives of God, unless it is for confirmation you have been seeking from God. Again, we are talking about borderline fruit. God will not reveal the sins of your past to anyone, once they are under the blood of the Lamb. He will not reveal them to any of His ministers by the Word of Knowledge, or by Prophecy, or by any other gift of the Spirit because God has chosen to forget about your forgiven sins. As stated in **Isaiah 43:25:**

> *"I, even I, am the one who wipes out your transgressions for my own sake, and I will not remember your sins."*

This means that if anyone begins to tell you that God has shown them something about your past that is under the blood of the Lamb, something that you have asked God's forgiveness for, then you can be sure that it is not God who is showing them your past unless it is for confirmation you have been seeking from God. Remember earlier I said that your past is like a history book for the enemy. Therefore, there are only a few possible sources for their information, if it is accurate, and all of them generally stem from familiarization. Some examples include gossip in the church, among family, or someone among your friends that has told them about you and some things in your past. This puts them in direct communications with one of the many sources from the enemy's camp. It can be done knowingly or even unknowingly.

Again, child of God, when you are forgiven, the only ones who remember your sins are you, those that were around you when it occurred, the devil and, sometimes, the church as God was delivering you. So, if anyone tries to tell you that God has revealed your sinful past to them, and if you know you have been forgiven for that particular sin, then be assured that they are more than likely not getting their information from the Lord. Get away from them and stay away from them. They are not fully serving the Lord who saves, delivers, heals, forgives, washes away and forgets repented sins. **God chooses not to remember forgiven sin! God forgives and God forgets!**

A true prophet of God is one who communicates or interprets messages from God as He has given them. No additives, no narratives, and with no personal side comments. A true prophet of God is a man or woman authorized by God to speak for God, on His behalf, to His people, just as an ambassador is commissioned to speak on behalf of the nations and he or she does exactly that. God's prophets have a ministry to the common man, that means me and you; and if a prophet taps into your past, it is for confirmation, submission, and then celebration in God!

Their assignment also has a "sent" component to it. Many miss this part. In developing our understanding in this area, we need to go more global in our outlook and discernment of prophets. In **Jeremiah 23** and **Ezekiel 12-14,** both emphasize that false prophets preach peace even though social injustice and immorality are rampant, whereas, true prophets of God seek to correct these situations. The prophet must serve as a contemporary voice of God in his particular generation. As the voice of God, the prophet is sent to point out religious and social sins and call for repentance. God's prophets are sent to confront and counsel "kings" and leaders and, at times, even direct battles.

Clear? I pray so. So, *let's move on* and gain a working knowledge of the enemy, his camp, his army and some other warring strategies and tactics that he wields at us.

The Enemy's Camp: Who is the Enemy and where did they come from anyway?

Before we go any further, we need to have a scripture based, common understanding about who the Enemy is, where he came from, why he is our Adversary and who are his original rank and file. There are two distinct situations mentioned in the Bible pertaining to the origin of the enemy's army of demonic forces. In both situations it is the result of angels choosing to leave their God given positions, thereby forsaking their divine purposes. What was driving them? The driving force was the desire to go in pursuit of their lustful cravings. Wow, the power of making choices outside of the will of God, our Creator! Anyway, at the risk of getting stuck on that topic, let's move on. The first incident can be best understood by looking at two key passages.

One is from the **Book of Isaiah** and the other is from the **Book of Ezekiel**. Let's first start with **Isaiah 14:12-15**.

> *"¹²How art thou fallen from heaven, O Lucifer, son of the morning! how art thou cut down to the ground, which didst weaken the nations! ¹³For thou hast said in thine heart, I will ascend into heaven, I will exalt my throne above the stars of God: I will sit also upon the mount of the congregation, in the sides of the north: ¹⁴I will ascend above the heights of the clouds: I will be like the most High. ¹⁵Yet thou shalt be brought down to hell, to the sides of the pit."*

Now let's also look at the second one, **Ezekiel 28:13-19:**

> *"¹³Thou hast been in Eden the garden of GOD; every precious stone was thy covering, the sardius⁽ʳᵘᵇʸ⁾, topaz, and the diamond, the beryl, the onyx, and the jasper, the sapphire, the emerald, and the carbuncle, and gold: the workmanship of thy tabrets and of thy pipes was prepared in thee in the day that thou wast created. ¹⁴Thou art the anointed cherub that covereth; and I have set thee so: thou wast upon the holy mountain of God; thou hast walked up and down in the midst of the stones of fire. ¹⁵Thou wast perfect in thy ways from the day that thou wast created, till iniquity was found in thee. ¹⁶By the multitude of thy merchandise they have filled the midst of thee with violence, and thou hast sinned: therefore I will cast thee as profane out of the mountain of God: and I will destroy thee, O covering cherub, from the midst of the stones of fire. ¹⁷Thine heart was lifted up because of thy beauty, thou hast corrupted thy wisdom by reason of thy brightness: I will cast thee to the ground, I will lay thee before kings, that they may behold thee. ¹⁸Thou hast defiled thy sanctuaries by the multitude of thine iniquities, by the iniquity of thy traffic; therefore will I bring forth a fire from the midst of thee, it shall devour thee, and I will bring thee to ashes upon the earth in the sight of all them that behold thee. ¹⁹All they that know thee among the people shall be*

astonished at thee: thou shalt be a terror, and never shalt thou be any more."

God created Lucifer for His glory. As our kids say today, Lucifer had it going on. Lucifer **was** beautiful in looks and sound! But he got the "big head" because of the magnificence of God's workmanship in creating him. In their ignorance, as time has gone on and even today, many people are deceived into thinking that Lucifer still has it going on. However, Lucifer deceived himself, and scores of others. He forgot **"Who"** created him and strayed from his original purpose, which was to glorify and serve God in Heaven. Lucifer was not to flip the switch and think that God would glorify and serve him. In **Ezekiel 28:18-19** from the previously mentioned passage, the Word tells us, when the people that have followed the enemy finally see Lucifer in his fallen state, they will be amazed at who and what he really is.

Also, we as the people of God must learn from Lucifer's mistakes! You, too, are created by God to glorify and serve Him on the earth, not visa versa. One more time: God is the Creator, we all are His creation! Lucifer, also known as Satan, the devil, morning star and Adversary, was created by God and is a fallen angel. The Adversary has three distinct traits:

1. he is immortal and therefore cannot die;
2. he is deceitful in his ways; and
3. he is evil in nature.

Lucifer got to be so rebellious in nature and persuasive in his thinking that he was actually able to convince a significant number of the other angels in Heaven to follow him in his foolish campaign to challenge God. Let's look at **Revelation 12:3-4, 7- 9**:

"³And there appeared another wonder in heaven; and behold a great red dragon, having seven heads and ten horns, and seven crowns upon his heads. ⁴And his tail drew the third part of the stars of heaven, and did cast them to the earth: and the

dragon stood before the woman which was ready to be delivered, for to devour her child as soon as it was born."

⁷And there was a great war in heaven: Michael and his angels fought against the dragon; and the dragon fought and his angels, ⁸And prevailed not; neither was their place found any more in heaven. ⁹And the great dragon was cast out, that old serpent, called the Devil, and Satan, which deceiveth the whole world: he was cast out into the earth, and his angels were cast out with him."

Wow to be in the very presence of God and still be so deceived! See how cunning the enemy is and can be? Never underestimate the enemy's power! Because of their blind allegiance to Satan, this group of angels was put out of Heaven and the very presence of God right along with Lucifer. However, always remember that we still have the victory and that there are far more fighting for us than against us! We know from **Revelation 12:4**, if we do the math, that there are at least two thirds more in God's army of angels than the enemy's. Also, we are told in **Hebrews 12:22** that that number can not even be measured!

"But ye are come unto mount Zion, and unto the city of the living God, the heavenly Jerusalem, and to an innumerable company of angels,"

In further developing an understanding of who the Enemy is, let's now look at the second occurrence of disobedience from another group of the heavenly angels. It happens in **Genesis 6,** which also deals directly with the wickedness and judgment of man. In **Genesis 6:1-4**, we are told:

"¹And it came to pass, when men began to multiply on the face of the earth, and daughters were born unto them, ²That the sons of God saw the daughters of men that they were fair; and they took them wives of all which they chose. ³And the LORD said, My spirit shall not always strive with man,

for that he also is flesh: yet his days shall be an hundred and twenty years. ⁴ There were giants in the earth in those days; and also after that, when the sons of God came in unto the daughters of men, and they bare children to them, the same became mighty men which were of old, men of renown."

We, as human beings, find ourselves in quite a predicament when we mingle and partner up with things that are not of God. This is the position that man was in because he had chosen to come under the influence of these angels. This led to cohabitation with this group of rebellious, fallen angels. The name of the leader of this group of angels is Semjaza, as stated in the **Book of Enoch, Chapter 6:3**. The added problem to this union was that these angels not only defiled themselves by uniting with the human women, they also taught man about charms, enchantments, and a host of other ungodly things.

These angels saw the beauty of God's creation in the woman and began to desire what was never created for them. These heavenly beings created offspring with the women. These offsprings, called 'Nephilims', were giants in stature, and were basically an abomination to God. This violation of the realms of creation greatly grieved God, and this act of rebellion brought judgment upon both the fallen angels and man. Our Creator was extremely angry with both the angels and man for their acts. So wroth, as the word says, was our Father that He condemned these angels to hell and flooded the lands destroying all human beings *except for* Noah and his family. They should have known better, and so should have man! For their act of rebellion, those angels that united with Semjaza, along with Semjaza, are locked up in hell until the Great Judgment Day as discussed in **Jude 1:6:**

"And the angels which kept not their first estate, but left their own habitation, he hath reserved in everlasting chains under darkness unto the judgment of the great day."

Further supporting this are the writings contained in the *6ᵗʰ* through *15ᵗʰ Chapters* of *the Book of Enoch*. Going another level in our understanding, when we further exam the origin of demonic spirits, we are told specifically in *Chapter 15:8* of these writings that, *"...giants produced from the spirits and flesh, shall be called evil spirits upon the earth, and on the earth shall be their dwelling."* We are further told the job description of these evil spirits from these unions in **Enoch 15:11**: *"they will afflict, oppress, destroy, attack, do battle, and work destruction on the earth and cause trouble and offenses and will rise up against the children of men and women"*.

This brings us to the next major point in understanding the enemy and his army. The majority of these fallen angels, even today, make up the commanding force behind Lucifer's army in the heavenlies and here on earth. This first group of fallen angels and evil spirits produced from the Nephelims possess the same three traits that Lucifer has that were previously mentioned. Additionally, they all have a devout loyalty to Satan, and willingly and unwittingly follow Lucifer even now in his unsuccessful rebellion against God to take over Heaven and His creations. However, take assurance in knowing that far more angels stayed to loyally serve God than those that were sternly put out!

Saints of the Almighty God, remember this too: just as Lucifer was created by God, so were all of these fallen angels. **Colossians 1:16** confirms this:

"16 For by him were all things created, that are in heaven, and that are in earth, visible and invisible, whether they be thrones, or dominions, or principalities, or powers: all things were created by him and for him: 17 And he is before all things, and by him all things consist."

These spiritual beings were not evil in nature until they rebelled against God, by aligning themselves with the plans of Lucifer and Semjaza. These fallen angels, also known as demons or evil spirits, are usually incorporeal beings. This means they have no body or form of their own.

Also, warrior be aware that within Satan's army, these beings have a distinction of rank and file. This designates the level of power and authority they have over the territories and areas they are assigned to. In other words, they are extremely well organized and capable of fighting this battle and taking over territories that we, as the Children of God, continue to allow them to inhabit. We are getting better at understanding our assignment. Right? **RIGHT!**

Just as all well trained soldiers we, as warriors of Christ, need to maintain a healthy respect for our enemy. Even Michael the archangel, as described in **Jude 9**, who was the head of the God's angels and full of the power and authority of God, did not fight or struggle with Satan under his own authority. Michael let it be known that he was *sent* under the authority of God and he *went* in the name of the Lord! Just as we must do to secure our victories!

Our assurance comes from the understanding that we are covered as Christians, because we are united in faith with Jesus, who sits at the right hand of our Father. Because of our Lord's position, angels, authorities, powers, everybody and everything else are in submission to Him. These forces and beings will not be victorious in their pursuit to overturn God's overall plan **or** overtake us as we are triumphant in this Battle!

The Enemy's Camp: Strategies & Tricks of the Enemy

To this point, we have developed a better understanding of who the enemy is and where they come from. Now let's look closer at who is leading the enemy's camp and who is in it spiritually. We can also be better equipped for the Battle if we know specifically what we are up against. So, now let's better understand, in and by the Word, the enemy's business and his job description. Satan's job description is the exact opposite of our Lord's and that can be seen in **John 10:10** as stated by Jesus:

"The thief cometh not, but for to steal, and to kill, and to destroy: I$^{(Jesus)}$ am come that they might have life, and that they might have it more abundantly."

Also, let's look at **Job 1:7** to see how Satan accomplishes this mission:

"And the LORD said unto Satan, Whence comest thou? Then Satan answered the LORD, and said, From going to and fro in the earth, and from walking up and down in it."

Satan's objective is given in **1 Peter 5:8**:

"Be sober, be vigilant; because your adversary the devil, as a roaring lion, walketh about seeking whom he may devour:"

Satan is called our adversary, which simply means he **is** our enemy. His job, which he has had centuries to master, consists of him walking throughout the earth to see what he can mess up. He is just like an atomic bomb waiting to explode. Get this picture in your mind. When one of these devices goes off, there is mass destruction and nothing is left standing. I am sure you have seen pictures of the huge cloud left behind after the impact of an atomic bomb hitting its target. In fact, you can not even recognize what was there once the smoke clears. That's exactly what the enemy and his alliances want to do to whoever and whatever they target that is coming into alignment with the will and purpose of God.

What our adversary does is very deliberate and intentional. Although at times it may appear to be, nothing is by accident. Walking and seeking are both very deliberate actions. You don't walk without purpose. You definitely do not seek without the intention of finding what you are in search of. This is how the enemy moves, this is how they focus in, and this is how they attack: deliberately and intentionally.

Upon getting to, or finding out what Satan has planned for his area of attack, his whole intention is to devour it. Devour means to eat greedily or ravenously. Have you ever seen a starving animal, especially a big dog, get his first meal in who knows how long? It's not a pretty picture! Devour also means to prey upon. Prey as an action verb means to attack or to stalk another as a target. To be "prey" means to be helpless or unable to resist or constrain the attack of another. To be "prey" literally means to be a victim.

When we are preyed upon by the enemy, the act is always violent and devastating. As the fight for life ensues, at the end of the Battle though we survive there are always scars. God never intended for us to be victims. We have been called to the military of the most High! We are not victims. We are overcomers that have been created to persevere even the most fierce, intense encounters.

Look Child of God: most of us allow ourselves to become prey because we have not **prayed**! Just as passionate and excited as we are in our pursuit of God and His plans for our lives, our adversary is equally, and in some cases even more passionate to see to it that anything that is God-related does **NOT** succeed or come to pass. So we must seek God on a daily and continuous basis to make certain that we are in alignment with His strategy for that very day and moment in time.

I often tell others that I mentor and counsel when the attacks are on to realize that Satan and his imps are only doing their job. Once we really understand their role, then we will never be surprised when attacks occur. We may not always fully understand why it happened, but we will not be surprised that it did!

The purpose of a battle is for one side or the other to win. If we really think about it, wouldn't we, as effective warriors, be doing his job with the same intensity in order to secure the victory. In fact, some of us would actually be doing even more severe damage to one another if we choose to fight on the side of the enemy. Be honest with yourself! Right? Yes, I know I'm right. Though we may not want to admit it, we would be more vengeful and violent than Satan himself.

Ah, yes but the Lord has hold of you now and it is the love of God holding you back and constraining you from your old nature and ways. Saints, though we lose sight of it from time to time, we are suppose to be just as intense in serving in the Kingdom as the enemy is in doing his job. But are you? Check yourself and make the appropriate adjustments, warrior!

Satan has been at this a very long time. Yes, he has mastered many strategies that can lead to our destruction, if that is what we choose. But why would anyone choose their own destruction? Hmmmm! Never forget the promises of God that are written throughout the Word and have been demonstrated throughout time to keep you! Know that Jesus has already taken, and proclaimed, the victory for you to lead a life filled and overflowing with Kingdom benefits.

Jesus tells us in **John 10:10** that we are to live an abundant life. Abundant means being marked by great affluence, wealth, and with ample supply. On the upside though, being marked means God has targeted and empowered you to live your life to its fullest original purpose. Your part in this is that you must boldly access God's instructions, submit yourself to His will and Word, and live your life obedient to His commandments. In other words, you too have to deliberately, intentionally and passionately fight in this Battle, in order to possess, maintain and claim the promised victory!

Being marked also means the enemy is aware of who you are. They know that when you get the full understanding of what you are capable of doing in the Kingdom of God, you will be a force to be reckoned with. You are capable of making significant impact in this world and doing major damage to the enemy's territory. Some of us may at times feel like the Lord doesn't know what Satan is up to or see what he is doing to us. However, know that the Lord's eye is always on the activities of Satan, all his imps and especially you. You may also be wondering why doesn't or hasn't God just destroyed him. I don't know, but I suspect it is because their time is not up yet.

Also, check this out Child of God: whether you realize it or not, or want to admit it, because I am sure the devil doesn't want to acknowledge it, his activities many times are the very reasons and circumstances that propel us more towards Christ and into alignment with God's purpose for us. As we are told by Apostle Paul in **Romans 8:28,**

> *"And we know all things work together for good to them that love God, to them who are called according to his purpose."*

Yes, even today, Satan and his followers' activities include opposing the will and work of God, counterfeiting the work of God, and by any means necessary, destroying all that is good. Why? Because all things work together for the good of those that love the Lord and have a predestined purpose to fulfill. And yes, this includes and means you!

Holding Your Position in Battle

Now you may be wondering how we can be certain what this Battle will look like in the end. To strengthen your faith in the matter of knowing that the victory is ours, let's look again at **Revelation 12:7-9** where the Word of God tells us what is to come:

> *"⁷ And there was war in heaven: Michael and his angels fought against the dragon; and the dragon fought and his angels, ⁸ And prevailed not; neither was their place found any more in heaven. ⁹ And the great dragon was cast out, that old serpent, called the Devil, and Satan, which deceiveth the whole world: he was cast out into the earth, and his angels were cast out with him."*

The enemy and his army are already defeated foes and opponents. However, this does not mean that the battle is still not raging on for us to get to the victorious state that we know is ours. What this does tell us though, is that we are to stay encouraged and be even more confident in how we fight this battle in pursuit of our corporate and individual victories. We should not be fighting as warriors that do not know the outcome, or like we only stand a 50/50 chance to win, or questioning the purpose or cause of the fight.

Look, this battle has already been won! The devil is not a negative God equal in power, he is **a fallen angel challenging his Creator**! Remember, it's not a fair fight because God has stacked the deck in your favor. God has already given you the victory in whatever you are doing or will go through. You shall be triumphant! Now this is a good place, and time, to give God a shout of PRAISE! Hallelujah! Now grab hold to the promises of the Lord and hold your position, soldier!

CHAPTER 6

Recognizing the Enemy Today: Reload & Focus Again!

Now, let's look at where the "man" power comes from to support the other side of the battle. Remember, a portion of the angels in Heaven followed Satan in his revolt against God and, because of their behavior; they were all evicted from God's heaven! This is the **same** bold uprising led by Lucifer in Heaven. Some of these fallen angels were put into bondage until Judgment Day as stated in **Jude 6**:

> *"And the angels which kept not their first estate, but left their own habitation, he hath reserved in everlasting chains under darkness unto the judgment of the great day."*

The others, well, they are the ones we have to contend with in our daily lives. The key thing to always remember when operating in this area of God is that this Battle is spiritual. It is not natural and it must be first fought and won in the Spirit realm before it can be successfully won in the natural or physical realm. Simply put: we win victories in the Battle in the Spirit Realm first through prayer and at times, prayer and fasting.

Look at what the Apostle Paul tells us about how we are to contend with the enemy and conduct spiritual warfare in **2 Corinthians 10:3-5**:

"³For though we walk in the flesh, we do not war after the flesh: ⁴(For the weapons of our warfare are not carnal, but mighty through God to the pulling down of strongholds;) ⁵Casting down imaginations and every high thing that exalteth itself against the knowledge of God, and bringing into captivity every thought to the obedience of Christ;"

Again, we are back to our main subject of hearing God in Battle, which is **both** a physical and spiritual discipline. We are to first recognize, believe and operate in a Godly manner, as we pursue the promised victory. This all begins in the Spirit realm. All conversations and varying viewpoints of men that do not exalt Jesus Christ as our Lord and that contradict the will of God, must be rebuked in the name of Jesus and destroyed in the Spirit realm, first. Then and only then, do we respond and take action in the natural.

Many of us react in the natural first. Wrong approach, warrior! This is exactly like our military forces rushing into the enemy's territory without checking in with their commanding officers first. They are ill-equipped because they don't know the overall strategy. This includes the territorial "safe" entry points, other supporting or challenging alliances, or worse yet, the divine timing and appropriate level of authority that they need to go forth. Therefore, they have entered into the Battle illegally! Fighting this way will assuredly result in some major losses and casualties! Continuing to do this will eventually result in death.

We win when we are able to, out of obedience to Christ; fight the Battle with the spiritual wisdom given to us by God. Again, fight the Battle and secure the victory in the Spirit realm **FIRST!** Get your Battle Plan. This is where God makes known the real cause of an issue, the true reason for the fight, the actual root of the battle and the most dynamic, operative way and timing for you to proceed. How do you access this Battle Plan? With prayer and a diligent heart inclined to hear the Spirit of the Lord's battle instructions by using the **B.A.S.I.C.S.** Here you will also be given the instructions you need to claim the victory in the natural. Step by step, in its due season.

Now, let's look into the enemy's territory and get some accuracy in our arsenal about the enemy, some of his staff members and their methods and tactics.

Who's in the Enemy's Army Today?

In this section, we will briefly look at some of the key players and devices that are in and utilized by the enemy's army: Familiar Spirits, Divination, Witchcraft, Sorcery, False Prophets and their relationship to demonic spirits and tactics.

Familiar Spirits

The term "familiar" is used to describe the alleged spirit of a deceased person or a spirit that is assigned to and therefore, belongs with a particular family from the perspective of the enemy's camp. Since this type of spirit is assigned to a particular family, this spirit is on intimate terms with the deceased person, and consequently it knows things about that person, their life, personality, events and surroundings. The bottom line is "a familiar spirit" is a supernatural being that knows specific, intimate and personal details about a particular person, place or thing.

Are they demonic in nature? Absolutely! How can you tell? Because they are not for God, they do not confess Christ as Lord, they are from the fallen angels, and eventually contact with them will bring confusion, chaos and destruction. Remember to use discernment at all times. There is no lukewarm area in this place of warfare. Every time, in time, the true nature of a thing will be revealed.

So do not get rattled here! We all have familiar spirits around us. They are spirits who are familiar with us. The ones that are familiar with me may not necessarily be familiar with you. But Lord oh Lord, they do get together and exchange information! They become familiar with you the same way you become familiar with someone. That is their primary assignment, to get to know you, what makes you tick, and what ticks you off. Their first objective is to challenge your faith in order to try to make you doubt the validity of God's Word, His existence and His promises to you for your life and the life of others. To accomplish this, they hang around and gather information that they can pass around among one another. Why? They do this with the primary goal in mind of separating you from God, and thereby hindering you from achieving your ultimate purpose in the earth.

Here's a simplistic example of how familiar spirits operate. You have been waiting for what seems to you a very long time for one of God's promises to manifest. Remember, there is a familiar spirit already assigned to you, and it also has many friends in both the spirit *and* natural realms. Now picture this: a conversation between you and someone else pertaining to that promise that God has made brings up the length of time you have been waiting. The friend innocently asks you are you sure it's going to come to pass. Hmm, if you are not on guard or steadfast you may inadvertently pause too long and in comes the question in your mind that could lead to doubt for a fleeting moment. Just for a second. You quickly recoup. But that was all the enemy needed to see. From that innocent reaction or conversation involving you or others about you, the "YOU" news flash in the spirit realm between spirits begins. This response then becomes information that is passed on to others both in the natural and supernatural realms. From this you will be challenged again on the same issue, until it is no longer an issue that can be used against you as a distraction or diversion. And all this trouble was initiated by the familiar spirit that was ease dropping on your conversation.

Now let's go another step because that is just the beginning. If you are not swift enough, as soon as a doubtful spirit finds that opening with you, either through your conversations or actions, he will begin to set up his camp around you. Setting up camp for a doubtful spirit sends out an invitation to a spirit of despair to also come join the party, which is on its way to gradually turning into a full blown battle in your mind! Then the two of them will start to build a fortified stronghold in your house. Once they finish building the foundation for a stronghold against you, they then send out an invitation to their friend, doom. Following fast on the heels of the spirit of doom will be the spirit of depression. All of these spirits in turn will act as though they have the right to take up residence in your house and around you. Before you know it, you are totally bound up, and an unwanted, but very necessary battle must be forged to reclaim your freedom. Again, all because of what a familiar spirit witnessed.

Can you recognize this as one of the enemy's strategy to bind you up? Most of us have been there. Let's look at one more example of the dangers of doubt from another perspective. As soon as you begin to doubt the truthfulness of God's Word, **despair** and **doom** are guaranteed to be on their way just as in the previous example. However, this time the potential fall out once they show up can also be a loss of hope. This in turn, can lead right into a state of depression that's gives a direct passageway to a state of hopelessness. It happens with such subtlety and cunningness, that you won't even realize it until it is upon you and all over your house. Before you know it, your joy is completely gone and the next thing you know, you are all tangled up in spiritual bondage not even realizing why you feel so "blah"! That is why it is so important to be faithful in maintaining your Spiritual Equilibrium and consistent in sharpening your discernment. A prayer partner is also helpful when you need help getting untangled. Whatever the case, as soon as you recognize the position you are in, immediately use the Sword of Truth to redeem your proper station in the Kingdom.

Listen to me carefully now because the point not to miss here is that **spirits do not die**! Yes, people die. But the spirits who operated in their lives will continue to try to influence the lives of the people that these individuals were around. This type of activity will continue until these spirits are overcome, evicted and defeated by the Word of God. There are some are common spirits that willingly team up with the familiar spirits around you. They can be found almost every place. Some of the more common ones are the spirits of fear, doubt, unforgiveness, selfishness and anger. There are also other types of spirits that can be territorial, such as poverty, famine, alcoholism, homosexuality and murder. Any one of these types of spirits can also be generational. They too can join forces with the familiar spirits around you and make your life absolutely miserable.

Remember, these spirits have one purpose and that is to defeat and destroy you in order to wipe out God's purpose for your life and those around you! They are determined to keep you down; trample all over you; make you feel inadequate, helpless, unworthy and inferior. They bring sickness, unhappiness, disaster, and every other evil thing that you can imagine, and some you have not.

Get the point? Now that you know why some things are occurring around you, aren't you tired of these spirits? This is why discernment is so critical. In order to fight effectively, you must be and stay closely aligned with our Father and the Word. Only by His Holy Spirit, will you be able to get to the root cause of any spiritual Battle you will face. The victory can not be fully claimed until you have identified the main demonic spirits in operation. These types of spirits are also known as strongholds and are invited in by the familiar spirits around you. Once you know who they are, you must evict them out of all the areas in your life where they have taken up residence, and then close the doors that they were permitted to gain territory in. The Lord is faithful and will lead you through this process. You only need to remember that the victory is already yours!

Some of them run in and out of the lives of God's people like they have a key to the front door. This open invitation can be thought of as a snowball effect. It usually starts by something as small as an unrepented initial thought contrary to one of God's promises. You need to stop and ask yourself: "Do unwanted things, people and situations like these come and go on in my life as they please?" **James 1:6-7** warns us about letting the spirit of doubt creep in.

> *"But let him ask in faith, with no doubting, for he who doubts is like a wave of the sea driven and tossed by the wind. For let not that man suppose that he will receive anything from the Lord; [8]he is a double-minded man, unstable in all his ways."*

Another word of caution: don't forget **doubt's** friend **unbelief**. These two together kept the Children of Israel wandering around in the wilderness for 40 years. When you find yourself operating in doubt, remember and meditate on **2 Corinthians 1:20**, which basically says **ALL** of God's promises are Yea and Amen.

"For all promises of God in Him are Yes, and in Him Amen, to the glory of God through us."

Our responsibility as His children is that we must know what His promises are. In others words, we must study His Word! Yes, there are times when it will be necessary for you to encourage yourself, by yourself, during the battle! Sometimes you have been set in the midst of the Battle to be the "example" that others can follow. Whether you think so or not - it is not really up to you. So, yes there will be times that you will need to go the road alone as a forerunner. Therefore, everyone should not be allowed in your house, or permitted to get close or too familiar with the people and things that are intimate and dear to you! You are responsible for protecting what God has placed under your watch and in your hands.

Always remember, spirits attract like spirits. They live wherever they are welcome or tolerated. If you allow them to flock around you, they will eventually influence you. Pay attention here, because this also applies to the people you hang around or allow to hang around you. The people you choose to associate with can make destiny-changing differences in your life and in your well being. How? Because the spirits operating in their lives will try to operate in yours!

Again, how do you evict these spirits and minimize their effects in your life? You must allow the Holy Spirit to lead you through this process. Familiar spirits will always be around you, just like they are around me and every other person on this earth, whether they believe and accept it or not. But by the authority that Jesus has given us, we are anointed and empowered to render them powerless!

This is also why it is so important to break away from certain people and situations when God tells you to! Many times, we choose our destiny by the people with whom we choose to associate. You must be mindful that bad company does corrupt good morals and the best of intentions are not always the righteous ones. It is vital that you understand this basic Spiritual Principle. If you associate with those who dabble in the things that God has told you to part with, or better still, not to be associated with at all, the spirits operating in these things and in the lives of those around you, will drag you down to their messy levels.

This reminds me of a commercial about a phone service that was out a couple of years ago. Their key motto was, "... and you tell two friends about us, and they will tell two friends, and they will tell two friends..." to get the word out. The impact of spreading the message this way is exponential; you cannot even calculate how fast the number of people, and in this case the number of spirits too that are picking up "news" about you and your activities over the air waves. You must watch over your heart with all diligence. You must put a guard on your mind, on your mouth, on your actions and yes, on your relationships and associations. You can really jack up your surroundings and destiny by selecting screwy companions.

So let me leave this section with one more word of wisdom for you to consider: to get rid of these spiritual deposits that decide to take up residence with you is no small task. Let's look at **Matthew 12:43-45:**

> *"43 When the unclean spirit is gone out of a man, he walketh through dry places, seeking rest, and findeth none. 44 Then he saith, I will return into my house from whence I came out; and when he is come, he findeth it empty, swept, and garnished. 45 Then goeth he, and taketh with himself seven other spirits more wicked than himself, and they enter in and dwell there: and the last state of that man is worse than the first. Even so shall it be also unto this wicked generation."*

This passage describes the enemy's reaction to evicting any one of his soldiers from what they have come to think is their rightful territory. This passage is speaking to God's process of Deliverance. Deliverance is a rough process, going through it is intense, and maintaining your freedom from these areas requires diligence. The enemy knows this and will fight viciously and continuously with his companions to try to wear you down in these areas where you are battling to be free. This will continue until he is convinced that it is a dead issue with you. How? Through familiar spirits and their acquaintances! Watchman, watch! Now, on to the next area of the Battlefield!

Divination

Now, let's go a little deeper in our understanding. Fraternizing and communicating with Familiar Spirits can also be referred to as using a spirit of divination. This includes those appearing to be of God **and** those that stress that they are NOT. Divination is the art or practice that seeks to foresee or foretell future events in order to discover hidden knowledge usually by the interpretation of omens or by the aid of supernatural powers. Originally divination meant the ritual hole or pit dug in the ground to give underworld spirits access to the practitioner for short periods of time. Later, the term was applied to the spirits who came up out of the hole, and also to the necromancer, which is one who calls up spirits to try and reveal the future, or one who speaks to the dead.

How does this work? Well, let's get a better understanding so that the enemy can't use this distraction on you again! A good example is in **1 Samuel 28,** when Saul sought counsel of a witch to try and contact the prophet Samuel, who was dead. The Witch of Endor, who was the mistress of a familiar spirit, expected to call up the spirit she was familiar with, known as a "control spirit". This control spirit is the natural being's contact into the supernatural realm. "Control Spirit" is an interesting term because it makes me wonder who's really in control here! Are they demonic in nature too? Absolutely! When Samuel appeared instead of her familiar control spirit, the witch was surprised and frightened, and it was only then that she recognized Saul as the king. Even she had enough sense to know she was out of her league when it came to God's people and His business with them.

To further grasp the seriousness of stepping into this area, let's look at an example of the consequences a person can reap by going to the Word. Let's look at **I Chronicles 10:13**:

> *"So Saul died for his transgression which he committed against the LORD, even against the word of the LORD,*

which he kept not, and also for asking counsel of one that had a familiar spirit, to enquire of it;"

Pay attention to the fact that this passage lists Saul's visit to the witch, the one who was in relationship with a familiar spirit, as one of the main reasons why King Saul was destroyed. Always remember that the punishment for breaking or ignoring God's laws can be far greater than you ever imagined. Thank God for His Grace towards us! On to the next area of the Battlefield!

Soothsayers, Necromancers, Mediums, Psychics

These "people" also operate by the use of familiar and demonic spirits. The key point here is that it is impossible for a Spiritualist, or a Medium, or a Necromancer, or even for a Prophet of the Lord, to speak to the dead. Those who try to deceive and act as if they can speak to the dead, speak to, and get their information from, spirits who are familiar with a particular person or a situation. Yes, it's a familiar spirit again. Busy little creatures, aren't they?

Remember a spirit that is familiar with you and has knowledge about you generally operates with a group of spirits that share and communicate this knowledge to those whom they serve. They're listening for historical, present, as well as any future information as it is spoken. We are not the only ones listening for what the Lord is speaking in to the earth. Therefore, don't be too quick to dismiss these contemporary soothsayers as fakes. Sometimes mediums, witches, conjurers, wizards, and some fortune tellers that have been dismissed as phony really work with familiar spirits, or control spirits, and can say with some accuracy what is going on with you.

You need to understand that in the Spirit World, your life is just like a history book. So do not be surprised if someone reads a chapter or two in your book and tells you some things that they have no natural way of knowing. So now that you know this, you should realize that everyone who has some supernatural knowledge about you is not always of God.

Also, when you take the time to examine the Word, you understand that no one can call up, or speak to, a deceased person or to their spirit. If one of these creatures shows up to visit you as your deceased Mom, Dad, great grandmother or who ever, tell them to go away. You don't have to rant and rave, and you definitely should not be afraid. Simply plead the Blood of Jesus over yourself, your family, and your living area and then tell them to go away. Most importantly be firm about it and use the Word of God. Sometimes it will take more than once because they want to know whether or not you really meant it. You must really mean it and know that no matter how harmless they seem, they are not your friends! Remember, things in this area are never as they appear to be.

Study the Word and maintain your Spiritual Equilibrium. We are told in **2 Corinthians 5:8** that while we are here, we are in our earthly bodies and physically away from the Lord. But once we die, we leave these bodies to become present with the Lord if we have been saved. If someone has not been saved, we as Christians know that Hell is the eternal alternative. In addition to **Genesis 3:19** and **Job 34:15, Ecclesiastes 12:7** says, *"Then the dust will return to the earth as it was, and the spirit will return to God who gave it."*

Again, know that when you die there are only two places for eternal residency: Heaven or Hell. Heaven, if you have accepted Christ as your Lord and Savior or Hell, if you have not. Only two options! **You choose by the choices you make in your life here on earth.** When your body goes to the grave, your spirit, the real you in you, goes to be with the Lord OR goes to the place of torment with the devil. The real you is your inner man, and the real you in you is going to live forever, if you are saved. You know Eternal life, right? Right! That is why Jesus came to redeem and reunite us with our Father; and this is why we **choose** to serve Him. Remember, a part of your inheritance is to live forever with the Lord in Eternity.

Which brings me back to the main point of this section: when you go to be with the Lord, no one can call your spirit or anyone else's spirit back and forth like some errand person. You will be rejoicing in the presence of the Lion of Judah or burning in the place of torment with the devil and his crew. You will not be running back and forth delivering messages or predictions to those that you left behind. Got it? Good. Now that we've dealt with the dead, let's look at some more of the living vessels in the enemy's camp.

Witchcraft

Witchcraft is a more subtle tool of the enemy and is another form of divination. Those that practice witchcraft as a lifestyle are known as witches. A witch is known as a Wicca (male) or Wicce (female). These are those who are credited with unusual malignant supernatural powers or black witchcraft often with the aid of the devil, a demon or familiar spirit. Are they real? Absolutely!

A warlock is another player in this category but at a much "higher" level in the ranks of Satan. He is one that breaks faith, clearly denounces God, and confesses Satan as his lord. He is a man practicing the black arts. Know that neither a witch nor a warlock will ever truly confess Christ. Christ is clearly not the head of their lives! If Jesus were their Lord, they would not be operating in this realm and calling themselves a name that our Father has such disdain for. Until they have received full deliverance by our Lord Jesus Christ out of this realm of the enemy's camp and confess Jesus as their Lord and Savior, they are our enemy.

Witchcraft involves the use of magic. Magic is the use of means believed to have supernatural power over natural forces that can result in giving one the feeling of being strongly influenced, compelled or attracted to a particular person, thing or situation. Magic, which is the key component of witchcraft, involves the use of spells and charms. Spells being a spoken word or form of words believed to have supernatural power, and charms being something worn or kept for its supposed magical power over a particular situation, person or thing.

We know, as soldiers in the army of God, and have been taught that our words have the power to give life to people and circumstances. Especially in **Proverbs 18:21**, where we are told that *"death and life are in the power of the tongue"*. Said another way, the spoken word has the power to do whatever we say, with an absolute guarantee behind it when it is believed and in alignment with the Will and Word of God. We take this for granted way too often. However, the enemy is well aware of this principle and wields it every chance they get as a mighty weapon of entrapment. Spells and incantations are absolutely perfect examples of this principle in action. Both are tools used in witchcraft.

Additionally we, as the people of God, must be careful in this area because even the smallest, most innocent encounter with "magic" can be both harmful and life changing. Dabbling in this area is a definite form of witchcraft and it can often open many unwanted spiritual doors that can take the person years to close! Pay attention the next time you are in the situation where an "illusion" is being presented. You will notice that the "magic" and its illusion will generally grab the attention of the majority of the group, but there will always be one or two that are especially drawn to it. It is usually the more intelligent ones in the group that think they can master the "trick" or figure it out even after others have lost interest. This is a screening process taking place right before our very eyes, and it is being done as early as possible to identify and tap "thinkers" and "leaders". Also included are games that challenge the youth to figure out war like scenarios like Dungeons & Dragons.

We have to get over the misconception that all the enemy's army is a bunch of mindless, slothful, horned monsters. Some of the most intelligent people on this planet are in major rankings in the enemy's army and hold powerful positions in the earth in government, businesses and the communities. Therefore we as parents and mentors over our youth have to be firm and guarded in who and what we allow to have access to our children. If our children are behaving rebelliously, we must check out their associates, games, activities, toys and TV programs they are watching. I promise you, if nothing else unusual is going on in the family, you will find your answer in one or more of these places. Then you must take appropriate action to change it, remove it, and when necessary as lead by the Spirit of God, destroy it! Believe me the effort and tough decisions upfront will save our children years of turmoil and future processing to get free. Be prayerful in all things no matter what they look like because with witchcraft and magic, things are usually never what they appear to be on the surface!

Be mindful that the key strategic technique here is deception and it functions on the foundation of presenting an illusion or distorted picture of the truth. Doing this sets up and creates trickery within the mind - challenging one's judgment on what is known to be true as a reality based on prior knowledge and experience versus what is not true or skewed facts based on what is being presented before one's eyes and into one's thoughts. The mystery of it all is why we as human beings are so drawn to this area and fascinated by it. Also, keep in mind that witchcraft is directly related to Divination, and therefore so is magic. Be prayerful in all things!

Another component of witchcraft itself is the communication with the devil, demonic, and familiar spirits in order to accomplish what it is purposing to do. Witchcraft's overall effect can be an irresistible draw, fascination or enchantment with something or someone that can harm you, and most definitely distract you from your assignment. Please don't minimize or dismiss this point because this "pull" can be so strong that it can lead to outright rebellion to specific instructions that God has given us. From this position the door to your heart and mind become wide open invitations for all Hell to break loose in your life!

Another major misconception that the world would have you believe, is that there is a difference between a white witch and a black witch, a good witch and a bad witch. Child of God, this is just another trick of the enemy. Just like a rose is a rose no matter what other name you may call it or what color it is, a witch is a witch is a witch! Let's look again at **Deuteronomy 18:9-14**:

> *"9When thou art come into the land which the LORD thy God giveth thee, thou shalt not learn to do after the abominations of those nations. 10There shall not be found among you any one that maketh his son or his daughter to pass through the fire, or that useth <u>divination,</u> or an <u>observer of times,</u> or an <u>enchanter,</u> or a <u>witch,</u> 11Or a charmer, or a consulter with <u>familiar spirits,</u> or a <u>wizard,</u> or a <u>necromancer.</u> 12For all that do <u>these things are an abomination unto the LORD</u>: and because of these abominations the LORD thy God doth drive them out from before thee. 13Thou shalt be perfect with the LORD thy God. 14Thou shalt possess, hearkened unto observers of times, and unto diviners: but as for thee, the LORD thy God hath not suffered thee so to do."*

God tells us here that all of these things are abominations to Him. Abominations are detestable things. God disdains them. What's "them'? First, horror scopes, I mean reading a horoscopes and reciting a zodiac sign. In addition to the fact that God hates it, as a child of God, why would you minimize who you are by calling yourself something God never said you are and that is less than human? Are they accurate? They certainly can be to a degree. How? This occurs because they are communicating with old demonic spirits. *Yes, it is that deep!* However it is not that complicated once you know the truth about what is really going on.

Next, any and all people that say they talk to "dead people"; any superstitious practices, like salt sprinkling; all forms of divination, like tarot cards, Ouija Boards, séances; magic of any kind, "black" or "white"; and any other kinds of ritual or gestures that involve sacrificing your children in *any way.* There should no longer be any confusion in this area for you. If I missed something here and you need further clarification, ask the Lord to give you the revelation on it, one area at a time.

We look at many of these areas as harmless. Many of us say, "It's not that deep!" But it is that deep. Any one of these abominations can open extremely dangerous doors and areas of exposure in your life! God's desire to restrict us from these things is not because He doesn't want us to know or have any fun, but because He wants to tell us the right paths to take, give us the righteous answers to our situations and, most of all, protect us from harm and the wiles and schemes of the enemy. His desire is for us to be victorious in all areas of our lives.

Just as we as parents tell our children don't touch a hot stove or play in the street. The dangers seem obvious, but just like our children, we have a tendency to dismiss the seriousness of the potential consequences that could result from involving ourselves in these matters. God is a God of love and would never harm us. He gives us this clarity because He loves us and we, each one of us, is precious to Him. Always remember that, Child of God. Now, let's go a little further!

Sorcery

Sorcery is another area of witchcraft yet can be more powerful in its influence and impact on your life. It is the use of power gained from the assistance or control of evil spirits, especially for divination. It especially includes necromancy, which remember is a person who practices sorcery, and involves "speaking to the dead." Those that operate in these areas are called sorcerers or sorceresses. A sorcerer is like a witch or conjurer, who practices illusions and summons spirits and demonic influences forth by incantations. Also, a sorceress is like a warlock and she functions as a charming and alluring girl or woman. Her motive is to influence and beguile.

My God! Do you recognize this stuff in most of the television and cable programs that are on TV? How powerful these vessels are! Also, pay attention to how hungry the world is for this type of power. The world entertains itself with this form of ungodly activity in attempts to find their purpose and answers for their lives and to their situations. This is also a direct indicator of the times we are now living in.

You need to ask yourself if you are addicted to chaos. Why? For the very simple reason that if you dabble in any of these things, you will be. That is exactly what these things and these people will bring you, the spirits of chaos, confusion and destruction! Now that you know what and who they are, you can safeguard yourself from them. Saints of God, you must take authority over these spirits and things in your life and in your household, and put them OUT!

Another key to remember is that the spirits that control or rule in your life will frequently control your children. Too many times, the manifestations of these spirits in the second generation are much worse than in the first, and so on! Along with the good traits, this also includes bad things like substance abuse, physical violence and even laziness. Praise God for the positive, and take charge in order to break the generational curses. Take full control. Use the authority that God has given you to rid your household and family of these influences and stay free in this area. It's hard, steady work but well worth the efforts.

Always remember that all of the entities discussed in this chapter are missing the FULL truth! Each and every one of them will reveal what they truly are, if you make sure that you are continuously being lead by the Spirit of God and are staying in the Word of God for yourself. Wow, that's a lot to take in, but remember this is a Battle. And we are building up our arsenal, so let's move on!

CHAPTER 7

Overcoming the Attacks of the Enemy: Staying Focused

So, how do you overcome all of these spirits, people, situations, and their potentially destructive tactics? By recognizing that the Lord really does have **all** of the power and authority needed to do whatever it takes for you to be victorious for His glory and the Kingdom. By recognizing that God is fully in control and submitting yourself totally to His will. By doing so, you will gain the authority and power you need to overcome and prevail. Begin to yield more and more to the Lord's leading and influence. This will build your confidence in Him, as you strengthen your relationship with Him.

People of God, now is the time that we must make a choice - either you believe the written Word of God from **Genesis 1:1** to **Revelation 22:21** and everything in between, in its entirety, or you don't. Partial belief is just like total unbelief, and living this way will eventually cancel out the promises of God in and over your life! And if the truth really be told: if you are a partial believer, you are really a nonbeliever! You need to repent and start anew by studying the Word of God so that you know the Word for yourself. Come out of those areas of doubt, wavering faith and mixed belief! This is the biggest trip up we, as Christians, have. The enemy knows the Word of God better than most of the followers of Christ and our enemies know that it is true! Therefore, we continuously give them the upper hand by not knowing our rightful positioning and authority in the Kingdom.

A principle to remember is that all warfare begins with the art of deception. The deception can begin with a very simple, seemingly innocent challenge to what you believe and know about a situation or person in any area of your life. I say "art", because it is generally done very skillfully and with extreme craftiness, like a "slight of hand" trick. This is why it is so critical that we stay grounded in God's Word. Even though **none** of us, despite what we may think, have it **all** figured out yet pertaining to the mind and workings of God. God has revealed enough of Himself to us for us to know that He is who He says He is. And that our Lord Jesus Christ, as His son, is our Redeemer and Savior as stated in **John 14:6**:

> *"Jesus saith unto him, I am the way, the truth and the life: no man cometh unto the Father, but by me."*

Following are some other things to keep in mind. First, know that the enemy does not have unlimited authority; he can not be in more than one place at a time; he does not know everything that is going on or that will happen; and finally, he can not create, he can only imitate. Just as our Father told Moses in **Exodus 3:14**, *"..I am that I am:"*. God alone possesses the following traits because our Father God is:

- Omnipotent, which means having unlimited authority.
- Omnipresent, which means being present in all places at all times.
- Omniscient, which means having infinite awareness, understanding, and insight.
- Omnificent, which means unlimited in creative power.

Yes, God is all that and then some! Second, remember that Satan and every other spirit is subject to the name of Jesus, and **every** knee shall bow. Third, the Bible clearly teaches that the devil cannot read your mind, nor does he know your future, so do not be intimidated by attempts to control your thoughts and actions. **1 Corinthians 2:11** tells us:

"For who among men knows the thoughts of a man except the spirit of the man which is in him."

Another good example to look at is this: The enemy did not know Jesus' future. If he had known the victorious significance of Jesus going to the cross, and the power that would come from the shedding of the Lord's blood, Satan would have done everything within his power to prevent our Savior from ever making it to the Cross.

The same thing holds true with your divine destiny. The enemy and his imps are not on attack because of anything you have already done or are currently doing. They are hitting you hard because of where you ARE going and the powerful impact that its fulfillment will have on the Kingdom of God. Again, neither the enemy nor anyone else can read your mind - they only know what you allow to come out of, or from you. They do not know everything - they only know what you have done and are currently doing. They do not have all power - they can only attempt to control you if you allow it. They cannot be in two places at the same time. The only things that they are capable of creating are hard times and tough situations. Satan is limited in time, knowledge, ability and space.

Now, don't get cocky though, because even though the devil does not know your future, he does know some things. He knows the tricks and the schemes he is going to try to pull on you in the future. He may even know the people and the circumstances that he is going to use to try to defeat you. But he does not know how you are going to react to the temptations he is designing especially for you!

The only thing that the devil knows about you for sure is your history. He knows what you say. He can see the way you act. Your life style tells him everything he needs to know about you and how to come after you for destruction, but he cannot read your mind! Only you and the Spirit of God that resides in you know your thoughts. Additionally, even though you may surprise yourself sometimes, God is never surprised!

So now, when utilizing the gift of discerning spirits God has given you, be sure to always recognize the Source for your escape and victory! Be yielded to God's Spirit and His voice in all things. Most of us are afraid of what we will have to endure when we step out on doing the things we have heard spoken to our spirit for God and the Kingdom. Get over it, and move on! The thought of the battles to come to get to the places that God has for us can overwhelm anyone. Even John the Baptist asked from prison **if** Jesus, the one he was following and devoted to, was really the One.

Some even say, "You know I don't even know if it's worth the tribulations." It **is** worth it! The closer you walk in what He has assigned you to do, the more of this "stuff" you have to deal with. As you go through more, the more you will be able to handle. From this, you will become stronger and more skillful in how to go through and fight the Battle victoriously. Eventually, this "stuff" will roll off of you and won't even break your stride or focus. Why? Because each time with each new trial, you grow and mature a little more spiritually and develop tougher Battle fatigues that will allow you to successfully handle life's situations and spiritual warfare. So, remember to listen for the "Amen" in your spirit. This Amen is an automatic, uncontrolled response when something is said or done that agrees with your spirit.

Never, ever forget that God is in control of **all** things. You better recognize and represent the King you serve. You overcome by submitting to God. How do you submit to God? You submit to God by submitting to His Word. You submit to His Word when you become a doer of the Word and not just a hearer. You submit to God when **His** word becomes **your** lifestyle.

Finally, we can not end a chapter as critical as this one without referencing the need to put on the whole armor of God for the Battle! Let's look at **Ephesians 6:10-18**. This is one of the primary places in the Word of God that specifically spells out who the enemy is, the activities of demons and what you must do to survive and be victorious. Understanding and operating in this passage of scripture must become a key part of your weaponry for warfare.

"¹⁰Finally, my brethren, be strong in the Lord, and in the power of his might. ¹¹Put on the whole armor of God, that ye may be able to stand against the wiles of the devil. ¹²For we wrestle not against flesh and blood, but against principalities, against powers, against the rulers of the darkness of this world, against spiritual wickedness in high places. ¹³Wherefore take unto you the whole armor of God, that ye may be able to withstand in the evil day, and having done all, to stand. ¹⁴Stand therefore, having your loins girt about with truth, and having on the breastplate of righteousness; ¹⁵And your feet shod with the preparation of the gospel of peace; ¹⁶Above all, taking the shield of faith, wherewith ye shall be able to quench all the fiery darts of the wicked. ¹⁷And take the helmet of salvation, and the sword of the Spirit, which is the word of God: ¹⁸Praying always with all prayer and supplication in the Spirit, and watching thereunto will all perseverance and supplication for all saints;"

As illustrated in **Ephesians 6,** we are at war. But, if we never recognize the fact that our enemy is real, if we never take our basic training in the Word of God, then we will never be effective warriors here on earth. Remember, spirits are just spirits. Every spirit, regardless of its name, rank or serial number, is subject to the Precious Name of the Lord Jesus Christ and every knee shall bow, every tongue shall confess that Jesus is Lord.

In closing out this critical part of the book, Sir Winston Churchill once said, "If you are going through Hell, keep going!" Why? You keep going through because you will most definitely eventually come out. And, with God, it will be with total victory. So go through the Battle and know that you will come out triumphant!

Part 3:

"Obeying with True Submission!"

CHAPTER 8

Submitting to God in the Midst of the Battle: Obedience

We have made significant headway in understanding the spiritual hearing process. Now the question for you could be: "I know I can, I know I am able, I know God wants me to, and I know why I need to. But what do I do with what I have heard from God?" You know, there is no better way to mess up or delay God's carefully designed plan for your life than by you not knowing what to do with what God has said to you or by you knowing what the Lord said to do, but doing it your own way. You must develop the ability and strategies needed to bridge the gaps between <u>what you hear</u>, <u>understand</u>, <u>know to do</u>, and finally, <u>actually do</u>.

Fill in and Close the G.A.P.S.!

We, as the Body of Christ, must become more accurate in filtering through what we receive in our spirits. Once we know it is the Lord, we must focus on what His instructions are and as needed, get clarity where we lack understanding. These areas of missing understanding are called "Gaps". Gaps are issues or breaches in our foundation that can unexpectedly interrupt and hinder us from accomplishing the things that the Lord has charged us to do. This includes doing it in the manner and timing that the Lord has given us to accomplish a particular thing.

A good way to think of "Gaps" is that they look and act like a series of Chicago pot holes. For those of us that have driven in the winter time on Chicago's roadways when the streets are covered with snow, you know exactly what I am talking about. You hit one of those covered up, hidden potholes, and depending on how deep it is and how many there are in the sequence of time, your whole car rattles, and everybody and everything in it are unexpectedly jolted.

As time goes on, you come to know where these obstructions are and plan your driving strategy to avoid as many of them as possible. Sometimes you find yourself even taking a detour, or shortcut, to escape the clutches of these obstacles. Also you already know in your mind that depending on the depth of the hole, you can sustain some pretty severe damages to yourself, your passengers, and your property! These are damages that can render you motionless and ineffective in getting to your destination as planned for a period of time. Which in turn, can throw you off schedule, and actually cause you, and anyone else with you, to miss being in the proper place at the proper time.

Can you imagine being the preacher charged with doing a wedding? Or worse yet, the bride or groom trying to get to the wedding, but having to stop and deal with a damaged tire or having to get a different ride to their destination as a result of hitting one of those monster pot holes? For some, this experience can pull out a few choice words of frustration from our old nature.

The main point here for us to recognize is that this part in building and solidifying our Battle strategy is crucial! If we, as the designated driver, get clear instructions that we understand about the best roads to travel, it is our responsibility to follow those directions. It is our responsibility to ask questions to gain clarity so that we don't get lost. Also once that is done; it is further our responsibility to follow the directions exactly as they are given regardless of all the short cuts we know about. Following this, we will be guaranteed to arrive at our assigned destinations in order, in tact, and on time.

Once we know where the definite "Gaps" or potholes are, we can go around them as we encounter them or better yet, we can avoid them altogether as we are instructed to do by the signs we see. This does not mean that we will never encounter any potholes.

But it does mean that we can learn to minimize the impact of these encounters. Therefore, the potential damage will also be less intense. Yes, missing these types of encounters can minimize our chances of running into the hindrances or interruptions that they would so freely give us. Thereby getting us off course and schedule, even if only for one frustrating moment!

Taking the time to identify and eliminate as many of these potential "Gaps" or potholes as possible **before** going into action will help keep you in your proper place, at the right time, and with accurate instructions. Get your instructions, get clarity, stay focused, and obediently do exactly what you have been instructed to do.

Are you still unsure? **Immediately** go back and get confirmation on the directions and timing before you move into action! Doing this will yield results that both glorify God, and help you persevere in the Battle! This strategy will sustain you during the Battle and help avoid battle fatigue! It will enable you to respond quicker to what you know to be the voice of God, and thereby empower you to be more effective in your actions. So, let's look at some additional things you need to do to close the gaps that can help you to better protect God's Word and promises in your life as you move on what He has spoken.

You want me to do what, Lord?

Needless to say, this brings us face to face with the area of Obedience. Why? This is done so that you, as a co-labor with the Lord, can bring forth the spiritual promises of God. Also, so that you can bear witness of God's word manifesting into **fruitful** results that you can see, feel, and touch in the natural! I know we all have heard more than a few messages on this subject and its importance in the life of the believer. Why again? Because obedience is another very necessary link for hearing God distinctly and clearly. The link of obedience is extremely important in all aspects of your spiritual walk if you want to get it right.

Obedience is the act or instance of obeying by following the commands or guidance of someone with authority. Obedience is the limit or territory within which authority may be exercised and it is the authority of a sovereign power over others to govern or rule. Our Lord Jesus has **sovereign rule** over all.

In the Old Testament, obedience in Hebrew means "sama", which is to hear, hearken, listen, obey and publish - or make known with action. "To hear", as it relates to obedience, means not only to hear what is said, but to agree with the intention or petition of what has been spoken. Nothing taken away, nothing added, but demonstrated obedience that comes from an agreeable heart!

An agreeable heart is one that responds to the Lord's directions with an unconditional "Yes". A "Yes" action! It is a submitting of your ways to His. It is a forsaking of your own agenda for His. "Yes" is agreement. "Yes" comes from the heart and in this meaning it is the total agreement and alignment of your mind, your spirit, your body and of course, your will with God's purpose for you.

Yes, the mind is subject to change based on the state or perception of your circumstances and based on your memories of similar issues and situations. When your "Yes" is not from the heart and more from the mind, it will come forth from you with conditions. "I will do this Lord, if You do this." Or, "If this happens for me, then I will help them".

This is the case, unless a renewing of the mind has begun to take place within you. This is a renewing that can only occur through the Word of God. A renewing of the mind will replace your ways by teaching you His ways. This can only be done by studying and knowing His Word for your self. Constantly remind yourself that the Bible is our Training Manual, and it is always the current edition! So, use it regularly.

Therefore, returning to the main definition, **"sama"** means to **hear and demonstrate** your <u>understanding</u> of what you have heard **and** your <u>obedience</u> to someone in power **by your actions** within the boundaries that they have been given you. Let's look at an example of this in **1 Samuel 15:22-23**:

> *"²²And Samuel said, Hath the LORD as great delight in burnt offerings and sacrifices, as in <u>obeying</u> the voice of the LORD? Behold, to <u>obey</u> is better than sacrifice and to <u>hearken</u> than the fat of rams. ²³ For rebellion is as the sin*

of witchcraft [1 divination], *and stubbornness is as iniquity and idolatry. Because thou hast rejected the word of the LORD, he hath also rejected thee from being king."*

This is the passage where God rejects Saul as king. God gave Saul very explicit battle instructions, through Samuel, for the destruction of Amalek. Saul was instructed earlier in the chapter in **Verse 3** to wipe out every body and every thing! Saul was given specific instructions on what to do in the battle. His obedience was to be demonstrated in carrying out what God had instructed him to do. Yet, Saul decided to keep the "best" because perhaps, in Saul's opinion, God didn't really mean get rid of it *ALL*. Hmmmm.

How many times have we received instructions from God, and thought, "I know what You said Lord, but didn't you really mean for me to......"? Watch out now, because you have just stepped into the realm of disobedience! Don't try and second guess God. If you are truly unsure of what He is instructing you to do, get confirmation!

Then once you realize you are off course and out of order, don't refuse to see your misjudgment for what it is. Change your course of action, starting with repentance and corrective action. To knowingly refuse to change your position, as Saul did, is rebellion. This continued, conscious act of rebellion is the same as dealing with acts of witchcraft. This form of rebellion is considered outward stubbornness. To be stubborn in this manner is a definite known form of sin to you. You are fully aware that you are overriding the decisions and desires of the Lord. It is crosses right over into the realm of putting yourself, other people and things **before** God and His commanded order for your life and purpose. Choosing and taking this position is giving these other issues, circumstances and your own self interests more consideration, place, and emphasis in your life and choices than you have given the Lord himself!

Furthermore, this way of thinking transcends into the worship of something you perceive to be greater than God. To knowingly refuse is flat out rebellion. To rebel is a sin of the same type as witchcraft which is attempting to illegally control a person, situation, or thing. Stay within the limits that God has given you! Always take the time to examine your decision and choices before acting on them. Know that there are always consequences for the choices you make. Good and bad!

Your actions, as a whole, will demonstrate where your heart really is. But you better recognize that you run the risk of being rejected by God for stepping outside the boundaries set by the Lord and His word. Yes, your choices and actions have consequences. The knowingly wrong ones will put you in a place that will could potentially cause the Lord to move you right out of the position He has established for you.

You must come to recognize who and what can cause you to kick in and override what you heard and know to do in God in exchange for doing your thing your own way. This applies to your thoughts, your ideals, your desires, your choices, etc. Unlike Saul, be careful not to think that you really know better than God what is best for you, and those around you.

Also, know that to do what the Lord instructs you to do is far better received by God than doing the most extreme act of giving up something. This passage in **1 Samuel 15** reinforces the viewpoint that religious rituals that are lacking both spiritual reality and a life in total allegiance to our sovereign LORD is worthless. In other words, don't just go through the motions, it's pointless in advancing you towards your purpose and God is definitely not moved by your actions alone! How can I say that? Let's look at **Jeremiah 7:22**:

> *'22 For I spake not unto your fathers, nor commanded them in the day that I brought them out of the land of Egypt, concerning burnt offerings or sacrifices: 23 But this thing commanded I them, saying, <u>Obey</u> my voice, and I will be your God, and ye shall be my people: and walk ye in all the ways that I have commanded you, that it may be well unto you. 24 But they hearkened not nor inclined their ear, but walked in the counsels and in the imagination of their evil heart, and went backward, and not forward."*

Punishment for disobedience, especially in this passage, was that they made no progress using their own devices and methods! Our Father is telling us that if we choose not to do the things that He is instructing us to do, we will not only be stagnant in our growth and movement in the Battle, but worse yet, we will begin to decline and regress in our position! However, when we do strive to walk in obedience to His will, then the areas of our lives and the things that matter to us will prosper.

Again, just as with Saul, the other critical point in this passage is for us not to get wrapped up in being so religious that we miss a true relationship with God. He didn't spend time discussing "traditions" with our forefathers when He delivered them out of bondage. But what was important then, and still is important now is that we **hear and obey** His Voice! We are to be obedient to His instructions because if we choose not to be, if we do not lean towards and become drawn to what God is calling us to, but instead stubbornly follow our own hearts, we will go backwards and not forward into our purposes.

Submit your way to His ways. Forsake your own agenda for His. Tell Him "Yes". But know that it will come a cost! "Yes" is agreement. "Yes" from the heart is total agreement, within the mind, body and soul. "Yes" from the mind is subject to change, unless a renewing of the mind has taken place. Your mind makes choices based on the state or perception of your circumstances when it is not from the heart. This type of obedience, or Yes, comes with conditions. Mind is the memories, recollection, and the way you know and remember to do things. It is not an easy, simply thing to understand. The mind is a complex set of elements in each individual that enables them to feel, perceive, think, will and especially reason through the matters of life. Lose your mind and take on the mind of Christ. How? Replace your ways by learning and doing His way. How? STUDY and KNOW His Word. It is our Training Manual and it is always the current edition!

Therefore, know that obedience is also connected to a willing heart. You have to choose to be obedient. Godly obedience comes about not because you have to but because you have been persuaded by your love for God and you choose this lifestyle. You desire to serve and please Him and you do it in His time, not yours. Why only partially follow after the Lord. What a tremendous waste of time and effort not to experience the fullness of Christ, yet call yourself a Christian! There's a walk we take in this Christian lifestyle that is greatly influenced by the choices we make. The outcomes and results of how we overtake the challenges that we encounter along the way are the true testimony of our relationship with Him. The more willing your heart is, the greater the manifestation of His glory in your life can and will be.

So, what is the style you have chosen for your life as a Christian? I cover this in more detail in my first book, "Breaking Through Towards Spiritual Maturity". However, at another level, we must close the gaps between how we are and should be living. The way we bridge the gap will clearly impact our lifestyle. Style meaning to call or designate by an identifying term, design, make, or in accord with a predominate mode. It is a distinctive manner or custom in which one behaves or conducts oneself. Lifestyle simply means the typical conforming, combining, demonstrative and essential characteristics of a group or individual. In examining your life, does the picture projected by the imprint of your lifestyle portray and demonstrate the nature of Christ? Hmmm. Continue to work on it, it's a lifetime process.

In pursuing after what God has charged you to do, there will be times when added measures should be used in understanding and confirming what you have heard. Why? This is to ensure that you are hearing and comprehending God accurately. Some things you can do when you get an answer from the Lord are as follows:

- Write it down. Keep it in a journal.
- Pray for confirmation on the answer or directive.
- Involve your prayer / accountability partner. If you don't have one, ask and let God lead you to one!
- Measure the answer or directive against the Word.
  - Is it in agreement with the Word?
  - Does it contradict the Word? If yes, then something is definitely wrong!
- Involve and discuss all major decisions with your Pastor.

Let me say that last one again. For significant, life changing situations, seek wise counsel. Be sure to use your spiritual hearing on a daily basis. During prayer and as you listen for the Lord's voice, strive to have at least one "conversation" a day with Him. That way when you do need the answer to a major situation, you will not be in a panic mode. Functioning in this state of panic draws in all kinds of voices and responses, including your own!

God speaks many things into our lives, like strategically placed blocks on a pathway. To see where the next block will lay you have to stay connected to the Architect that's constructing the road. Can you imagine being on a road that all of a sudden takes an unexpected detour or the road just runs out? Stay in contact with God, He's your Navigator and He knows what best for you! Your only obligation and responsibility is to be willingly obedient to what the Lord has spoken to you and demonstrate your obedience through your actions.

We need to realize that willing obedience will also bring peace in your mind and heart. This peace is the strength to stand still and know He is God. You just need to have the courage to lay all of it down at His feet and move in obedience when the Lord tells you to go! No murmuring, no complaining, just focused, willing obedience.

So now it's time to build a strategy for maintaining God's peace in the midst of the Battle as you press towards and walk into your victory. In order to do this, let's:

- ♦ Identify some of the key hindrances that keep you from clearly hearing God;
- ♦ Give some recommendations for how to obediently move with the peace of God from one position to the next in order to bring discipline into your life; and
- ♦ Discuss some strategies for maintaining God's peace as you continue your Christian walk in obedience.

So let's get started!

CHAPTER 9

Failing Communions with God in the Midst of the Battle: Breaking Through The Barriers!

Lord, why can't I hear You now?

Have you ever felt like, "Lord, you are not hearing me." or "Lord, you are not listening to what I am saying here about this situation."? Because what you see happening, in your opinion, is **not** adding up to what you were expecting. You may even want to say sometimes, "Man, Lord, You are taking away stuff I don't want to give up, giving me stuff I am not so sure I want, and then the stuff I want to give You, You don't want, or You take something else in its place.". Wow!

The bottom line is, you are just not sure where the breakdown in reception is occurring! This condition is called "failing communions". What do I mean by that? Well, "communions" are actions that involve the sharing of a common purpose between those united in an intimate relationship. "Failing" is the absence of something essential. Lastly, "intimate" here meaning the deep closeness that we have to someone that we care deeply about. So in other words what's going on here is that intimate fellowship is missing between the Lord and you! Consistent, daily communion with the Lord is either lacking or just not there in your life. Ouch, I know. This is the condition that allows barriers to form between you and the Lord.

In our terms today, this is also called a "failure to communicate"! This break down in the information flow between you and the Lord is the direct result of us encountering known and unknown hindrances in our daily walk. Many of us have major blockages that keep us from hearing God clearly. So much so that some of us can not hear Him at all. Additionally, your very intimacy with God is suffering! Yes, there are times when God will do or allow the unexplainable to remain unexplained. However, most of the time it is us and the choices we have made that cause issues to be clouded.

So what are the hindrances these blockages can cause? Let's look at some of the key ones below. These hindrances are:

- Unbelief
- Disobedience
- Hidden Sin
- Immature Spirit
- Stubbornness
- Negligence, and
- Lies, Deception, and more Lies!

Yes, I know that's quite a list. I am also sure each of us can identify ourselves having been in, or are currently in, one or more of these states of spiritual hearing impairment. So, let's take some time to better understand each of these issues so that we can grow and overcome them when they attempt to manifest and disrupt our spiritual reception.

Unbelief

This is the first biggest hindrances for being able to hear directly from God for ourselves. **Unbelief!** Unbelief is simply being unwilling to admit or accept what is offered as true or having an attitude of doubt. Remember we talked earlier about the severity of the consequences of letting doubt creep in. If you don't believe God will, then usually He won't!

You know, with Christians it is not so much that we don't want to be obedient to what God is saying; it is more that we are not sure it is Him speaking. According to Webster, unbelief means skepticism especially in matters of religious faith. In unbelief, there is an unwillingness to admit, or accept what is offered as true. Even to the point of taking a "do it first, **then** I will believe it" position towards the Word and promises of God. Ouch! We will look closer at the area of Faith in **Chapter 13**. But for now grasp the fact that you can not please God when you allow unbelief to enter into your relationship with Him.

Another thing that influences this area of hearing is that we are listening to too many other sources that want to speak and impact our decisions and daily activities. Stop talking and listening to strangers! There is a danger in allowing strangers to influence your beliefs, thoughts, and heart. A stranger in this case is someone that does not share the faith in Jesus Christ as our Lord. Let's look at **Hebrew 4:1-2,** which talks about this type of faith and the dangers of unbelief.

> *"[1]Let us therefore fear, lest, a promise being left us of entering his rest, any of you should seem to come short of it. [2]For unto us was the gospel preached, as well as unto them: but the word preached did not profit them, not being mixed with faith in them that heard it."*

Talking to and listening to strangers can and will eventually lead to unbelief. The result of this is called mixed faith. This happens when you allow your faith to become confused by what those of the world are speaking into your mind and spirit. Additionally, in **Matthew 7:18-20**, the Lord answers a very significant question about the link between unbelief and spiritual power for the Disciples:

> *'[18] And Jesus rebuked the devil; and he departed out of him: and the child was cured from that very hour. [19] Then came the disciples to Jesus apart, and said, Why could not we cast him out? [20]And Jesus said unto them, Because of your unbelief:" for verily I say unto you, If you have faith as a mustard seed, ye shall say unto the mountain, Remove hence to yonder*

place; and it shall remove; and nothing shall be impossible unto you."

The Disciples wanted to know where they missed it in this particular battle. Even though they had witnessed the miraculous works of the Lord first hand, they did not fully believe that this power and authority applied to them.

Listen, it does not have to be a real deep experience every time you seek God and are able to hear Him clearly. What is required is that you believe the truth fully and supernaturally, which means beyond what you know as truth naturally. Even if developing this process initially is done a little at a time. Over time with each new circumstance that you trust God with, your level of belief in these areas of your life will grow and strengthen. Just like you believe the sun and moon are going to rise and set each day whether you see it occur or not, is how steadfast you must be in accepting the promises and guidelines in the Word of God as the necessary truth for living.

Know that hearing from God is not a miracle, it is a gift. Stop looking for sporadic or one time miraculous events. Your spiritual hearing is a gift that will last you a life time and that you can use whenever you desire it. So take care of this gift, treasure it, and take the time to nurture it so that it will develop and become the sharpen weapon that God intended it to be in your arsenal. Why? Because we are to do greater, or more, works than Jesus did in His time on this earth. Believe it!

Disobedience

The next big hindrance to getting accurate instructions from the Lord is **Disobedience.** Disobedience can cause you to be rejected from the very position He has established you in! Disobedience is the refusal or act of expressing oneself as unwilling to act on something. It also means to neglect or give little respect to the commands, guidance, conformity or compliance with someone in authority. **Deuteronomy 8:20** tells us the consequences of not being obedient to the things God has spoken to us!

"As the nations which the LORD destroyeth before your face, so shall ye perish; because ye would not be obedient unto the voice of the LORD your God."

In the above passage, we are told the consequences for disobedience are the death. This is letting us know that when we walk in disobedience to His voice we are willingly making the decision not to do what He is instructing us to do. For this act, the consequences will eventually result in spiritual and natural death in the same manner that the Lord has destroyed our enemy. What "manner" is this? This is the same ways that we have been witnessed God's hand moving in judgment against our enemies, and it will not be a pleasant experience at all!

You need to know that disobedience can also cause a spirit of deafness. If you willfully rebel against the Word of God and what He is saying to you, you violate your heart and open yourself up to voices of deception. Let's look at **Matthew 13:10-15:**

"10And the disciples came, and said unto him, Why speakest thou unto them in parables 11He answered and said unto them, Because it is given unto you to know the mysteries of the kingdom of heaven, but to them it is not given. 12For whosoever hath, to him shall be given, and he shall have more abundance: but whosoever hath not, from him shall be taken away even that he hath. 13Therefore speak I to them in parables: because they seeing see not; and hearing they hear not, neither do they understand. 14And in them is fulfilled the prophecy of Esaias, which saith, By hearing ye shall hear, and shall not understand; and seeing ye shall see, and shall not perceive: 15 For this people's heart is waxed gross, and their ears are dull of hearing, and their eyes they have closed; lest at any time they should see with their eyes, and hear with their ears, and should understand with their heart, and should be converted, and I should heal them."

Simply stated here you are told that doing things your own way will dull your hearing, understanding and perception to the things of

God. In these days and times, you need the upper hand of knowing and seeing the plots of the enemy well advance of the attacks so that you can be properly prepared to be victorious in the Battle. The Lord and His Word are the only true sources for accessing these Battle plans and your strategy clearly.

Be steadfast and obedient to the will of God. The way you are guaranteed to overcome these situations is to freely give your heart to the Lord. You do this with a surrendered mind to the Word. The Lord will then open your spiritual discernment and hearing so that you are empowered to know the mysteries and answers of the Kingdom of Heaven for this Battle, and in your life **now**.

Hidden Sin

The third biggest hindrance is **Hidden Sin**. Hidden means being out of sight or not readily apparent. Hidden sin clogs up your heart and in turn, your spiritual hearing. It directly ties itself to the desires of your heart, mind and physical body. These issues that are known and unknown to you must all be dealt with over time, in God's time. Remember, whatever state your heart is in directly reflects your ability to hear God. The result of hidden sin can be seen in **Isaiah 57:17**:

"For the iniquity of his covetousness was I wroth, and smote him: I hid me, and was wroth, and he went on frowardly in the way of his heart. "

Here, God tells us if we continuously chose to live a lifestyle full of chasing after excessive desires for **more** stuff than we need or even deserve, we are living in sin. Our persistent pursuit after both of these types of conscious and unconscious choices will eventually really "tick" God off!

How will we know for sure? We will know because He will hide Himself from us! No access to the King or His throne! What an awful position to be in. Worse yet, the Lord will allow us to continue on in our own ways if we persist in pushing down that road.

Our Father says three small yet powerful words here that can literally change the course of your life. God says, *"I hid me"*. Again, be careful Child of God, because the Lord will do this when we display behaviors that are focused aggressively on driving us away from Him and towards gathering more than we need or should even possess. So be aware of when this is happening to you.

How can you tell? It is when you begin to behave in ways you really can not explain when it comes to going after things that are outside the will of God. It is when you put yourself in situations that you swore you would never be in again. Any type of behavior done to satisfy these excessive desires will put and hold you captive in a place of hidden sin.

So, how and why does that keep happening? It keeps happening because of those hidden areas of unresolved sin. You know these areas exist in your life. You know that God knows these areas exist in your life. Yet you chose not to let Him deliver you from these messy, chaotic habits. What are these habits? You know, the same things that you are doing that you don't want anyone to find out about, especially since you know they are wrong in the eyes of God, those that you look up to, and worse yet those that look up to you!

Look, you also need to realize that there are very real consequences to living this way. You, in actuality, force God to turn against you. We are told here that in addition to continually making these types of lifestyle choices that make God angry with us, we also pressure our Father's hand to act against us! One of the major things you better recognize is **if** God is not there, He has also removed His protection from you on the Battlefield!

God says He Himself will cause injury and affliction to you for living this way by *His* very hand. Wow, judgment is not a pleasant position to be in. Imagine being on the Battlefield and the Admiral is gone, the battle plans are gone, your fellow warriors are silent and all your armor has been removed. To make matters even worse, the enemy also has spotted your vulnerability and is eagerly in pursuit of you! All because of living in the area of hidden sin that you refuse to recognize and deal with.

Listen, you don't ever want to be in the position of God turning His face away from you because whether you know it or not, you cannot recover from these areas permanently without Him! So deal with these areas that are in conflict with the Word and Will of God as soon as you become aware of them. Besides, what do you think you could have possibly done that He does not already know about anyway! Trust me, there is nothing about you that He does not already know. Better yet, He even knows the things you have chosen not faced yet. The Lord knows, He knows, yes He knows.

So, Child of the Almighty God, if this is you, I beseech you to return to Him. Turn these areas of hidden sin over to Him so that together you can renew your heart. Ask the Lord what these areas are and pursue after the deliverance He has for you so that you are not a wounded or exposed Warrior on the Battlefield. Remember Warrior, whatever state your heart is in directly reflects your ability to hear and respond appropriately to God. So allow the Lord to strengthen your heart and your spirit by submitting to His process of growth. Together, you can clean up these areas of your life!

Immature Spirit

The next hindrance to hearing directly from the Lord is an **Immature Spirit** and this will definitely hinder your ability to hear clearly from God. Our Father is not referring to the babes in Christ here. He means the grown folks in the Church that should know better because they have sitting under the Word of God. **1 Corinthians 13:11** tells us to grow up! Let's look at it:

1 *"When I was a child, I spake as a child, I understood as a child, I thought as a child: but when I became a man, I put away childish things."*

Having an immature spirit will cause you to become desensitized to the things of God. You can become comfortable with religious tradition and the way things have always been done because you have become used to being lead and fed like a babe. This is still the case even though you have been in the Church long enough to be a legal 21 year old adult. Yet in still, you are one of Jesus' warrior that is capable of making righteous decisions, living a holy life, and even mentoring others through this Battle.

Warrior, never become too relaxed or dependent on anyone or anything other than God in your spiritual walk! Never forget this is a war. Not only are we held accountable for developing our gifts from God, but we are told by Apostle Paul in **1 Thessalonians 5:23**:

> *"And the very God of peace sanctify you wholly; and I pray God your whole spirit and soul and body be preserved blameless unto the coming of our Lord Jesus Christ."*

This means you are to protect and seal within yourself what you already have been given by God. This sanctification serves as one of the building blocks in your foundation of faith and relationship with the Lord. Don't get so use to what's going on around you that you become desensitized to when God has changed direction and methods. True, His Word does **not** change. However, you must continue to mature as a Christian to discern when and where the seasons and methods of the Lord are progressing. This will allow you to be flexible enough to quickly adapt to His movements in order to achieve your Kingdom assignments. To do this effectively, you must continue to develop and refresh what He has already given you.

Also in **Romans 8:14-16,** we are encouraged not to be afraid of the changes, but to be led by the Spirit of God!

> *"For as many as are led by the Spirit of God, they are the sons of God. For ye have not received the spirit of bondage again to fear; but ye have received the Spirit of adoption, whereby we cry, Abba Father. The Spirit itself beareth witness with our spirit, that we are the children of God."*

Your knowledge of the Word greatly impacts how much you can be led by the Spirit. The Holy Spirit bears witness to your spirit, which means He will confirm what you sense you are to do based on what you have heard from God. Remember, the deeper levels of effectiveness and discernment within your spirit are based on how well you have prepared yourself in God's Word. This training and preparation will provide you with sure guidance from God as you journey throughout this world. When the Holy Spirit bears witness to your obedient and God-sensitive heart, you will have a safe and sure guide to the will and purpose of the Lord and what He is saying for your life. Grow up Warrior; strive to mature in the ways of the Lord so that you can live the life He purposed for you!

Stubbornness

Stubbornness is the state of being unreasonably or perversely unyielding. Worse yet, it means that the things you do are performed or carried out in a viscously obstinate and persistent manner. Therefore, you and the things associated with you become very difficult for others, and even you, to handle or manage effectively in a God like manner.

Stubbornness is the extreme opposite of Submission. And please stop lying to yourself by saying that you are just very determined. Recognize your behavior for what it really is. Stubbornness is not to be confused with having determination! Stubbornness is second only to defiance, which will eventually put you into the state of a reprobate mind. A reprobate mind means having the mindset to live your life without God, the Lord and the knowledge of God. It is the complete turning away from our Creator by His creation. As stated in **Romans 1:28**, God will let you live that way if you chose to! Take a look at the path that can follow unresolved stubbornness:

" *[28]And even as they did not like to retain God in their knowledge, God gave them over to a reprobate mind, to do those things which are not convenient; [29]Being filled with all unrighteousness, fornication, wickedness, covetousness, maliciousness; full of envy, murder, debate, deceit, malignity; whisperers, [30]Backbiters, haters of God, despiteful, proud, boasters, inventors of evil things, disobedient to parents, [31]Without understanding, covenantbreakers, without natural affection, implacable, unmerciful: [32]Who knowing the judgment of God, that they which commit such things are worthy of death, not only do the same, but have pleasure in them that do them."*

Yes God is talking to His children here. Those of us that knew Him and His Word, but for whatever reason have chosen to turn away from all knowledge of the Father. Wow, how dangerous! Just as all things and matters in life have a way of maturing into something else, if you are not careful in not letting stubbornness be an ongoing issue, you will end up walking in defiance and after your own methods. This in turn, will not only put you right out of the will of God, but into direct conflict with Him! Believe me, God is not an opponent you want to take on as your enemy. You will lose! Sooner or later, now or then, you will eventually lose out all together on the life that God has purposed for you.

Furthermore, stubbornness is equivalent to what God refers to as being "stiff-neck". Boy that even sounds painful! **Jeremiah 17:23** tells us:

> *"But they obeyed not, neither inclined their ear, but made their neck stiff, that they might not hear, nor receive instruction."*

The first thing to note here is that they made a choice not to be obedient. Since it was a conscious choice, they were functioning in the realm of committing an intentional sin. Next, they chose not to listen. Not only did they choose not to hear, they were *determined* not to be told what to do. As though their ways were better! Wow again. The thing about becoming stubborn, or stiff neck, is that it is not only visible to God, but it is a physical posture and behavior that is visible to others!

Whew, three strikes by choice: deliberate disobedience, intentional deafness and willful defiance. An example of the consequences of choosing to be this way can be found in **1 Samuel 15:23**:

> *"For rebellion is as the sin of witchcraft, and stubbornness is as iniquity and idolatry. Because thou hast rejected the word of the LORD, he hath also rejected thee from being king."*

Again, stubbornness is another area that will move you right out of your divinely appointed position. It puts you in the realm of thinking and believing that you, everybody and everything else can do it better than God. It is making God the choice of least preferred!

Not until people and situations important to you begin to fail do you turn and say, "Oh well I tried everything else, I guess I'll try God now.". Too wait to long because there does come a point in time where God's grace runs out, and He will say to you no more of your foolishness! Submit yourself, everyone and everything that is important to you under the mighty hand of the Lord! Do it submissively, quickly, and willingly.

Negligence

Another big hindrance to hearing the voice of the Lord is **Negligence.** Negligence is the failure to exercise the care that a prudent person usually demonstrates. Care meaning expending and showing diligent effort or watchful attention to a particular person or thing. To be prudent means to have the innate ability to govern, and discipline your self by using logical reasoning. The bottom line here is this: when you allow your relationship with the Lord to suffer because of issues, circumstances, people and even yourself, you are jeopardizing your very standing in the Kingdom. You are taking a stance that states that you do not value *your divine purpose and future* enough to invest the required time *in the present* needed to build and sustain a solid relationship with God.

Hmmm. It is not reasonable for you as a Child of God and a disciple of Jesus Christ to try and live your life according to your own reasoning and abilities. It is not reasonable for you as a servant in the Kingdom to not only leave the King out of your daily life, but not even know your headship. It is not reasonable for you as a soldier in life's Battle not to know who and what you are fighting for on a daily basis, not to mention which side you are on and whose attacking you. You and I both know you know better by now.

We invest in what we believe in and what is important to us. You need to stop and ask yourself, "How important is the Lord to me, really?" If you want to know how to be prosperous and victorious in all aspects of your life, start now investing yourself daily in your relationship with the Lord. Invest your time, effort, focus and heart! We are reminded of the correlation between the heart and what's important to us by Jesus in both **Matthew 6:21** and **Luke 12:34.**

"For where your treasure is, there will your heart be also."

So, why would a "reasonable" person live their life as though everything else in the world matters more to them than their Savior? That is the same as trying to figure out why a "reasonable" person would not drink water, if he or she is thirsty, from a filled glass sitting in front of them versus ignoring it and going out to the store to buy some water? Why overlook the Eternal Source for all that you could ever need or want, and Who is so freely available to you for the mere cost of your willing heart and obedience? Simple conception, but tough for us humans to adapt to!

So Soldier grab hold of this: to really know God's voice and drink from His cup, you must intentionally seek to spend time with Him! Let's look at **Philippians 3:8-15**:

> *"⁸Yea doubtless, and I count all things but loss for the excellency of the knowledge of Christ Jesus my Lord: for whom I have suffered the loss of all things, and do count them but dung, that I may win Christ, ⁹And be found in him, not having mine own righteousness, which is of the law, but that which is through the faith of Christ, the righteousness which is of God by faith: ¹⁰That I may know him, and the power of his resurrection, and the fellowship of his sufferings, being made conformable unto his death; ¹¹If by any means I might attain unto the resurrection of the dead. ¹²Not as though I had already attained, either were already perfect: but I follow after, if that I may apprehend that for which also I am apprehended of Christ Jesus. ¹³Brethren, I count not myself to have apprehended: but this one thing I do, forgetting those things which are behind, and reaching forth unto those things which are before, ¹⁴I press toward the mark for the prize of the high calling of God in Christ Jesus. ¹⁵Let us therefore, as many as be perfect, be thus minded: and if in any thing ye be otherwise minded, God shall reveal even this unto you."*

The Lord has given us the power and authority to know how to survive victoriously and live a prosperous life. However, it must be in Him, with Him, and through Him! At times we act as though we have either forgotten this wonderful fact or never knew it at all. God is always doing a new thing in our lives, and if we are not paying attention we will really miss it!

We, as Christians, go through situations and deal with issues in life so that we can know Christ even the more. We are instructed in this passage to press towards God at all times. Don't be just a "Sunday only" Christian. Don't go places you can't take Him with you or get involved in things that you will have to be ashamed of sharing with Him! Staying free of these issues can only occur when we continuously press in our relationship with Him even the more. The better we know Him, the **more** we desire to know Him; thereby leading us to an unveiling of ourselves to ourselves. Let's also look at **Isaiah 43:18-19**:

"Behold, I will do a new thing; now it shall spring forth; shall ye not know it? I will even make a way in the wilderness, and rivers in the desert."

This inner revealing is exactly who we are in the Kingdom, to Him and to one another. As we mature as Christians in our relationship with the Lord and in our purposes, a miraculous transition begins to occur. This "new thing" is visible. It is also visible to others as we go through our most trying situations. And its full potential is only possible through a consistent relationship with God.

Also, as we come into a closer relationship with the Lord, we as brothers and sisters in the faith begin to act alike, speak the same language, and think the same thoughts as Christ. Wow, we will behave just like a real family. Imagine that, Christians fully displaying lifestyles in the image of their Creator! Glory to God! However, remember that this can only be accomplished fully by intentionally devoting time to your relationship with the Lord.

Take comfort in knowing that God wants to be involved in your life. Make it easy for Him and you to spend time together focused on things that will help you develop, grow and prosper. In case you forget something, God promises to help you remember. Once in Christ Jesus, remember saint that you are only alone if you choose to be. His arms are always open, so choose to enter in and dwell in His presence!

Lies, Deception, and more Lies

The last big hindrance that we will cover is the one of Lies, which is the deliberate misstatement of the Truth. It is essentially **Deception**. Deception is covered in various chapters throughout this book. But just as a reminder, deception here means the art of using ingenious ways to persuade or dupe someone away from what is true so that they can not receive what is rightfully theirs.

In everything that is made available to us today to pull our focus and affections away from God, following are the more prevalent lies used by the enemy. These deceptive devices and thoughts almost always include one or more of the following lies!

- God does not care about you, or have the time to deal with your issues. He is too busy!
- Jesus is not the only begotten Son of God.
- There are many paths to Eternal Life.
- We all have within us the power to become God.
- Satan, demons, and the Spirit Realm are not real and NO one will believe you if you say or think differently.

Also, to help you identify and dismantle the five most common lies of the enemy, here is some strategic information to put in your arsenal and heart.

First, God does not care about you, or have the time to deal with your issues. He is too busy!

To disprove the first falsehood by the Word of God, let's look at what God tells us in **Luke 12:22-24:**

"²²And he said unto his disciples, Therefore I say unto you, Take no thought for your life, what ye shall eat; neither for the body, what ye shall put on. ²³The life is more than meat, and the body is more than raiment. ²⁴Consider the ravens: for they neither sow nor reap; which neither have storehouse nor barn; and God feedeth them: how much more are ye better than the fowls?

If God, our Father, continues to provide for birds as scavengerous as the ravens, and the Lord considers and calls us priests and kings in the Kingdom, how much more will our Father do for us than He does for the other living creatures? Even in the natural, don't you take care of who and what is precious to you, especially your children? Of course you do! Then, how much more is our Heavenly Father willing and capable of doing for us as His Children? We are reminded to keep this in the forefront of our thoughts in **Matthew 7:11**.

"If ye then, being evil, know how to give good gifts unto your children, how much more shall your Father which is in heaven give good things to them that ask him?"

Yes, child of God, know that God does care about you and those things that concern you. You only need to ask the Father in prayer. Discuss with Him all that is in your heart and on your mind. All that matters to you, matters to Him. In fact, the basics are already promised and we are therefore told not to give any thought to them. Additionally, let's look at **1 Timothy 6:17**:

"Charge them that are rich in this world, that they be not highminded, nor trust in uncertain riches, but in the living God, who giveth us richly all things to enjoy;"

Here, we are further told that even if you are already doing exceptionally well in life, don't lose sight of the True Source. And whether you are humble enough to admit it or not, you still have issues and need God's help. Rather it be matters of your heart, physical body, mind, or spirit, you still definitely need the help of the Lord. Even if you think you have "everything", you are more than likely still empty. You must come into the knowledge of the fact that this emptiness can only be filled by a personal relationship with the Lord. Know that our Father will even supply to you, as His child, blessings beyond not only your immediate needs, but also well beyond where you are already excelling in order for you to enjoy life even the more.

One more step as we close this first falsehood, note that though you may get tired in your struggles and pursuit of your destiny, God never does! Let's look at **Isaiah 40:28**:

"Hast thou not known? hast thou not heard, that the everlasting God, the LORD, the Creator of the ends of the earth, fainteth not, neither is weary? there is no searching of his understanding."

So you stay encouraged in this life, and remember that our Father never tires. He knows everything from the beginning to the end including everything that concerns you, and will NEVER lose strength or power in the attainment of your victory in the Kingdom. We are also told that we will not be able to understand how He does it. So stop trying to figure it out, and rest in His promises to be our Keeper, Protector, Provider, Strong Tower, Creator, and Counselor, Who is our every thing! Rest and prosper in that wisdom.

Listen, we have divine purposes and Kingdom assignments to achieve. Don't get wrapped up in the little stuff. Let God handle the necessities of your daily living and meeting your needs in the days to come. Yes, bad things do happen to good people sometimes. But always remember what we are told in **Romans 8:28**:

"And we know that all things work together for good to them that love God, to them who are the called according to his purpose."

It does all work out and as you grow in your relationship with the Lord, you will look back and find that all your concerns were taken care of and, going forward that all your needs are being met! Amen.

Second, Jesus is not the only begotten Son of God.

The next deceptive issue to be dealt with is the myth that Jesus is not the only begotten son of God, the Father. Let's go directly to the Word of God to disprove this statement by starting with **1 John 4:9:**

> *"In this was manifested the love of God toward us, because that God sent his only begotten Son into the world, that we might live through him."*

Jesus is the only begotten Son of God. He is not just another prophet, not just a teacher or master that lived on the earth centuries ago. In fact there is no denying the reality that Jesus did live, and is a very real contributor to the history of mankind. However, now we are at the point where your faith comes in. As a Christian, you must know, by faith, that Jesus, as the only begotten Son of God, was sent to earth in order to rightfully restore our fellowship with our Creator and Heavenly Father. Again, this is where your faith is required and should not be swayed based on trendy doctrines and naysayers! So what does that mean to us today? Look at **Hebrews 4:14:**

> *"Seeing then that we have a great high priest, that is passed into the heavens, Jesus the Son of God, let us hold fast our profession."*

Jesus Christ, who is the Son of God, is our Savior and Redeemer. We are told to hold on tight to our faith and what we confess as our belief. Further support comes from one of our biblical pastors, Timothy, who admonishes us to always be on guard against false doctrine and exhorts us to become more mature in our spiritual walk. He is able to ***summarize who Jesus is*** in one small passage in **1 Timothy 3:16:**

"And without controversy great is the mystery of godliness: God was manifest in the flesh, justified in the Spirit, seen of angels, preached unto the Gentiles, believed on in the world, received up into glory."

Yes, our Savior Jesus Christ is the Son of God, he has already come, and it is a finished work! We'll talk more about the fulfillment of His purpose in **Chapter 11**. For now, marinate in the fact that as a Christian, this is what our faith is based upon, and this truth helps us become and stay victorious in this life. Know the Word of God for yourself so that you don't get tripped up in this area. Know the background of your Savior, the one that is the head of your life.

Third, there are many paths to Eternal Life.

The next deceptive issue to be dealt with is the misteaching and mixed faith issue of having a lot of options for reaching Eternal Life. Again, let's go directly to the Word of God to disprove this statement by starting with **1 John 2:22-25.**

"²²Who is a liar but he that denieth that Jesus is the Christ? He is antichrist, that denieth the Father and the Son. ²³Whosoever denieth the Son, the same hath not the Father: (but) he that acknowledgeth the Son hath the Father also. ²⁴Let that therefore abide in you, which ye have heard from the beginning. If that which ye have heard from the beginning shall remain in you, ye also shall continue in the Son, and in the Father. ²⁵And this is the promise that he hath promised us, even eternal life."

We are told in this passage that if you deny Jesus as God's Son, you are also denying God, the Father. There are no equals and there are no substitutes! Jesus, and Jesus alone, is the way to God, the Father and thereby, the path to eternal life. There is no other way! As Christians, you have to firmly believe and stand on this truth for it is one of the key foundational trues of our faith.

No more wavering on this. Though we are not to judge and condemn others for their lack of knowledge, we are to stand flat footed and upright when it comes to the truth of what we are staking our Eternal Life on. If you still have doubts, get into studying the Word of God for yourself, get back in Church, and get out to Bible Class! If you are still unclear, search out where your faith got shook and resolve those issues as soon as possible! Don't be deceived any longer because this deception could cost you your life and position in Heaven.

Let's also look at **John 3:15-16** which addresses both facts that: 1) we have Eternal Life through the Son of God, and 2) how God further proved to us His love by allowing His Son to be the necessary sacrifice that allows us to be rejoined to our Creator in a personal relationship.

> *""¹⁵That whosoever believeth in him should not perish, but have eternal life. ¹⁶ For God so loved the world, that he gave his only begotten Son, that whosoever believeth in him should not perish, but have everlasting life."*

In this passage, it clearly states that the only way to the Father and Eternal Life in Heaven is through our belief in Jesus Christ, as the Son of God. Believe it or not, it is still the Truth. Choose to live your life believing any other way, you better be right because in the end it will mean eternal death for you.

So, you may be wondering, what else is going on on the way to Eternal Life, and what does that have to do with you on the Battlefield? Well, to further understand why God sent His Son we must look at the love our Father has for us as seen in **1 John 4:10**:

> *"Herein is love, not that we loved God, but that he loved us, and sent his Son to be the propitiation for our sins."*

Propitiation here means being the atoning sacrifice that ensures the re-establishment of our personal relationship with God. Jesus was our atonement. Atonement means the reconciliation of God and man through the sacrificial death of Jesus Christ. The bottom line is

Jesus Christ paid the price in FULL for us to be restored and gain access to God the Father. Again, by the Word of God, *only* Jesus, the Son of God, can give you Eternal Life because He is the only atoning sacrifice that has enables us to willfully and individually restore our relationship with God and regain the grace and favor of God, our Father.

Furthermore, this sacrifice covers **all** of those that have the desire to come into God's Kingdom; yesterday, today and all the tomorrows to come. This is further supported in **1 John 2:2:**

"And he is the propitiation for our sins: and not for ours only, but also for the sins of the whole world."

This ultimate demonstration of love by our Father means that Jesus has *"Paid It Forward"*! Point blank, this sacrifice serves as the under girding for our ability to be able to seek and receive God's forgiveness, grace, and mercy for all that we have done, and will ever do against the Father. Only the Son of God, Jesus Christ made amends on our behalf that resulted in us being able to reconcile with God after the break in fellowship between God and man caused by Adam.

Realize, Child of God that the matter of "Reconciliation" is a whole other book and excellent individual study time for another time. For now, accept the truth that this is all a part of God's Divine plan for man to have a personal relationship with Him, Jesus His Son, and the Holy Spirit was the only acceptable sacrifice to accomplish this reconnecting of divine fellowship.

Fourth, we all have within us the power to become God.

The fourth is a lie that is spreading in the world through false teachings is the one that appears to have the innocent overtones of "positive thinking", "mind over matter" and "taking matters into your own hands"! How? You believe, wrongfully I might add, that you are just as intelligent and mighty as God. We have all heard them right? They also sound really good, right? They all sound harmless enough too, right? Wrong! Let's look at **Romans 1:25:**

"Who changed the truth of God into a lie, and worshipped and served the creature more than the Creator, who is blessed for ever. Amen."

Here we are asked who changed the Word of God anyway. The Word of God is what it is; the truth for living this life the way the Lord says it is to be lived. Do you even realize that when you move away from this truth, that not only are you moving out of your position, but you are also leading others.

There is no taking away from the Word of God, adding to it, or ignoring it all together. How can the creation possibly show you a better way than the actual Creator? Yes, we are to live Godly lives, but we are not capable of being God Himself. As we are told in **Isaiah 43:15**:

"I am the LORD, your Holy One, the creator of Israel, your King."

Just in case it is not clear, YOU are a part of Israel. To go directly to the basics of creation, look at **Genesis 1:27** which further confirms our identity for us:

"So God created man in his own image, in the image of God created he him; male and female created he them."

Everything that has life, God has allowed. I know I am trending into deep waters here, but we as Christians must stand on our faith. Therefore, everything that has breath, God has given it. Regardless of the amount of intervention or invention by man's hands, God is the main ingredient for life and we would not be here if it were not for Him. Yes, we need Him to survive, to wake up each day and go to sleep every night. It is not and will never be the other way around! We are also reminded in **Colossians 1:16-17:**

[16]*"For by him were all things created, that are in heaven, and that are in earth, visible and invisible, whether they be thrones, or dominions, or principalities, or powers: all*

things were created by him, and for him: [17] And he is before all things, and by him all things consist."

In this area of hindrance, they all give the message of us exalting ourselves at the same level, and in some cases, even above God! Watch it and be careful! Remember what happened to the devil for behaving and moving in this same way of thinking. The enemy and those that thought similarly were cast out of the very presence of God and heaven.

God is the Creator of those that don't even believe or accept that He created them. Here are also the inroads into the fact that this walk that we live and Battle that we fight are spiritual first based on the initial creation of God. Again, this is truth whether you believe it or not! It is still true. There is only one true God and He is our creator as stated in **Genesis 1:1:**

"In the beginning God created the heaven and the earth."

God, the Father is the Creator, we, the people and everything living are His creation. Each one of us being set into Eternity by Him; and given a divine purpose to be accomplished within His Kingdom Plan. Some may stumble into achieving their purposes without coming into the knowledge of the truth of God. But they never fully achieve all that the Lord has in store for them. And even still, He allowed them to stumble and thrive in it. Whether they acknowledge it or not, this was not accomplished by them without Him.

This revealing of full purpose for man comes once the reconciliation through Jesus Christ has been made with God. This is what is referenced in **Colossians 3:10:**

"And have put on the new man, which is renewed in knowledge after the image of him that created him:"

The process of transformation begins at the point of reconciliation. The renewing of the mind is an ongoing process. The newness comes from the understanding of man's need and desire to be reconciled with His Creator. This is what gets us back to His original purpose for us .

Last point in this area is that our God is alive and well, and so is His Son, Jesus Christ! He is our living God as stated in **Matthew 22:32:**

> *"I am the God of Abraham, and the God of Isaac, and the God of Jacob? God is not the God of the dead, but of the living."*

We serve our Father who is the living God, not a statue, or a historical dignitary that has long ago past away, but the one and only Almighty God. So why do we struggle and not do as we are instructed in **Matthew 6:33** which states:

> *"But seek ye first the kingdom of God, and his righteousness; and all these things shall be added unto you."*

The Lord knows your beginning all the way to your end, especially in this natural life. So why would you not seek Him for advice and direction versus attempting to live without Him? For those of us that know better this is truly mind-blowing when we think out how senseless that logic is, isn't it!

Finally, observe this truth: He is the Creator, we are the creation. Please don't miss that truth. In your natural family, where you respect, obey and love for your natural parent(s), you would never jump up and out right neglect their instructions, disobey their guidance and disregard their provisions. No not if you were raised properly. So consider this, how dare you knowingly do it to our Heavenly Father! As **Jude 1:25** says:

> *To the only wise God our Savior, be glory and majesty, dominion and power, both now and ever. Amen.*

We have dominion and power because our Father and Lord have chosen to share it with us. Stop taking it for granted and reverence the true Source. Recognize and use this God given power and authority accordingly!

Fifth, Satan, demons, and the Spirit Realm are not real and NO one will believe you if you say or think differently.

The last lie brings to the table the reality of all that is spiritual, including our Father, our Lord Jesus Christ, the Holy Spirit and the enemy. The Spirit Realm is very real and ever present rather you acknowledge it or not. Stop letting the enemy mess you up in this area. As we are told in the Word of God, in **John 4:24**:

"God is a Spirit: and they that worship him must worship him in spirit and in truth."

There is a divine order to everything. God, the Father, is the head. The triune is God the Father, Jesus the Son of God and the Holy Spirit. "Being made in their image" means that all of their aspects and nature are present in you as a human being. You have a physical body that houses your soul and spirit. Your soul is your will, your mind and your personality. Your spiritual being is in the image of God. Since this is the case and we are connected by the spirit, your spirit allows you to speak God's language, hear God's voice, feel the Lord's presence, discern the movement of the Holy Spirit, know the will of God for your life, and live your life to the fullest in achieving your divine purpose. Your spirit man allows you to manifest spiritual things in the natural. Yes, your spirit man allows you to come into the presence of His and communicate directly with our Father. As we stated early, all human beings are created in the image of God. So stop dismissing 1/3 of your very being. The Lord desires that you be whole!

Also in **1 Corinthians 2:12**, we are told as Christians that it is the Spirit of God in us that distinguishes us from the world. His very Spirit is what allows us to know Him even the more!

"Now we have received, not the spirit of the world, but the spirit which is of God; that we might know the things that are freely given to us of God."

Know that this lifestyle is a spiritual walk and the Battle is a spiritual one as we are told in **Ephesians 6:12**:

"For we wrestle not against flesh and blood, but against principalities, against powers, against the rulers of the darkness of this world, against spiritual wickedness in high places."

Our battle does not originate in the natural realm against man. It never has. It begins in the Spirit Realm, in the Heavenlies, and it manifests in the natural realm. All battles are fought and won in the Spirit Realm first. Then they unfold in the natural realm which is here on earth. This is why it is so critical for us to stay connected to the Lord and live in the truth that we are victorious! Know your Word so you can fight victoriously. In fact, knowing your Word and stay connected to the Lord daily will give you advance warning to when the attacks are coming so that you can be better prepared!

Yes, the Spirit Realm and spiritual beings are real. They do exist. Don't be scared of them, don't dismiss them as fiction, and don't doubt this truth! Because again, it is true rather you or I believe it or not. But you now know it is, so prepare yourself for Battle by putting on the whole armor of God as we are instructed in **Ephesians 6:11** and **Ephesians 6:13**:

"11 Put on the whole armour of God, that ye may be able to stand against the wiles of the devil."

"13 Wherefore take unto you the whole armour of God, that ye may be able to withstand in the evil day, and having done all, to stand."

Lastly, after reading **Part 2** of this book surely this is still not an unanswered question for you in this area of whether or not the Spirit Realm exists! If so, please go back and reread it because it is all very real and ever present rather you acknowledge it or not. Don't let the enemy trick you! Remember anything that conflicts with the word of God or exalts itself or you at the same level or above our Lord is a lie of enemy! It must be put in check with the word of God immediately!

So now that we have exposed the biggest hindrances to hearing God, let's deal with how to come into alignment with the will of God based on what you have received and heard from Him!

Aligning with God in the Midst of the Battle: Yielding to God's Agenda

Aligning yourself with God in the midst of the Battle is one of the most critical steps that you can take in the Kingdom. As a matter of fact, it is not an option but a strategic choice of life over death. This choice impacts your life both spiritually and naturally. It ultimately involves the long term commitments that you will make for every aspect of your life. Yielding to God's agenda begins the process of bringing you into a place of victorious living. Recognizing the full benefits of being a Kingdom heir happens as a result of you aligning yourself with King Jesus.

"Aligning" is the action of being in, or coming into, precise adjustment or relative position with a specific party or **cause**. To do this effectively one must yield their own wants and desires for that of another. To dig a little deeper, "to yield" means to give over control to another, or render one's rights because this action is fittingly owed or required by someone else. "Yield" also means to give up or cease resistance and contention to a given situation. Because yielding control of your life and your way of making choices is not an easy or desirable position to be in, aligning yourself with the Lord is considered to be a personal sacrifice.

Ouch! I know we don't like saying or even hearing that word, "sacrifice". But you need to realize that "alignment" is an intense thing, and yes, aligning yourself with the will of God requires a tremendous personal sacrifice. This is a sacrifice that costs you something that you would not easily want to give up. In fact, you would even offer some other **really** good "stuff" in its place before surrendering your final rights up for that "special" situation, precious item or endeared person. Yes, you know instinctively that you are really going to feel the impact of the lost and it is NOT going to be a warm and fuzzy adventure. Uh huh, a sacrifice is the category that it fits in.

When God asks us to come into alignment with His will for us and make that sacrifice, we fight Him tooth and nail! This occurs sometimes knowingly, and sometimes unintentionally. But warrior of the most High God, don't you know that He is not the one that your fight is really with? So what do you do?

First, you stop fighting against the Lord's process. That's the wrong battle. Stop resisting the change. Second, you fight the good fight of faith as Apostle Paul tells us. How do you do that? By submitting yourself to the will of God and yielding your agenda for His. With the Lord's guidance and protection, know that this type of sacrifice will begin the process of getting you aligned with the will of God and ready to serve on the Battlefield as a well trained military soldier. Its ground level preparation for each and every level of maturing that you will go through in life. So get ready and expect it to happen!

The Blessings of Alignment

I want to share a testimony with you about the blessing of alignment that comes from yielding your life to God's agenda. As many of you know, we live in an era where there is no guaranteed job security, even for the best performers. Companies of all sizes and industries find themselves down sizing at one point in time or another. Well, though I had seen many take place, this time I had the wonderful opportunity to be one of the "chosen" ones. I was offered a package to leave my position with IBM, or stay and find another position in a different department. Now, working at IBM had been an early career desire. Wow, to be at one of the top ten - I knew I had arrived. And for that season, I had! However, God had different plans for my life at that point in time. So, I was face with a major decision that would change the very course of my life and my family's.

The notification date came in 2004, and my manager was more broken up about it than I was. In fact, I was encouraging him the entire time, and telling *him* it was going to be all right. I told him that God knew this was coming even if I didn't and that He would take care of me. After I hung up the phone, yes of course I got my cry out as the sting took effect. Man, I hadn't been without a job and steady income for over 25 years. At the same time I knew a major shift was at hand. I knew I had to talk to the Lord to find out what was going on and what I needed to do next. Time was of the essence! I had bills that needed to be paid, tuition for our sons that I was responsible for, and I was clueless on what to do next. But I did know that God had a strategy.

It just so happened that I was already scheduled to head off to Washington DC for an engineering competition that our oldest son was competing in. So the Lord and I would have several days to get on the same page. I should have known it was a "divine set up", right? Exactly! As I prayed for direction during that time, the Lord spoke clearly, firmly and specifically on what I was to do over the next 12 months.

This time of revelation only came after I surrendered my agenda for His. I asked what I should do, and He answered, "What is your desire?". Shoot, my natural mind was yelling, "My desire is not to be unemployed. I like working, and IBM pays very well! Are you kidding me?" But my spirit and heart knew that the right response was to do what pleased Him. Even though I knew God would have honored my choice, I wanted to be certain that I was in alignment for His will for the direction of my life. It just makes life so much easier that way.

See, Warrior, you have to learn, just as I have learned, to watch for those multiple choice questions that lead to more processing (smile). All jokes aside though, truly in my heart, my desire was to do whatever would bring Him glory through my life. So immediately by making that choice, I knew the cost would be tremendous to walk in.

Upon my return, I told my manager I would be returning to school and would accept the termination package. God as my witness, my manager was determined to find me another position. There were at least 30 jobs that I easily qualified for, including some overseas as a Project Manager/Senior Business Analyst. Even having been informed of my choice, my manager, God bless him, kept sending job information to me right up to the very last day!

In the midst of this, came the time that I had to let my family know of my decision. My Mom immediately said, "You will be OK". I think there were only five people on the entire earth that did not think I had lost my natural mind, and I was one of them. People will not understand when you make this type of decision that is not understandable to the world or natural mind. Truth be told God had been preparing me for this for a number of years. He had been telling me all along that this point in time would eventually come. In fact, I would have to say that I was given several extensions! I chose not to acknowledge it, and therefore I did not take full advantage of the preparation time. Anyway, I got off the fast track in corporate, which was a senior position and status that I had worked the last 25 years of my life to accomplished; and got on the Lord's straight and narrow road for my life.

Now station break here: this choice **is not** for everybody and when the Lord leads us to do this type of transition, it is rarely "suddenly". So don't go saying, "Dr. Paris confirmed in her book that I am supposed to quit my job right now." The devil is a lie! If this is a confirmation for the place you are in with God, right now - then Amen. But for the majority, it is not the case. For many, the day to day working world is where your ministry. Be it to your manager, supervisors, colleagues or employees. Know your place, the season and timings! The season and timings are critical to being in proper alignment with God's will. The **key** concept that I am confirming here is that there is a definite need for us, as God's people, to *come into and stay in alignment with His Will and purpose for each of our lives in every season, at any given point in time.* Only when we do this as individuals can we help the Kingdom collectively.

What coming into alignment accomplished during this time is immeasurable. I grew up a lot. Even though I thought I was already grown. I finished my doctorate degree, which I might add was paid for in full by IBM as an added benefit for separated employees. (*2 Blessings!*) I finished and published the first book, "**Breaking Through Towards Spiritual Maturity**". *(Another Blessing!)* I was invited out to Stanford University to do a speaking engagement to many young, impressionable minds! *(Major Blessing #4!)* I went to the Holy land fully paid through the kindness of others (thank you - you know who you are!) *(This counts as an innumerable Blessing!)* All of these significant blessings occurred within a 12 month time frame! Though it was tight, I am far stronger spiritually and more secure in who God called me to be from to the overall experience than if I had stayed at IBM and continued on my personally developed life destination.

My coming into alignment with the will of the Lord for my life has ultimately caused me to know Him the more in many ways that I may never have known Him in. He is a provider. He is a strong tower. He is a healer. He is a protector. He is a miracle worker in finances and relationships. He is definitely a keeper! For me, being in alignment with His will, allowed me to experience life changing events and opportunities. Doing this has made me a living testimony to what it can look like walking in the fullness of Him. If I my choices had been different, then I may never have experienced this aspect of the Lord. Yes, I am one of His living testimonies with much more still to be accomplished. And you can be too, just come into alignment with His purpose for you!

Knowing the Heart of God in the Battle

Remember part of the definition of alignment is to get in a position of importance with a specific **cause**. We talk more about the **Cause** in **Chapter 11**, for now we are going to continue to focus on aligning ourselves with the will of the Lord for our individual lives. In order to do this, the first step involves reconciling your heart with the Father. Let's look at **Jeremiah 24:7**:

*"And I will give them an heart to know me, that I am the
LORD: and they shall be my people, and I will be their God:
for they shall return unto me with their whole heart."*

"Return" in this passage refers to coming into proper position,
into a right standing. It literally means reconciling ourselves with
the Father. Our Father created us to have a heart that is **one** with His.
Remember, spiritually our heart is our spiritual ear for hearing the
voice of the Lord and communing with Him when ever we desire to.
The desire part is the element that ties directly to reconciliation. Our
reconciling with our heavenly Father is a matter of personal choice.
Yes, here we are put full circle back to the choices we make.

Within each of our individual life times, it is necessary to come
to the realization that we must have a heart that is surrendered to
Him as we discussed in **Part One** of this book. He created us with
the ability to walk in His ways, speak and decree His Words, know
and declare His Will in earth, and be in direct relationship with Him.
This ability validates that we belong to Him. Access to this ability
validates the position when we choose to do it willingly. This is the
essence of the spirit of reconciliation and it pleases the Father even
the more when we do it of one's own free will!, from this position
you are given the insight, power, authority, and strength you need
to endure and stand victoriously in the Battle. Yes, reconciliation is
a key! Once we give our hearts to the Lord and reconciliation takes
place, our relationship with our Father is restored.

Then what? I'm glad you asked! We, as His sons and daughters,
are then prepared for battle. How? Well let's look at **1 Chronicles
28:9**:

*And thou, Solomon my son, know thou the God of thy father,
and serve him with a perfect heart and with a willing mind:
for the LORD searcheth all hearts, and understandeth all
the imaginations of the thoughts: if thou seek him, he will be
found of thee; but if thou forsake him, he will cast thee off
for ever.*

In this process, as God searches our hearts and minds, He teaches us to search for Him in all matters. The Lord already knows you. The processing is to develop and mature you so that YOU know you! You don't want to surprise yourself in Battle and become your own "best" enemy. Do you? Warrior, go through the process!

Make the commitment to reconcile with the Father and serve Him with your whole heart and life. To do this, you must be willing to make the choices that glorify God and prepare you even the more for your destiny. You must want to know the Father's will for your life. Some of us really don't want to know fully. If you really did, would you still say, "Yes Lord, yes to Your will for my life."? We need to do just as King Solomon did. Know the Lord, serve Him, and allow Him to mature your heart. Above all else Warrior, do it willingly. Soldier, you've already come too far!

For most us, if you are reading this book, you REALLY have come too far to get out of the will of God. If you are stuck, which we do get from time to time, here's the strategy to keep in mind. You must KNOW God in order to SERVE God in ways that glorify Him in the earth and in your life! You can only fully serve someone if you know them. You can only truly know them by the experiences that you have with them. Based on the experiences you have in your life with the Lord, you begin to know Him for who He is.

Now I know this is going to be an interesting statement. But I will venture to say that you will only know Him for who He is based on the level you have allowed Him to be to you and the amount of access you have given Him to your "stuff". Our Lord Jesus is more than enough. But you have to ask yourself when you get stuck in your stuff if you have really tapped into the fullness of God to access all the privileges of freedom available to you as a child of the King. The skill of knowing how to recognize that you are "stuck" and even when to ask yourself this question is level of maturity that develops with each experience that you have with the Lord. As God matures your heart, you will begin serve Him without question or doubt or even regret. This process of a maturing heart will allow you to come into full alignment, one step at a time.

Remember, coming into alignment puts you into your rightful position within the Kingdom. This is where access to the blessings can and will overtake you! Some of us only have a foot in the doorway and can't or won't come any closer. You are missing out on what God has in store for you. These blessings are just sitting there with your name on them, all beautiful and ready to go! Yet they have a huge "inaccessible due to lack of preparedness" or "deferred release" signs on them. Get into alignment, Warrior! You have come this far so you might as well come all the way in willingly! The other down side to this is that once you know better and still choose to reject Him, there will come a point that you will not be invited or allowed in again to gain access to the knowledge of His heart or the attached blessings. Let's not allow that to happen! You've come too far and you know too much about Him. So how do you continue to get into alignment for the Battle? Read on.

Lord, how do I do what You want me to do?

There's a walk we take in this Christian lifestyle that is greatly influenced by the outcomes and results of how we overtake the challenges that we encounter along the way. What is the lifestyle that you have chosen as a follower of Jesus Christ? The way we bridge the gap between what God says we are to do and what we actually do will clearly impact our lives. Many times we are ready and prepared to move, but do not know how to take the next steps. So, in this section we will look at a few ways to increase our level of obedience. Let's start with **Jeremiah 7:21-23**:

> *"²¹ Thus saith the LORD of hosts, the God of Israel; Put your burnt offerings unto your sacrifices, and eat flesh. ²²For I spake not unto your fathers, nor commanded them in the day that I brought them out of the land of Egypt, concerning burnt offerings or sacrifices: ²³But this thing commanded I them, saying, Obey my voice, and I will be your God, and ye shall be my people: and walk ye in all the ways that I have commanded you, that it may be well unto you."*

We are told here by God via His prophet Jeremiah that we must not only hear the voice of God, but we must also OBEY! There is a condition applied here in that to receive the blessing of God our Father, we must hear *and* obey. By doing so demonstrates that we belong to Him as His people. Obedience to the Lord is very visible and demonstrative in your spiritual walk. Lack of it is also very visible to others as they watch you live your life. The act of obedience highlights your desire to serve the Lord willingly, and because of this God is inevidentably glorified through your life.

These verses call attention to the importance of the need for the believer to live a life of total obedience and devotion to the Lord, first and foremost. The scriptures consistently teach us that religious observances devoid of spiritual reality are worthless. Listen, God earnestly longs to meet us in communion and fellowship with Him and continuously He finds that we do not keep our appointments with Him! On the flip side, even though we "diss", (*meaning ditch, disrespect, or disregard*), God for other things, some of us get beside ourselves when others do to us what we do to God by not keeping their commitments to us. Wow!

The most important thing to realize here is that they don't wake us up in the morning, they don't supply our needs, and they don't give us breath. God does! So why can't we keep our appointments with God as He beckons for us to come closer? Hmmmm. So to help us with to focus and turn this situation around, following are some keys to help you become more discipline in this area in your life.

Obedience requires a Submissive Spirit

Here is where we started the chapter. True submission is when your obedience to the Lord is in alignment with your total agreement with what the Lord is saying and doing in the Kingdom, with nothing else in between. No hidden agendas, no ulterior motives, just pure humility with the desire to serve. To be submissive means humbling yourself to others. It is the act of yielding to the authority or the control of another. Submission is the sacrifice of your choices for someone else's choices for you. However, please be aware that submission is not to be confused with a position of weakness! Having a submissive spirit is willingly giving your will, which is your power and authority to choose for yourself to another "freely" to make decisions for you. This is the position we are to be in at all times with the Lord. And this is a position of true power and authority in the spirit realm. We are to walk with a submissive spirit yielded to the Spirit of the Lord.

Let's look at **1 Peter 5:5-6:**

"⁵Likewise, ye younger, submit yourselves unto the elder. Yea, all of you be subject one to another, and be clothed with humility: FOR GOD RESISTETH THE PROUD, AND GIVETH GRACE TO THE HUMBLE. ⁶Humble yourselves therefore under the mighty hand of God, that he may exalt you in due time: ⁷Casting all your care upon him; for he careth for you."

This is the position we are to be in at all times with God. This passage also tells us the order of submission one to another. Having a submissive spirit moves us into a higher level. It's beyond the humbled will. How? Because developing a humbled will leads to a change in your "old" lifestyle and ways. The humbling of one's will is God's initial processing of His children. In this process, each of us has to willingly submit to it. Some have not fully understood its purpose, many have chosen not to go through the process, and even some others have been occasional trainees. But for those of you that endure the initial processing, there is a level peace that can not be explained to others that have not experienced it.

Once you are at this level, it's difficult to go back to the ways of the world and the way you used to do things. Why? This is because a **Submissive Spirit is the result of a disciplined heart**. A discipline heart is developed from leading a life that thirsts after the righteousness and heart of God. This is a heart that has been transformed by the Spirit of God. In **Romans 8:6** we are encouraged to grow to this level of being lead by the Spirit of God and, thereby developing a lifestyle pleasing before God.

"For to be carnally minded is death; but to be spiritually minded is life and peace."

Remember, you are God's glory in the earth, so act accordingly!

Obedience requires Patience

All of God's promises are Yea and Amen! God will often reveal strategic events and issues just as He did in **Joshua 6**. When He does, it doesn't always mean act on it right away. Some of us get the plan, (the what) and instructions (the how), but don't wait to hear the "when" (the season and timings). We figure we can handle it on our own in our own time. We say, "OK God, that's an awesome plan, I got it from here". But, as He told Job in **Job 37:14:**

> *"Hearken unto this, O Job: stand still, and consider the wondrous works of God."*

If God can handle the heavens, earth and all that's in it, surely He can handle you, and your situations. If He hasn't given you the time, its not time for you to know the "when" yet. With this in mind, being patient also requires that you seek His Timing. Allow the things of God manifest in their fullness of time by being patient and letting God be God. Know that there are other situations and issues being worked out and put into place for the completion of your purpose.

While you wait, let the Holy Spirit teach and prepare you for what's to come, each step of the way towards accomplishing your purpose. **Psalm 25:4-5** tell us what we are to do while we wait for God.

> *"Show me thy ways, O Lord; teach me thy paths. Lead me in thy truth, and teach me: for thou art the God of my salvation; on thee do I wait all day."*

We are to watch for God's move and be led by His Spirit and Word. Remember your Spiritual Equilibrium, and wait on Him; no matter how long it takes. You must remember, He knows your beginning and end! Therefore, He knows the timing for each move in your life. Allow the things of God to manifest in their fullness of time.

Obedience requires Discretion

Obedience requires that you use discretion with the information that God has given you. Patience and discretion are closely related in everything that God will instruct you to do. You must take the time to gain understanding and clarity about what God has spoken to you. To do this, you must put some thought into what God has spoken to you. Ponder it! To ponder means to think about, reflect on, and consider quietly and deeply. In **Luke 2:19,** we are told:

> *"But Mary kept all these things, and pondered them in her heart."*

After the angel of God visited Mary, Mary first kept everything to herself that she had been told and then she pondered what had been said to her. There will be many things that God will say to you that are for you and you only. God will tell you things to come if He can trust you. As you prove that you can be discrete with what He has given you, more will be revealed to you. Why? This is so that you can tend to them in the earth. How? Through prayer and your obedience to perform what He has given you in the manner and timing that He tells you. In other words, when God releases you!

Obedience requires Total Alignment

Total obedience requires that your heart and will be in alignment with God's heart and will. Your attitude about doing what God has asked you to do is critical in determining what your level of blessing will be and how much God will say to you. Let's look at **Isaiah 1:19-20**:

> *"¹⁹ If ye be willing and obedient, ye shall eat the good of the land: ²⁰ But if ye refuse and rebel, ye shall be devoured with the sword: for the mouth of the LORD hath spoken it."*

God tells us if we are willing **and** obedient, we will eat the good of the land. He also tells us what will happen if we are not. Not doing so, you are in rebellion. And how many of know, partial obedience is still disobedience, which is rebellion. Obedience in action alone is not enough to please God. God wants you to carry out His spoken word with the desire to serve Him with your whole heart. No matter what He has asked of you, you are to do it with a joyful heart, to the letter, when He tells you to do it.

Obedience requires Godly Counsel

Complete obedience requires that you seek Godly Counsel. God will tell you who and when this is. Don't ask everybody and unqualified people for advice about your situation. In the Word, we are told in **Psalm 1:1-2:**

"¹ Blessed is the man that walketh not in the counsel of the ungodly, nor standeth in the way of sinners, nor sitteth in the seat of the scornful (ungodly or wicked) ² But his delight is in the law of the LORD; and in his law doth he meditate day and night."

As stated here, do not walk in the counsel of the ungodly. When you seek counsel, it should be someone seasoned with the Word of God and liked minded in the faith. You wouldn't see a mechanic for a tooth ache, would you? And your purpose is far too important to God for you to let "bad" advice change your course! God will lead you to who you need when you need them. How? **Verse 2** tells us: by the continuous meditation and study of the Word!

So what else is keeping us from getting there?

Obedience requires Stepping Outside of the Box

Surrendered obedience requires that you step outside of the box of the natural realm and walking in the supernatural. This is called living in the realm of Faith! Faith is the currency for the Kingdom of God! This is the same as the Star Trek theme: "To boldly go where no man has gone before!" This leads me to challenge you to do this as you live day to day: instead of saying or thinking what God would never do, begin to think and say, *"I have faith to know that God will do all things that will bring me into alignment with His perfect will for my life".*

Stepping out of the box requires that you do something that you may have never done before. When the Lord speaks, it will always require your faith to hear Him. What He says will require courage to follow Him. Warrior, you must remember that what He speaks will sometimes go against all natural reasons and rationalizations of the world, your family, friends, and yes sometimes even yourself. That is why it is called "stepping outside the box". Obedience to God many times requires that you get out of your comfort zone. Otherwise eventually you will stop growing!

The safety net in area is to remember that God is a confirming God! If you are unclear or unsure in what has been spoken, ask Him for confirmation. Another most important safeguard is to know that what He speaks to you will **ALWAYS** line up with His written word. This is important! Remember in all things, the Rhema Word, which is the spoken word, will be supported by the Logos Word, which is the written Word of the Bible.

Don't be afraid to get into the spiritual flow required to recognize the seasons of God for your life. Then, you will know to move when He says move, and be still when He says be still! There is a time and season for EVERYTHING as **Ecclesiastes 3:1** tells us:

"To every thing there is a season, and a time to every purpose under the heaven:"

Stay in alignment, listen and respond in a timely and orderly manner to the voice of our Savior. Remember my testimony mentioned earlier about my career move from IBM. Recall that I knew the "general" outcome was to leave IBM almost 3 years prior and that my season there would end soon. As I spent time in the hotel room on Capitol Hill fasting, praying and seeking the Lord, I wanted and needed to know the what, how, and why.

I know that when God gives a Vision, He will also provide the provisions. That's not just a cliché'. The provision in this case included **both** clarity in direction and financial means. When you hear instructions from God, especially the ones that are life changing and impacting, you must take the time to fully understand them not only with your natural hearing, but especially with your spiritual hearing, your heart. By the time the competition was over, the Lord had revealed and clarified my next steps with such clarity that I could not say I was uncertain. I must also say that though it may not been the way and manner that I was accustom to, the Lord sustained me and my family totally during the transition! ***Thank you Lord.***

You see, God "had need of me", just as He does you. Was I afraid? Absolutely! However, I was not doubtful on what I was to do after taking the time to seek the Lord to be certain that I was in season, with His time and alignment. Ponder each major move. There is always time for reflection, divine clarity and natural prepa-ration. You have to take the time to get in God's presence and get it, especially for the major events and issues. It is also important that you do this on an ongoing basis. As I mentioned earlier, I knew 3 years prior that that decision would have to be made. Most of us get the end result, but get ahead of God's timing. Though He had prepared me for what would come, I still waited for the divine season. I can't say I was in love with the ideal, but I knew I wanted to be within His will and timing.

Moving too soon is like stepping off an unfinished bridge. Now I am not talking about the ones that are struggling, or that don't like your manager, or those that disagree with the company practices. All of these are good reasons to quit a job, I guess, but don't blame it on God, when it is really you making the decision. Do not forfeit the promises of God by getting ahead of God's plan and moving out on your own agenda. See who is talking to you because it certainly could be your own pride, bitterness or angry dressed up really nice and convincingly attractive. Remember; don't doubt what you hear, BUT discern who's speaking when you are stepping outside the box!

Again, looking at the flip side to this, I have heard a number of God's people say, "God told me to quit my job." My response gener-ally is, "Really? And what are you going to do?". "I don't know." Can't you just hear the screeching brakes? Many times, when I am allowed to speak on this area to the person, I say, "Um, excuse me, but what do you mean you don't know?" Discern my brother, discern my sister. Discern who's talking and once you have confirmed that it is God, WAIT for the instructions for what you are to do once you walk out the employer's door. God is a God of ORDER! Generally, He is not going to have you, or your family, be without the provisions that come from working. Get the strategy! Get your instructions! If He is really telling you to leave that job, He will tell you clearly when, how, why, and what to do **next**.

Lord, You promised me Peace in the Midst of the Battle!

Finally, aligning yourself with the will of God will guarantee you peace in the valley, in the wilderness and in any battle. Strive to keep your peace in tack because to fight an effective fight, your heart and mind must have peace. Don't try and make something work when you don't have peace about it. But make sure it is inner peace that's missing and not fear, which is doubt, uncertainty, or confusion running rampant! Ask yourself what you are afraid of. Check how you feel and what you sense about the situation or issue.

Allow the Holy Spirit to teach and lead you. He will teach you how to hear Him. **Philippians 4:6-9** tells us exactly what this peace looks like.

> *"⁶Be careful for nothing: but in everything by prayer and supplication with thanksgiving let your requests be made known unto God. ⁷And the peace of God, which passeth all understanding, shall keep your hearts and minds through Christ Jesus. ⁸Finally, brethren, whatsoever things are true, whatsoever things are honest, whatsoever things are just, whatsoever things are pure, whatsoever things are lovely, whatsoever things are of good report; if there be any virtue, and if there be any praise, think on these things. ⁹Those things, which ye have both learned, and received, and heard, and seen in me, do: and the God of peace shall be with you."*

Verse 6 and **7** tell us how to obtain God's peace. **Verses 8** and **9**, tell us how to keep it. In order to keep God's peace, we must occupy our minds and hearts with the right things and busy ourselves with the right activities. The peace of God is that inner tranquility of the heart and mind freeing the believer from fear and worry. It is peace divinely bestowed in times of anxiety and yes, war! It guards and protects you! It gives you the ability to maintain a clear mind so that you can keep your focus on what's **really** in front and ahead of you. Remember the things we covered in **Chapter 4**!

What did He promise? We grow faint and weary in long Battles and lose sight of what the Promise is. When we lose focus, there is a danger of indifference setting in. The "whatever" or "it is what it is" perspective can take hold quickly. Stay focused on the things of God. He tells us in this passage those things to concentrate on. Though they may seem "sappy" or too warm and fuzzy, even for the toughest of Warriors, mediating in these areas of previous victory and blessings will keep you in the midst of the wilderness. Especially when you feel like you are fighting all alone. The building of your testimony is not always for the future generations to see. *The building of your testimony is also for you to understand the past and stand stronger in the present, so that you can be better prepared for the future!*

You sustain your peace in the Battle through prayer and letting God know what you are in need of. As He grants your requests, alignment will come! Alignment gives us the ability to stay focused and obedient to the will of God. Knowing the will of our Lord under girds our faith when we yield our will for His. As we get through each battle, big and small, we may not always understand how it happened, but we know that it was because of God's controlled hand over your life. Know what He has promised you directly so that the cause for fighting is personal and clear to you!

CHAPTER 11

Living in Obedience: Surrendering Totally for the Cause

What's a "CAUSE" anyway?

You may be still wondering what this is really all about! Is there really a "Cause" for all this intense preparation and fighting? To get to that answer, we need to break this down into manageable pieces. To do this, we need to first understand and agree that "Yes, there is a Cause!" But what exactly does that mean to you and me? Let's start by getting a better understanding of what the meaning of "Cause" is. Simply stated, cause is a reason for a specific **action** or **condition**.

Cause is an important matter of question to be resolved through visible activities or efforts. As an action, cause compels us to do something. It is why we do what we do, and it is what drives and motivates us to act. At the same time, cause is the antecedent for the posture we must take in following and standing on what we believe. Our outward countenance is how others are convinced that we are who we say we are. In our specific case as disciples of Jesus Christ, the demonstrative action within the Cause is provoked by our desire to live within the boundaries of the Gospel in our daily Christian walk.

Cause as a condition for us as the people of God gives us an overwhelming, indistinctive desire to consistently strive to uphold it. This condition is a way of life driven by our openness to receive and give the love of God. By this, I mean the cause is where our passion initially lies thereby becoming the place where we invest our hearts. This condition is established and illuminated in our Christian lifestyle by our love for the Father, our Lord, and one another. In other words, as Christians we must *walk the walk* **and** *talk the talk* in bearing up and living successfully within the realms of the Cause through the love of Christ Jesus! We are therefore able to create, influence and control the environment we live in moment by moment based on how we utilize this life sustaining ingredient called "LOVE".

The question that is being pressed for resolution surrounding the Cause is, "Will we be victorious in our pursuit of God's divine purpose for His people and Kingdom?" According to **Revelation 19** this question has already been resolved and the answer is a resounding, "YES!" YES, we will be and are victorious in our pursuit of fulfilling the Cause. The passion behind our day to day actions and the travailing conditions of our hearts to induce God's will in our lives and in the earth are the driving forces that carry us through this Battle triumphantly. **2 Corinthians 2:14** further confirms this:

"Now thanks be unto God, which always causeth us to triumph in Christ, and maketh manifest the savour of his knowledge by us in every place."

Our heavenly Father will always cause us to be triumphant as we live a life that is Christ focused. We must know this as fact and live it as truth with gratefulness and an appreciation for who He is and what He has said. As we go forth in this wisdom, this life sustaining knowledge becomes even the more precious to us in all we do issue by issue, day by day, situation by situation, and battle by battle.

So, what's our Cause?

Now that we have a basic parameter of what the Cause is, let's get even more specific to what it is to us as Kingdom Warriors. Precisely stated as followers of Christ, a cause means to have a reason for action in order to bring about a specific condition. In the Kingdom of God, *"The Cause is fighting and winning the Battle in ways that glorify God, our Father"*. The truth we must walk in is that we are warriors of the Lion of Judah and the fight for the Cause has already been won. We must keep in mind at all times that *we are fighting for the manifestation of the joint results of the Cause that bring Salvation and Redemption to all of God's people for all eternity.* That's our mission in supporting the Cause. At the core of the Cause is the Harvest of the Kingdom of God as we are told in **Matthew 9:37:**

> *"³⁷Then saith he unto his disciples, The harvest truly is plenteous, but the labourers are few;"*

Each battle fought and won is over territory in the Harvest. This can be in your life personally, another person, family, neighbor, job, finances, home or any particular area or realm that the enemy chooses to wage war. To be overcomers on the battle field, we are to take our rightful places and walk with authority in our purposes within the Kingdom. The victorious fight is **all** about the glorified Kingdom of God as described in **Revelation 21**. Oh, yes, there is a Cause and it is a matter of life and death, both naturally and spiritually for the people of God! But before we go further I would like to take a few paragraphs to address the importance of the **Book of Revelation** since it is critical to our study of the Cause.

Why is the Book of Revelation Important?

This chapter deals quite a bit with the book of **Revelation**, so before we go any further I think we should briefly address the issue of why these particular writings are so critical to our faith, the Kingdom of God and this Battle. So come on, let's get busy and address this very important foundational question of *"Why is the Book of Revelation important?"*

To do this let's look at the what, who and why. First, this book's proper title is: **"The Revelation of Jesus Christ to John"**. It is the result of John the Apostle's divine encounters with the Lord while he was in exile on the island of Patmos. These divinely inspired writings lay out God's strategy for us as His people to live in the present and go forth into the future. It is His prophetic program for the world. That's the "what".

Now, let's deal the "who". This book gives us the revelation of the "person" of Jesus Christ, our Lord. It is the revealing of what *had not* been previously revealed to us about Him fully in previous writings. Now, look at the "why". It is the full unveiling of Jesus Christ to His people by our Savior for us to know Him even the more. To know Him the more enables us to live an abundantly empowered victorious life! As we are told in **John 10:10** this is one of the main reasons He came!

Also, let's dispel the stronghold of some traditional teachings. You are **not** to be afraid of this book of divine knowledge! In fact, you should want to know the truth and know it for yourself. Don't think the enemy hasn't check out the **Book of Revelation**! Don't let them continue to have the upper hand on you because they know more about your destiny and purpose than you do. Know your *HIStory*! As we are instructed in **2 Timothy 2:15**:

> *"Study to shew thyself approved unto God, a workman that needeth not to be ashamed, rightly dividing the word of truth."*

Foundation Knowledge that Supports the Cause

Now we are ready to dig a little deeper. Let's put another layer of foundation on what's really going on because God has given you the authority to know. Recall that discernment is the ability to skillfully grasp **and** comprehend a specific issue or circumstance. Remember to use it regularly! Especially in this present day when it is becoming even more critical for us not just to fight the good fight of faith, but to discern what we are fighting for! Therefore, the questions that we seek answers for to strengthen our understanding of how to support the Cause are:

- "Why Jesus Christ?"
- "Who is He that leads us?"
- "What are we fighting about?"
- "Who are we to the Lion of Judah and the Lamb of God?" and
- "How do we surrender to fight victoriously for the Cause?"

To get to the answers we are seeking, **Revelation Chapter 5** is an excellent starting point. This passage will be referenced throughout the rest of this chapter. This particular passage also helps us get clarity on how the Cause relates to our relationship with our King and our overall spiritual walk. So let's get further into our investigation.

Why Jesus Christ?

Starting out as a preface for understanding and submitting to the Cause we need to understand why Jesus is the "One", so let's start with **Revelation 5:1-4.**

"¹And I saw in the right hand of him that sat on the throne a book written within and on the backside, sealed with seven seals. ²And I saw a strong angel proclaiming with a loud voice, Who is worthy to open the book, and to loose the seals thereof? ³And no man in heaven, nor in earth, neither under the earth, was able to open the book, neither to look thereon. ⁴And I (John) wept much, because no man was found worthy to open and to read the book, neither to look thereon."

We are told here that there were major tasks of monumental importance that needed to be fulfilled. However, among all the living creatures that God created there was no one that qualified for the job. In God's perfect plan for mankind, He knew a sacrifice was needed. Therefore, He sent a part of Himself to reconcile His family back into relationship with Him. This atoning sacrifice of the Lord for us is seen in **1 John 2:2:**

"And he is the propitiation for our sins: and not for ours only, but also for the sins of the whole world."

Our Lord Jesus paid the price for all of us to be restored and gain intimate, direct access to God the Father. As a Christian, and follower of the Word, we must stand firm on the fact that the only way to be rejoined in this holy relationship with the Father is through His Son, Jesus. There is no other way. Again, by the Word of God, only Jesus, the Son of God, can give you eternal life because He was, and is, the only atoning sacrifice that enables us to restore our relationship with God and regain the grace and favor of our heavenly Father.

A major key to realize here is how important God's love is towards all of us. Let's further look at the love of our Father for us as it is seen in **1 John 4:10***:*

"Herein is love, not that we loved God, but that he loved us, and sent his Son to be the propitiation for our sins."

You may be asking well why Him still? Well don't take my word for it, let's continue to back it up in the Word. **Philippians 2:8-11** tell us this:

"And being found in fashion as a man, he humbled himself, and became obedient unto death, even the death of the cross. Wherefore God also hath highly exalted him, and given him a name which is above every name: That at the name of Jesus every knee should bow, of things in heaven, and things in earth, and things under the earth; And that every tongue should confess that Jesus Christ is Lord, to the glory of God the Father."

Jesus alone paid this price with His natural life. He didn't have to do it, but he did. How many of us would give our life willingly, for all these people, who some you know, some you don't, some you like, and some you don't. Better yet how many of us, with the weight of the world upon us, would not lift a finger to alter this course of destiny if we had the power to do so? Because remember now, when He came, Jesus came as a part of the God head wrapped in flesh. He had the power to destroy all of them that opposed Him with just a glaze or simple thought. How do we say it, "Just say the Word and it's handled."! My natural father knew people like that, in fact, he was one of those people. Anyway, you get my point, right?

So, why is Jesus the only one worthy to be King and answer this proclamation from heaven? Jesus is the answer because he alone fulfilled the sacrificial requirements that were required for rejoining us to God, our Father. What other man, being or whatever has the power, ability or even the authority to do this? There is none. No, there was, is, nor ever will be any one else. He did it and this is who we are following into battle. Why? What do we gain? We gain Eternal Life with Our Savior in Heaven.

Now the next real question here is: **"Who has the right to judge the world?".** That is, who has the authority to reveal what is hidden in this scroll and **to execute what is written**. No man, literally, "No one", not among mankind, and not among the angels. In **Philippians 2:8-11**, which is provided above, we are told His very name has power to change and impact any situation at a moment's notice. More often than not, we as His warriors hesitate to use this power at a moment's notice!

The most righteous judge is the one that paid the price and has been given the authority to have sovereign rule within and over the Kingdom. In this passage, He is presented both as a Lion from the tribe of Judah, which is symbolic for "supreme ruler", and as a Lamb, symbolic for the full payment of the debt we owe our Father. The vision of our Lord Jesus Christ here brings together the twofold aspect of His first coming as our Savior and Redeemer and his expected second coming as our Sovereign Ruler. Yes, Jesus has the right to judge, possess, and rule the earth because of His submission to a natural death on the Cross.

So who is He that leads us?

The identity and qualifications of the One leading us in pursuit of the Cause are in **Revelation 5:5-7**. Let's check it out.

⁵And one of the elders saith unto me, Weep not: behold, the Lion of the tribe of Judah, the Root of David, hath prevailed to open the book, and to loose the seven seals thereof. ⁶ And I beheld, and, lo, in the midst of the throne and of the four beasts, and in the midst of the elders, stood a Lamb as it had been slain, having seven horns and seven eyes, which are the seven Spirits of God sent forth into all the earth. ⁷And He came and took the book out of the right hand of Him that sat upon the throne.

Let's start by gathering some additional information on what is happening here in determining who is leading us. We are given both the heavenly and earthly identification of the Son of God in this passage by a divine counsel. This counsel consists of the elders that sit in Heaven with our Father. Our Leader's heavenly identification is that of both the **Lion of the tribe of Judah** and the **Lamb** in this passage. This is an unusual combination, isn't it? A lion - fierce king and conqueror of whatever territory he goes into, and a lamb - one of the most gentlest natured creatures on the earth. Hmm, sovereign power and strength balanced with complete love and humility. This is a dual reference for His divine role in helping us understand the magnitude of the Cause. His earthly identification is that Jesus is the **Root of David,** who was an earthly king and a "man after God's own heart". Jesus' unique DNA, rich heritage, and legacy, empowered Him to overcome the Battle for a victory in both the heavens and here on earth. Given these distinguishing traits, Jesus is further qualified by the heavenly counsel to both open the book and loose the seals.

The "book" referenced here is a scroll with seven messages, each of which has been sealed with the authority of God. The breaking of the seals will reveal the message inside each part of the scroll. This scroll contains the Tribulation judgments of God. This is a whole series of lessons in itself. If you want to study it later, it correlates to the Books of Ezekiel and Daniel. For now let's stay on understanding the Leader of the Cause. What's going on in this passage is that the question is being asked **who** can open the book or scroll of God's Judgments on the world.

This is a critical moment in eternity because only the One with the proper authority can open the book by removing the seals. Each seal contains a powerful judgment, such as the world wide conquest of the Antichrist, War, Inflation and Famine, Death to a fourth of the population, martyrdom of the Tribulation saints (these are those that will come into the faith after the Rapture), natural disasters of all kinds, and the awesome seventh seal that contains the seven trumpets. This final component is rough all by itself in that just by the very opening of this seal there will be a long silence followed by the unleashing of another whole set of End Time Judgments. None of which are pretty or pleasant. As I say to my sons and daughters, be afraid, be very afraid! Am I scaring you? Good! If you are out of alignment or without covering self teaching yourself - I beseech to return to our Father God today!

This is an awesome responsibility. To be found worthy by God to perform a task of this magnitude is a staggering thought. If you, as a true Christian, in your heart even think that you are capable - you need to think again because you truly do not understand the immensity of this role! According to Webster's Dictionary, worthy means to be important enough, being honorable, or having merit or excellence. According to Vine's Expository, "worthy" in this passage means *"axios"*, which means the weight or worth of a person **and** their deeds have been found flawless. Hmmm, yes, we are to strive to be flawless and without blemish just as our Savior is. Both their character and personal actions are placed under intense scrutiny in order to place this specific qualification upon the person. The actual personality of the person is under close examination. How many of us could withstand such an intense examination? The full outcome of this search finds the One that is truly worthy to be our Lord Jesus. Jesus has withstood this examination, and He has been found flawless by Heaven!

Another consideration here is that it is not just the act of opening the Book, but also being empowered to handle each and every consequence that will follow as a result of this act. In both major roles, Jesus has prevailed and overcame the tremendous dimensions of testing and preparation that no man could withstand. As a result, our Father has given Jesus the authority to both open the book and loose the seals - and manage everything that follows.

As you ponder this note that we are told here that **no man** is capable or qualified for the task. How many people do you really know that can make you a king and priest, give you true dominion over the earth, and fully empower and equip you to serve our God in His Kingdom? Certainly, no man or creature other than our Lord, Jesus Christ! The overwhelming magnitude of this entire situation is why I believe John began to weep.

Have you every made a major decision in your life and wished that you could have taken it back? Well this is one of those decisions that once it is put into motion it will have a waterfall effect and there is no turning back. Who else could be more certain than the most Righteous Judge, Jesus?

So exactly who is He that He is the only one worthy of opening the book as our Ruler? As our Ruler, He is called the Lion of Judah over the tribe of Judah. His forthcoming into this position can be trace throughout the Old Testament. And how many know that a Ruler has the authority to do whatever he wants to do in his kingdom. His desire for those of us that stand for His purpose is revealed in both the Old and New Testaments. In the Old Testament, in **Isaiah 11:10** we are foretold that:

"And in that day there shall be a root of Jesse, which shall stand for an ensign of the people; to it shall the Gentiles seek: and his rest shall be glorious.

This is not complicated. We are told that Jesus will stand as a symbol for us as His people, to where we will search Him out, and find rest in His kingdom. Historically, people look for a place to establish their lives in order to live a good life. Well, we are told here, Jesus is the good life and we only need to find Him! Find Him means accept Him as ruler over our lives! When we do this fully, the benefits are immeasurable. The discipline of this lifestyle is not always easy, but the benefits are tremendously rich and far out weigh our individual sacrifices.

Tying this back to **Revelation 5:5-7**, this promised land of rest and prosperity is symbolic for Judah. We know Judah means Praise. It also means a fierce, purposeful, favorable judgment of a situation or circumstances. Never forget that Jesus has already given us the victory over all our situations and circumstances. Yes, the report is yea and amen!

In the New Testament, let's look at **Matthew 19:28:**

"And Jesus said unto them, Verily I say unto you, That ye which have followed me, in the regeneration when the Son of Man shall sit in the throne of his glory, ye also shall sit upon twelve tribes of Israel."

Regeneration here is referencing a renewing of all things in heaven and earth. It is the kingdom of righteousness yet to come. As His people, we shall sit and lead among rulers in order to fulfill the accomplishment of His glory.

As the Lion of Judah, our King is the sovereign ruler over His Kingdom. Symbolic with the lion, know that a lion is always the king of his surroundings. He can deliver blows powerful enough to break a zebra's back, and hunt and kill even a crocodile. The adult lion also has a keen sense of sight, smell and balance. Interesting too is the fact that the lion cubs are born blind. As they grow and mature, they develop a keen sense of sight and discernment for their environment. We too are born blind, until we are born again by the Spirit into the marvelous light of our Savior and King, the Lion of Judah, at various points of time in eternity. Remember the aspects of our spiritual equilibrium? We get this from our Ruler!

Another important trait of the lion is his voice, also called his roar. It has multiple, magnificent purposes in battle. First, this roar serves as an alert that danger is present and that it is time to fight. Second, it is also called "singing" since it serves as a form of bonding within the Pride, which is a tribe of lions. Third, the piercing sound of the roar can literally paralyze the lion's prey. Even more interesting is that the lions roar can have such a powerful force behind it that it can raise a cloud of dust that cloaks Him coming. He doesn't have any enemies that can withstand the attack of Him and His army.

Therefore, they are just prey! Interesting isn't it? His voice and the response of His tribe is how we must hear and respond to our King's voice. Though His voice may be quiet at times, it is never powerless or without purpose. Oh how majestic is our King!

As the head of the "Pride", the Lion is also very protective over his family and will fight to the death to defend them and keep them. Even during battles, the Lion protects his warrior males as needed. Note that the pride actually has a family structure and the "family" members know and live by this. Within the family of the Lion, battle strategies for hunting are devised by the Leader and have been studied and proven to be ruthless and scientific in their deliverance! The Leader plans out each fight, and the attacks are extremely well organized.

So to fully understand "who is leading us", we must grasp and embrace both Jesse's divine and natural order of leading. From the natural aspect, Jesus is the Root of David. As our reigning King, Jesus has the preeminent role of dominion and power to prevail on earth. From the spiritual aspect, Jesus is the Lion of Judah. As our Ruler, He is Sovereign, all Powerful, the King of Kings, our Lord of Lords, and He is mighty in Battle. This means ALL battles and any type of battle, be it relationships, medical, financial, etc. He is the Root of David, our King and the Lion of Judah, our Ruler! That's who He is, that is who is in control, and that is who is leading us. We only need to get in alignment and follow!

What are we fighting about?

The Cause that we are fighting about and for is in **Revelation 5:8-9**.

> *⁸ And when he had taken the book, the four beasts and four and twenty elders fell down before the Lamb, having every one of them harps, and golden vials full of odors, which are the prayers of saints. ⁹And they sung a new song, saying, Thou art worthy to take the book, and to open the seals thereof: for thou wast slain, and hast redeemed us to God,*

by thy blood out of every kindred, and tongue, and people, and nation;"

The prayers of the righteous are another layer at the center of this Battle. The prayers for family members, loved ones, personal purpose, the nation, the foreign nations, the list goes on and on. All are done to gain the Lord's counsel pertaining to particular situations and how to get into proper alignment with the plans of the Father. The key to getting this accomplished, on the earth in order to start and complete the plans of God, is accessing and laying up prayers in the heaven. This literally invites and involves heaven in your daily walk. Jesus' responsibility towards us is to intercede on our behalf's to ensure that the will of God is manifested in our lives as we strive to glorify Him in the earth. Joining up with the spiritual power of heaven only makes good sense! In this case, more help is definitely better.

We are also reminded of the fact that we have been bought and paid for with a price. The "price" was the natural life of our Savior, when He was slain, as the Lamb of God. Keep in mind that this sacrifice has redeemed us back unto the relationship we once had with our Father God. Not one person will be left out that accepts Jesus as Lord over their life. Remember the Harvest is at the core of this Battle! This sacrifice was the means for reestablishing our personal interdependence with our Creator. Additionally, His sacrifice was the ultimate key to restoring us to our rightful place in God as kings and priests with the power and authority necessary for ruling over everything in the earth for His glory in the eternal Kingdom.

Our Savior and Redeemer paid us in advance for our lives to be used for His glory for Kingdom purposes. He came so we could live our lives more abundantly in spite of the opposites we will face according to **John 10:10**:

"10 The thief cometh not, but for to steal, and to kill, and to destroy: I am come that they might have life, and that they might have it more abundantly."

At the same time we begin to move in the things that the Lord has for us, we will be challenged on every side as we go forth to do this! However, our role is to demonstrate before others what we truly believe is the truth through a lifestyle of praise and newness in Him. To enable us to do this, again the good news is that Jesus is our Chief Intercessor as we are told in **Hebrews 7:25**:

> *"Wherefore he is able also to save them to the uttermost that come unto God by him, seeing he ever liveth to make intercession for them."*

To also be considered in the realm of intercession is that we are only vessels charged with praying that the will of God be done in the earth. Let's take a look at **Romans 8:34:**

> *"Who is he that condemneth? It is Christ that died, yea rather, that is risen again, who is even at the right hand of God, who also maketh intercession for us."*

As warriors in God's army, we must be careful with our words, thoughts and actions when flowing in the gift of intercession. He is the HEAD Intercessor. We must come subject to His authority and must be mindful that people's lives are at stake. He knows their beginning and ending and everything in between. We do not. So we must be strategic in our asking and be sure that we are asking with the heart and mind of God. We must be lead by our Leader during these crucial times.

The passage asks "Who condemneth?" Wow. Are we as His people not His to do as He chooses as we are so strongly reminded in **Matthew 20:15?**

> *"Is it not lawful for me to do what I will with mine own? Is thine eye evil, because I am good?"*

We must not forget the Harvest belongs to the Lord. We are ONLY caregivers! Who are we to say who can enter the Kingdom of God and who can not? Who are we to say what their kingdom purpose is and what it is not? Who are we to stand in judgment of anyone and make a final determination about their soul and eternal life? Who are we to say what God's overall plan and strategy is for His people? He only gives us pieces of it and our specific parts to be fulfilled. How dare we stand in the way of what the Lord is doing in the earth and in His people! As we are told in **Psalm 24:1:**

> *"The earth is the LORD'S, and the fulness thereof; the world, and they that dwell therein."*

In everything we do in our lives and with the Harvest, we must submit to the Lord and seek Him out for the strategy on how to proceed as we are told in **Proverbs 16:3:**

> *"Commit thy works unto the LORD, and thy thoughts shall be established"*

The Cause that we are fighting about is to ensure, today and forever more that the opportunity for full restoration be made available to anyone of God's people that desire to come into this covenant with Him. Why? So that we can reign with Him in the earth in order to accomplish our roles in fulfilling His eternal purpose. No one is an island by Himself. In other words, you can't do it alone nor is it ever God's will for you. We, as His people, are mandated to fulfill our destinies together towards the realization of His purpose in the earth. It is His desire that **not** ONE be lost, forgotten or left behind. That is the Cause!

Who are we to the Lion of Judah and the Lamb of God?

Our leader in the pursuit of the Cause is further clarified in **Revelation 5:10:**

> *[10]And hast made us unto our God kings and priests: and we shall reign on the earth.*

We are a chosen generation. We are the Redeemed! As His people, we are given a twofold promise: that we shall reign here on earth and in Heaven with Him. So who are His people? We are a chosen generation, kings and priests, and the tribe of Judah.

What do we do NOW going forward with this knowledge? We listen for instructions from our ruler, who is the Lion of Judah, to lead you through the Battlefield. Yes, we are the tribe of Judah, people of praise and victorious in this quest. Staying in alignment with the Lord means that victory is inevidentable and guaranteed.

Our principle responsibility for all eternity is to serve God. You could have been born in a time or place different than when you were. But you weren't. Just as **Ecclesiastes 3** tells us there is a season for everything. Therefore, determine what season it is for your life and get about the Father's business! If you can't do it for the short time you are here on earth, why should He let you in heaven? Hmmmm. We must live our lives focused around listening, hearing and submitting to the will of God and the Lion of Judah as our Ruler.

We are told He is listening to us in **Revelation 5:8**. He has the odor, or easier said the essence of our prayers. The essence here is being and having His nature versus our own nature. In this capacity it has been described as God's response to the prayer of the saints, which is a cry for revenge against our enemies. So we should be getting our Battle instructions from Him to be effective in this Battle, and more specifically, in our prayer time.

Tucked away in **Revelation 5:10** is another one of His promises to us as heirs, and that is that He has rejoined us into relationship with God, our Father as kings and priests that will reign in this new world and on earth. Oh yes, Jesus is worthy and He is the only one with the power to Rule over us and with the authority to open the scroll of judgments to progress us into the new world. With all this in mind, what's next? Our full surrenderance! So let's go further.

How do we surrender to fight victoriously for the Cause?

The power of praise and worship are two key weapons to securing victory during a Battle. In **Revelation 5:11-14**, Heaven says. We are to mirror heaven, in our praise of the Lamb of God for all He has done. Our leader in the pursuit of the Cause is seen again in **Revelation 5:11-12**.

> *"[11] And I beheld, and I heard the voice of many angels round about the throne and the beasts and the elders: and the number of them was ten thousand times ten thousand, and thousands of thousands; [12] Saying with a loud voice, Worthy is the Lamb that was slain to receive power, and riches, and wisdom, and strength, and honor, and glory, and blessing. [13] And every creature which is in heaven, and on the earth, and under the earth, and such as are in the sea, and all that are in them, heard I saying, Blessing, and honour, and glory, and power, be unto him that sitteth upon the throne, and unto the Lamb for ever and ever. [14]And the four beasts said, Amen. And the four and twenty elders fell down and worshipped him that liveth for ever and ever."*

In **Revelation 5:8-14**, there are 3 outbursts of praise and worship which are directed towards our Lord and our Father. The first is that the beasts and the elders praise the Lamb for having redeemed them through His blood and for giving them future authority to reign in the earth. The second is the myriad of angels also praising Jesus for His glory and wisdom. The last is that every area of creation worships both our Father and our Lord. This is done continuously and it is done in every atmospheric possibility! This is the ultimate form of surrenderance; the deliberate and intentional praise and worship of our Lord.

To know how do something effectively, I am a firm believer in the fact that you have to understand what is expected. So, for us to actually surrender to the Cause and then fight for it, we need to know what "surrender" means. According to Webster's Dictionary it means to yield to the power, control, or possession of another upon compulsion or demand. It also means to give up completely or agree to forgo especially in favor of another, or to give oneself up into the power of another especially as a prisoner. When we surrender, we relinquish control and we give ourselves over to something or someone as an influence or course of action.

Know that the compulsion tied to surrenderance is the condition of being compelled to go further. Take the time to know yourself and know when you do what you do. Know and recognize the triggers for doing things that you know are not the will of God for your life. Make sure that you are submitted to His cause and not your own. Remember, Jesus is our King and we owe Him our very lives because He gave His life for us. This is a very powerful defense weapon to have in your arsenal against the enemy.

Also be aware that His love is the power that keeps us. His love drives us to living and responding to life and one another in His way, and with His thoughts and heart. Do you need a real life example? OK - Say someone said something to you that made you very angry. Our way is to retaliate with an even sharper response. Some may even say - cuss the person out with some very unnecessary words. However, as a follower of Christ, if you are surrendered to Him and allow Him to lead you, His love will embrace you, restrain you, help you refrain from acting inappropriately, and give you a Christ like response to the situation. His love is the power that keeps us!

Let's look at **2 Corinthians 5:13-15**:

"13For whether we be beside ourselves, it is to God: or whether we be sober, it is for your cause. 14For the love of Christ constraineth us; because we thus judge, that if one died for all, then were all dead: 15And that he died for all, that they which live should not henceforth live unto themselves, but unto him which died for them, and rose again."

The Warfare side of this can be seen in **2 Corinthians 10:5,** which says:

"Casting down imaginations, and every high thing that exalteth itself against the knowledge of God, and bringing into captivity every thought to the obedience of Christ;"

We are to take no credit for the progression of the Cause. All the glory belongs to God our Father. Do not overlook the fact that to truly surrender to God actually puts you in a position of power not one of weakness. When you give the Lord complete control of your life and thoughts, the outcome is without limits in every area of your life; wisdom, resources, finances, health, family, etc. Every area is covered. Therefore be sure in your heart that His Cause is your Cause. **Ephesians 4:8** tells us:

"Wherefore he saith, When he ascended up on high, he led captivity captive, and gave gifts unto men."

If we really let the truth be told, sometimes we don't always feel as free as everyone is telling us we are in this Christian walk. Side comment here: if you do all the time, amen - and please pray for those of us that are doing the best we can in this area. Along the way, you must also keep in mind that as you flow in your purpose in support of the Cause that each result and outcome of every Battle you face must be obtained strategically and in order.

To flow strategically, you must understand and embrace Our Father's Word daily. Though we are bound by our relationship with Him, we are freer than we could ever be in any other lifestyle. Whether you admit it or not, you are following and being lead by something or someone. This very thing or person could never have your best interest at heart at all times. But Jesus can and does! So to flow in order, you must understand and embrace our Father's ways.

To flow with the Cause, you must know the will of our Father. Knowing His Word and understanding His will only come from surrendering to Him. Doing so will help you live freer, keep you balanced and prepared for any attack that come your way. As you submit to serving in the Battle for the Cause of God's Kingdom, victorious living is a guaranteed promise. So surrender totally to the Cause, warrior! Now let's continue to put some final substance on our foundation!

Part 4:

"Staying Victorious in The Faith!"

CHAPTER 12

Receiving from God in the Midst of the Battle

Some may think that it is strange that I would put the chapter on 'faith' last as oppose to first. I did this because I wanted to give you the tangible matters and strategies of our faith first before drawing you into the 'intangible' component of who we are as Christians.

This is the last link needed to complete our journey in discovering and obtaining the gift of hearing spiritually. Faith leads us directly into the hearing aspect of our relationship with the Lord. Remember the key: *in order for you to hear God, you have to believe you can in your heart.* As stated before, it all begins and resides in your heart. Your faith has to be at the level of knowing that He can and will speak directly to you, clearly on all matters. You must also come into the revelation that Christ didn't come so that we could just get by or live a life of commonality. The Lord came so we could live life more abundantly. We must come to the revelation that this abundance manifests from various dimensions of our faith. So let's move forward in our study of this area in God.

As stated earlier, I have been sent to confirm that the Lord **will** initiate, begin, and conduct a conversation with you. Are you are now to the point that **you think** that too? Before you answer this question, notice I asked you a "head" question about what you believe. I asked, "Do you "think" God will speak to you?". You should be in agreement at this point because we have just covered all the "logical, mind" issues needed to bring your "head", or natural understanding, into agreement. By the written Word of God, we have backed up everything that has been needed to prove to you that you are able to, and should be hearing from God for yourself in your daily walk and in the midst of the Battle. A resounding "amen" should be ringing in your spirit and heart by now.

To ensure that you are equipped to function and stand in the war in this alliance with our Lord, we will now look at ways to maintain and receive strength and endurance in the midst of the Battle. To accomplish this, we will first develop an understanding of the final component for hearing God, which is our faith. So let's move on.

The Necessary Link of Faith for Hearing God

As stated earlier, the last component needed to hear God clearly is the link of faith. It is the final link required for synchronizing your spiritual hearing. Faith is closely intertwined with obedience in this area, and obedience is dependent on focus. Focus allows you to see and concentrate on the results of what you have been standing in agreement with God about. Total, willing obedience to the Lord will compel you to move towards accomplishing His purpose for your life. This applies to any given area, at any given time. Faith is the underlying foundation that brings and holds all the things of God together in the life of a Christian Warrior.

Living your life with the combination of all the three components, Obedience, Focus, and Faith, will cause you to come into alignment with the strategy and direction that you need to go towards every time you hear from the Lord. Additionally, faith is mandatory for serving well in the Kingdom of God as we are told in **Hebrews 11:6:**

> *"But without faith it is impossible to please him: for he that cometh to God must believe that he is, and that he is a rewarder of them that diligently seek him."*

At this point, you should be well past the issue of whether or not all of this is a 'reality'. Increasing faith systematically removes the impossibilities of man, and allows the infinite possibilities of God to reign in your life. Simply put, you ARE because He IS! This is a foundational statement that you must take hold of in your heart and your mind. Yes, this is the reality of who we are as divinely created human beings. Whether you recognize it or not, doesn't make it any less true or real. We are who He says we are! Therefore, doesn't it make sense to access every aspect of Him that the Lord has made available to us? Of course it does! So don't leave anything on the table unused just because you haven't taken the time to learn what it is and how to use it for His glory. Diligently go after Him so that you can live a victoriously abundant life.

Fighting the battle victoriously without hearing and knowing the voice of the Lion of Judah is like trying to operate a complicated piece of machinery without the instructional booklet and proper training. You may be successful on a hit or miss basis. However, worse case scenario is that you may lose a limb or even your life in your trial and error stages. Our Father never intended for you to go through the battle of life this way. Doing so, you will **never** recognize or possess the fullness of life that God planned for you. This approach to life can be avoided, and you can live far more victoriously if you take hold of listening for the voice of the Lord, and then doing as He as instructed.

It is your responsibility to search out the heart of God in all matters of your life, and then receive by faith the life sustaining answers that you need to live victoriously. How do you do that? Read on for further instructions because it is time to figure out how to transition this head knowledge into the manifestation of God's will for your life. Everything that you were created to accomplish is possible through accessing and utilizing this intangible thing called "**faith**". So let's take the time to examine this necessary component of our Christian Walk even closer. We will do this by first looking at *what faith is*; then *what faith is not*; next *how faith works*; then *what faith does*; and finally, *how to put faith fully to work* in your life.

So, what is this thing called "faith"?

Faith, in its root form, is in the Word of God 231 times. If we begin to add the variations of this word, faith, it is in the Bible 78 additional times as faithful and 49 more times as faithfulness in the Old Testament alone. By definition, faith according to Webster's Dictionary is an unswerving allegiance to God, a duty or person. Per Vine's Expository Dictionary, in the Old Testament, the Hebrew word for faith is faithfulness, or *emunah* which means certainty and is often used to describe the relationship between God and His chosen, favored people. Based on the definition of faithfulness, it is very interesting to note that in the Old Testament, we, as God's people, are expected to live in a state of unquestionable faith to and in God!

In the New Testament, the word for **faith** in Greek is *pistis*. As we mature in God, His desire is that we become *pistos*, which means to be called or thought of by the Lord as faithful, trustworthy and reliable. On the other hand, the Greek word used by Jesus to describe us as having "little faith" is *oligopistos*. This is a tender rebuke for having anxiety as given in **Matthew 6:30** and **Luke 12:28,** and for fear in **Matthew 8:26, 14:31** and **16:8.**

For us as the Lord's Warriors, faith is our steadfast belief, trust in, and loyalty to God. To operate *"in faith"* is to move through this life with certainty, without doubt about the things pertaining to the Lord and what He has purposed for our lives. Though man's concept of faith is considered to be an intangible area, to us as Christians, *faith is* the tangible arena that we must master and strive to live in. So let's continue on. At this point we are well past the level of soul saving faith, which is the gift that is described in **Ephesians 2:8,** which says:

> *"For by grace are ye saved through faith; and that not of yourselves: it is the gift of God:".*

We, as maturing Warriors in the Kingdom, must also understand that faith is relational, and it is personal. Therefore, faith requires a close, ongoing alliance between the Creator and His creation, which is you. God, our Father is the original source of our faith. **Faith is relational and should always be between you and the Lord, first and foremost.**

With that said and the foundation laid, let's look at faith even deeper as the major, most sensitive component to hearing God. To take a closer look at what faith is in the Word, let's start with **Matthew 17:19-20:**

> *"[19]Then came the disciples to Jesus apart, and said, Why could not we cast him out? [20]And Jesus said unto them, Because of your unbelief: for verily I say unto you, If ye have faith as a grain of mustard seed, ye shall say unto this mountain, Remove hence to yonder place; and it shall remove; and nothing shall be impossible unto you."*

Listen, **faith** is a very serious strategic tool to living this life in Christ on a daily basis. The continuous nurturing of this gift is critical. It is obvious in this passage that even some of the most "elite" followers of Christ struggle with it, even today. Jesus is letting us know that we are accountable for our faith and the results that it is able to produce in our lifetimes. This will happen once we begin to comprehend what faith is and stop doubting its possibilities. We are charged to develop and walk in faith on a daily basis. Doing this will allow us to not only move hindrances, but actually destroy them! We will look closer at how faith works and what faith does later in this chapter. But for now, know that taking responsibility for the development of your faith gives you the power that you need to live victoriously in Him as an overcomer in every battle that you will ever face.

For us as Warriors, faith is the life sustaining dependency on the presence and promises of the Lord. We, ourselves, are sometimes our greatest enemies (mountains) because we just don't believe we can. We often find ourselves once again struggling in the same areas of unbelief as the disciples in this passage. We know God is able, but we do not always think the role that He has assigned to us fits our level of expertise. We know that He must be talking to someone else. In a sense we are half right, because without Him we can not do it alone and still expect to obtain the full benefits of the matter. For that very reason, we must stay aligned with Him in all situations with that life line called faith. Warrior of the most High God, always remember what we are told in **Philippians 4:13**:

"I can do all things through Christ which strengtheneth me."

In looking closer at this promise, we must receive it by faith. This will allow us to walk in the realization that our greatest power comes from taking hold of the revelation that Jesus Christ is the source of our strength, and that our *faith is* because *He is*! An added gift to that revelation is that just knowing that gives us even more power. Again, we are able to receive this revelation and the ability to move in it by that thing called faith.

Now, let's look more at the spiritual aspects of what faith is. *Faith is* the energy that allows us to move in God supernaturally. *Faith is* the key element for your spiritual sight. It contains the vision of your destiny and links up with your spiritual hearing through your obedience and focus. *Faith is* the activity flowing from where your focus is as your destiny begins to manifest in the natural. There are many aspects to our spiritual hearing that link up with what we are able to see.

This sight gives clarity, but it can also be deceiving. That's why discernment is important in all aspects of this Christian walk. Remember that there must be agreement in the spirit between your visible and audible senses in order to have clarity in your next movement in the Lord. Maturing *faith is* that ingredient of certainty. It empowers you, as a Warrior of the Most High God, to walk in purposeful authority in every assigned spiritual dimension within the Kingdom.

Also, Warrior, know that there is an even greater level in the arena of faith. It is a deeper depth to a very powerful weapon to be used in the Kingdom. This level of faith is the third realm of the gift of faith. Recall that the first realm is associated with the gift of salvation and the second is associated with our daily Christian walk. As a Warrior, faith, in this capacity, **is** the supernatural ability to stand boldly on the promises of God on your behalf, and even more powerful, on behalf of others! As a Warrior, the Lord Jesus often allows us to operate in these extraordinary realms of faith to produce miraculous results. Yes, moving and operating in this realm manifests miracles, signs and wonders. This is the realm where the stuff that dreams are made of becomes reality. When you receive and operate in this supernatural empowerment, you can literally impact, change and propel yourself and others into the very destinies that God has established for us. This supernatural gift of faith is the power that under girds the wondrous works of the Kingdom. Yes Warrior, you too can operate in that realm once you take full hold of what **faith is**!

Let's look at an example that represents a good balance between faith, focus, obedience and our spiritual walk. Let's look at the *battle as a storm*. There is a relationship in the natural between the actual storm, lightening, and thunder.

The lightening is the first sign of an approaching storm. It is *visual* notification that something is brewing. The brighter the lightening is the more severe the storm. The lightening, which is equivalent to your spiritual sight, is always the forerunner for a storm heading your way. If you are on your watch and paying attention early enough in the battle, you will see the attack coming in the spirit by the flickers of light. This could be in a dream or vision. As time passes you will also recognize the forth coming natural signs in the spirit. The lightening signals that your immediate obedience is required.

The thunder is the *audible* alarm that something is approaching. It is equivalent to your spiritual hearing. The louder the thunder, the closer the storm is. These thunderous types of warnings can also come forth through a rhema or logos word. The thunder occurs to get you to focus on a particular situation. It will sound out and solidify the directions you are to move in once you have heard from God. If you are listening for God's voice, you will be fully aware of the proximity of the enemy's approach.

The storm itself is the actual manifestation of all the elements, or situations, that the lightening and thunder have been jointly announcing. In anticipation of the impending battle, or storm, you can prepare by grabbing your proper garments like an umbrella and coat, or go out with no protection at all. To be noted here is many times we miss the first warning signs. We are literally looking every where else. So God will send another warning; another lightening bolt or thunderous jolt to get us to look in a particular direction. Yet, we still blink which puts us in need of another warning. At times, even with all the advance warning signs from the heavens, we don't take the time to grab the things we need to endure the oncoming storm.

As our situations intensify because of a lack of focus and obedience, we find that we missed some prep time and signals to be used for strategy. Now a louder sound will be given from the heavens. However, it is difficult to tell which way the storm is coming from now just by hearing the thunder. It's difficult because we missed the initial, visual warnings and now we have to play catch up! A "louder" more thunderous warning will hit again! Very rarely can you ignore the sound of thunder, especially as it gets closer to you. Think of the last time you were asleep and a loud clap of thunder sounded off. Didn't it get your attention; didn't it wake you up?

Worse yet, sometimes the storm is the actual wake up call for some of us. Don't be caught completely off guard. Build up your faith, so that you can be on watch, Watchman! As Warriors, some of us are even assigned to be storm chasers! Which in the Weather Industry, are the top notch experts that literally go after where the storm is brewing and report on its progress. To operate at this level, you better be built up in faith!

Sight and sound, which are jointly fit together, lead the way and announce that the storm is on its way. Your spiritual sight and discernment work the same way as the lightening and thunder as long as *you stay focused, obedient and stand in the faith* for the incoming storms in Battle. You should rarely be caught off guard, soldier!

So, what *exactly* is faith? It is the immediate minimizer to the impact of the storm. *Faith is* the directional current that you need to endure and overcome the storm! How? By the way you go through it. The lightening symbolizes focus. It draws your immediate attention, especially if it hits something on earth, or in your world. The thunder symbolizes obedience. It drives you to stay within close proximity of the parameters of your assignment that the Lord has established for your life. Our protection comes from heeding both types of warnings. How well we prepare for the storm and respond to the lightening and thunder is determined by our levels of faith. *Faith is* the forerunner for where we place our focus and obedience. Our faith in the revelation that the Lord has already secured the victory on our behalf grows stronger and more mature with each storm we go through; and how well we focus and obey based on this knowledge.

Our spiritual gift of faith joined with discernment will give us several signals. It shows us by the Spirit that it's time to begin whatever it is that God has purposed us to do at that specific time. All of this working together will cause us to experience the blessings and fruitfulness of being in alignment with the Lord. All of this is the under girding of our faith! *Faith is* the power available to achieve and succeed right now because *faith is the intangible evidence of our NOW and the things to come*!

What faith is NOT!

Let's go directly to exposing and resolving three major misconceptions pertaining to faith for us as Christians. They fall in the areas of origin, discipline, and image. Not fully understanding the two areas as they apply to faith can lead to us misunderstanding God's original intention for our growth in Him and our ability to fully achieve our purposes in Kingdom. Our ability to thoroughly comprehend the fact that God is our true Source for all things is critical to fighting this Battle successfully. This includes having a child like trust in Him to the control of our lives, temperaments, and appetites. To gain this understanding let's take a look at both issues.

First and foremost, God is the originating Source of our faith. We are not the creators of our faith as it applies to us as Christians. Yes, we are accountable for what we do with it, just like the servant with his talents in **Matthew 25**. Yes, we are responsible for it's development as stated in **Jude 1:20** which says, *"But ye, beloved, building up yourselves on your most holy faith, praying in the Holy Ghost.."*. But we are not the Creator or Originator of it. We are the recipients of a very precious, life sustaining gift. God, our Father, is the Originator, and **Romans 1:20** let's us know this truth. Therefore, we can no make excuses for why we are not taking possession of this precious gift called faith.

> *"For the invisible things of him from the creation of the world are clearly seen, being understood by the things that are made, even his eternal power and Godhead; so that they are without excuse:"*

Again, one true that we need to grasp at this point is that we are not the Creator of faith. Faith is a seed planted by God. Faith is a gift given to us that we are charged with nurturing and developing under His watchful eyes. Faith is one of those original things we spoke of earlier as a key to accessing the Kingdom of God. We are told in **Hebrews 12:1-3**, that He is the author, which is the beginning source and resource of our faith. God is the starting point, so why do we want to start in the middle of a situation like we are in control?

Look, Warrior, we bring God joy when we live a life filled with assurance that is established in who the Lord is and what He says is to happen in our lives, and then boldly pursue after it. What are we told to do when we run into brick walls and barriers that boggle the mind and challenge our endurance? We are told to consider, reflect, and weigh what the Lord has already overcome for us. Doing this out of obedience will keep us focused and will build us up in our faith in what's to come. Just as our strength to war on comes from Him, so is our faith *established in Him*. Not in ourselves, but in Him.

This is further confirmed in **Hebrews 12:2a** which says: *"Looking unto Jesus the author and finisher of our faith;.."*. Yes, the Lord is the author. This means that he created, designed and gave His final approval. Yes, the Lord is also the finisher. This means that we are to have an glorious expected end as we go on living this life with hope and expectancy. Additionally meaning that when we reach our destiny, He will not be surprised, and as we walk closely with Him, we will not be either!

Secondly, in the arena of faith, faith and discipline are not the same. Faith is NOT how well we can discipline ourselves, or say 'no' to the addictions and habits that have kept us from being free, or able to manage our attitudes, opinions and dispositions towards others.

Faith is not in any shape, form or fashion the same as self discipline. The critical key here is that with self discipline we are still in control. Often times we want to fight with our own strength and make decisions within our own intellect without prayer or inquiry of the Lord. These are the primary results of confusing faith with self discipline. We are fighting our flesh with flesh, not controlling our flesh through the spirit. ***Living by faith allows the Lord to be in full control of our lives***.

The symptoms of, or signs that show up with self discipline include thinking and believing that *we* are the source of our faith. This is a real danger for those of us that are already highly disciplined within ourselves. It becomes very easy to misplace our faith in our own abilities to obtain and fight in the Battle. Yes, we can be mildly victorious. However, the fullness of the Lord is never obtained or manifested.

Developing our faith through the Word of God and prayer are the only proper ways to nourish our spirit. You can believe what I tell you here: *'if your spirit man is weak, it is due to neglect in your study time and prayer life'*. How can the spirit sustain a lengthy battle between our flesh and the outside worldly influences too if we have not spent time building up our faith? Hmmm. Faith is just like a child that God has blessed you with. You have to feed it, overseer it, and utilize it to its maximum potential with the proper food, which is the Bread of Life. In order to utilize it to its maximum potential, you must understand it, nurture it and put it into action!

When you live by faith, you give the Lord permission to do what ever needs to be done in your life in order for you to live victoriously. Remember, we are striving to live abundantly, not just survive. Though discipline is a major part of faith, it is not the seed God has placed in you that will allow you to access the matters and things in Him. Faith is your direct hook up to the heart of the Lord, which in turn allows you to be transformed by His love for you.

So see, we really can no longer have any excuses! By this I mean that we can no longer give any reasons for missing the mark in the area of operating in faith. We are commanded and expected to be transformed into His likeness, meaning in our thoughts, by our actions and even in our desires. We can only come to this realization of creation and control by completely embracing the elements of faith as prescribe by God in His Word. In **Genesis 1:26**, we are told that:

> *"And God said, Let us make man in our image, after our likeness:.."*

As Warriors in this Battle, our goal must be to become as one with the Lord. Not make Him one with you, but become one in Him. By that I mean, we must strive to speak the same language, have passion for the things that please Him, and handle matters in the same way that the Lord would. Being conformed into His likeness gives us the ability to manifest His glory in the earth.

Did you ever wonder what is meant by God in **Genesis 1:26** when He said, *"**let us make man in our image, after our likeness,...**"*, and God's purpose for us in this matter? Most of us assume we have the revelation on this, but have missed this for years. Therefore we continually struggle with the issues of our spiritual essence and physical nature. We more often than not place our faith in our own capabilities thereby allowing our physical nature to dominate over our spiritual being. This very point causes us conflicts in our lives and prevents us from progressing forward in the blessings and victories that God has predestined for each of us. Again, it is not about what you are able to do, it is about His desires for your life.

Finally, note that it is not our physical traits that are to resemble God, but it is our spirit man. We are not trying to look like Him by our outward appearance. Even though over time your outward appearance may change, this is not where the true transformation and eventually, maturation occurs. Therefore, all the things about how a person looks on the outside, including dressings and coverings have nothing to do with our Godliness or relationship with Him.

The one on one personal relationship with our Lord originates within our hearts. The evidence of this contact shows up as a quickening in our spirit that trains our spirit man to think and respond as our Father would. What is transformed from within us will eventually show up in our outward appearance. The simple key to remember is that our spirit is the part of us that has been made in His image. We are spiritual beings, living in physical body. Therefore, it is out of Kingdom order to allow the "house" to rule over the "inhabitant". The spiritual shaping of who we are begins as we yield control over to Him, and lessen our hold on our own perceptions and ways of thinking.

Yes, we are created in His likeness. This includes every one of us; even those that are trying to deny who their Father is. At the beginning of this thing, He is the Father that gave all of us life. Therefore when He looks upon His creation, we are to reflect back to Him who **He** is in the earth. Each of our reflections is to become a pure image of who He is as we mature in the faith. This image only becomes distorted or clouded when we are out of alignment with Him. Remember we get out of alignment when we don't study the word, are not focused, or have not had regular contact with Him in prayer.

One more time, His likeness means that He is looking at His very essence within us. Warrior, pay attention here: since we are created for and after such greatness, how can we not be victorious once we totally grasp hold of *why and how* we should walk in faithfulness to our Lord? To do this well can not be out of any our physical characteristics, but must be out of our maturing spirits through our developing faith. *Faith begins and ends within Him!* So how does that happen? Read on.

So now, how does this intangible thing called "faith" work?

So, how is faith suppose to work actively and with power in our daily lives? How do we build ourselves up for the battle in the area of faith? Good questions. Warriors, first and foremost, always remember that faith is the energy that allows us to move in God supernaturally. Let's examine how faith works closer.

First, here's how **faith** develops within us in a very simplistic view. This process of faith starts with a certain belief about a particular thing, person, or situation. This belief begins in your mind as a simple thought or perception. As you take hold of this belief, it takes root within you and becomes a reality, or truth to you. As this belief continues to form a truth within you, it moves to becoming established in your heart. As you experience and receive other "information" about that particular subject matter, you begin developing a 'support system' around why you believe what you do about that matter. This belief support system begins to become a reality to you as you continue to receive even more 'concrete' data that advocates your point of view. Over time, almost no one and nothing will be able to change what you believe in your heart to be true about that particular person, matter or situation because the 'support system' will have become established in your mind as a reality.

Now let's go a little deeper. These same "beliefs" are what now begin to form building blocks that strategically shape your perceptions of how you see the world around you. They represent your reality, and the foundation for how you think, feel, make decisions, interact with others, and live your life. "Beliefs" are where these issues leave your mind and begin to dwell in your heart. It becomes a matter of *"I don't why, it just is and I believe it to be true!"* Once this shift occurs, you know you have just moved from the area of things being processed mentally to them becoming matters of the heart. You have now begun to operate and live in the realms of **"faith"**. Isn't that **"faith"**? You don't know why something is or how it happened the way it did, but you can not and will not be told that the cause was any different. Isn't that **faith**? Yes, it is.

However, child of God, be aware that whatever you have **faith** in is where you will look to draw your strength from, place your trust in, and rely upon for direction and guidance in pursuit of the answers to the "things" in your life. Therefore, you must be careful about where you let your faith reside.

So now that we looked at the initial formation of faith, let's look at how it relates directly to us as the children of God. Let's go deeper in our comprehension of this area and how we can move from our faith in the "things" we think we have control over to developing and keeping our faith in the Lord! We can do this by looking at the **Book of Hebrews** and specifically **Hebrews 11:1-3.**

The book of **Hebrews** itself is an exhortation to all Christians to hold fast to our faith in the Lord Jesus Christ. Fast forwarding to **Hebrews 10**, we are told to embrace the new covenant of faith, including the fact that Jesus is the new and living way by which we believers have direct access into the very Holy place of God, our Father. We are told to hold firmly to the affirmation of our faith without wavering because the One that we are in covenant with will be, and is always, faithful towards us. We are to love and encourage one another individually and in joint assemblies as a part of our commitment to this covenant. The concept to take away here is that this book, and specifically this passage, gives us insight into how faith actually works!

As we move from the natural aspects of faith to the supernatural realms, we are told in this passage that faith is really our spiritual eye because it gives us insight into the matters of God. We know now that hearing God absolutely requires the participation of your faith. But what else is required to make it work as God intended it to in our lives?

Recall that faith, according to Webster, is a firm belief in something for which there is no tangible proof. As my Pastor, Bishop Simon Gordon, often says, "Faith is **not** something that can be taught, it must be caught.". Caught means to see and recognize the meaning and importance of a particular person, place, thing, or issue. Have you ever heard someone say, "Oh OK, I caught that, I know exactly what you mean."?

In looking at **Hebrews 11:1-3**, we can begin to see how to make the connection of the tangible elements of what we believe with the intangible ingredients of faith. We can begin to catch hold of the substances under girding faith. Additionally, we begin to recognize the link between the natural and the supernatural, and the preexisting bond between our Creator and His creation. This is a very familiar passage of scripture that many quote freely but have never taken the time to fully understand what God is saying to us here about faith and what it is capable of fulfilling. Prayerfully, by the time you reach the end of this chapter, not only will your faith be increased, but you will have caught a whole new revelation of the matter that will propel you to your next!

So let us study faith even closer to gain a better understanding of the process and how it can be built up in us to operate victoriously in the Kingdom. In looking at **Hebrews 11:1-3**, we are going to "catch" a better understanding of this process called faith as it applies to us as Christians. It reads as follows:

> *"¹Now faith is the substance of things hoped for, the evidence of things not seen. ²For by it the elders obtained a good report. ³Through faith we understand that the worlds were framed by the word of God, so that things which are seen were not made of things which do appear."*

To press on, let's now develop a common reference point for the key words in this passage.

- **Substance** is the fundamental, essential nature or essence of something. It is the ultimate *reality* that underlies all outward manifestations, and it changes and overrules all practical importance. Substance means that whatever that specific thing is, it is what is real, tangible, and yes, you will be able to see, feel, hear and touch it. Substance is the beginning foundation, or layer with unlimited potential.

What am I saying? In the Kingdom, the 'substance' that God is referring to is our full revelation of what is real in the Kingdom and accessible in the earth in God's time. Substance is the seed of the thing that you are standing in agreement with God about to happen in your life. Furthermore, this seed is nurtured and developed by what you feed it. In other words, 'substance' is *your next* that was set in time at the beginning of time by God. It has already been established in your heart, and now must be settled in your mind. To join the two, substance is also always to be prayed for in *your now*.

- **Thing** is a matter of concern; it is the aim of effort; or a separate and distinct individual quality, fact, idea, situation or entity. 'Thing' is something that makes a strong appeal to the individual, it gets one's attention.

- **Hoped for** is to have cherished a desire with expectation; or the belief that the desire will be successfully fulfilled. Hope is faith relating to the future. Hope points you towards *your next.*

- **Evidence** is an outward sign, something that furnishes proof; and it is a testimony. Evidence is something legally submitted to get to the truth of a matter or thing. Evidence is for *your now.*

- **Through** is the process from its beginning to its end. In this context, it is your progress and process from *your now to your next!*

- **Not seen** refers to being invisible; meaning being incapable by nature of being seen. However, remember that in the spirit God often allows us to see our next if we are open to Him. Some other examples include dreams, visions, and prayer.

- **Framed** is to prearrange evidence so that a particular outcome is assured. In other words, it does not matter what it looks like right now, God can and will stack the deck in our favor for His glory and our victory.

- **Worlds**, also ages, refers to the movement of time, it is a generation of the inhabitants of the earth distinguished by living together in the same place, or at the same time. What you are transitioning from / going towards is also for those around you to see in order to help established their faith in what our Lord is capable of doing in their lives.

- Finally, **appear** means to become evident, manifest, or to come into existence. This is the manifestation of *your next*! Now, let's work through this passage!

First, note at the beginning of **Hebrews 11:1-3**, we must recognize that the word **"now"** lets us know that faith is immediate and ever present. We have to operate in the reality of the fact that faith is always accessible and useable. Though faith requires patience, we never have to wait for it, and it is a fact in the Kingdom of God that better is available at this very moment, right NOW! How so? Because remember this is a part of the process of working our faith. This is a key element where faith taps into the very nature of God within us in order to enable us to endure and accomplish the impossible.

Looking closer, the answer to fully comprehending how faith works is right there in **Hebrews 11:3**.

"³Through faith we understand that the worlds were framed by the word of God, so that things which are seen were not made of things which do appear."

Catch this truth and run with it Warrior! *The Word of God set everything* in place at the beginning of time for all generations to come. That means you, me, generations before us, those here now, and those yet to come. Paris, do you really mean everything? Yes, **EVERYTHING**! Everything that you could ever possibly need, want, and desire to accomplish your mission and purpose in the Kingdom has already been strategically placed by God on a path in your "world". Everything! Every financial need, every divine connection, every healing, every miracle, every relationship, every resource! Yes, everything - even if I didn't list it here! Why? This has been done so that we can be victorious in this Battle and in our daily lives. God has already preordained us to be victorious by prearranging our appointments with our divine destiny. All we have to do is desire it and work towards it, in Jesus name! Isn't it awesome to know that you were on the mind of God right from the beginning of time? The power in that revelation is phenomenal; so much so that you need to confess that out loud. Take a minute and just say it - "I was on God's mind in the beginning.", "I've been on God's mind since the beginning of time!"

How do you get faith working in your life? The answer is right there in **Hebrews 11:3**, *THROUGH FAITH*. Faith in knowing that everything you will ever need to be victorious is just waiting on your arrival. Victorious meaning obtaining the good report mentioned in **Hebrews 11:2**. Warrior, half the battle to be won is God waiting on *you* to arrive. It is you overcoming the issues of faith. So how do you arrive? By working your faith trial by trial, test by test, situation by situation, issue by issue, relationship by relationship, etc. Are you getting the picture?

Wow, can you imagine how awesome our lives will be once we catch and begin to live with this revelation as a driving force for our daily walk. We have been created unstoppable, undeniable, and irresistible. In the Lord's terms, that's victorious, sure, and highly favored. Listen Warrior, the degree that we are able to access the things of God for our lives, which is our divinely created substance, depends on our level of understanding of how faith works. If we allow God to operate totally unrestricted in our lives, the creativity of our faith will yield unlimited possibilities and opportunities. Again, everything is already prepared and waiting for our arrival.

Warrior, once God says it, you are going to see it happen! Why? He said so in the beginning of time. He said it would "appear" and that you would be able to tell others about it! Remember that this substance will be the substantiating evidence of your faith. This evidence is the continuous manifestation of your now! It is undeniable proof that God is real and WHO you say HE is in your life to the world. This process becomes continuous for us as Warrior through obedience, focus and of course, faith. Faith is our edge on the enemy! With faith working in our lives, there is absolutely nothing that we can not do in the earth for God's Kingdom.

To go further, we need to fully grasp the fact that the process of building up our faith deals with the issues and concerns we have along with the desire and belief that they will be resolved by the Lord favorably. When we live by faith, the Lord gives us the authority to speak on His behalf directly to the things, situations and decisions in your life that are not yet known by us. As He reveals and resolves these "things", the hand and foot prints of His work build testimonies in our life and becomes evidence for why this 'faith' should be desired and can be accessed by others. Yes, this is a part of the process of faith. Yes, this is faith at work. And yes, going through this process establishes and builds up our faith. Ahhh, but the distinction here is that our faith is being established in Him and built up on a foundation in His ways.

The fact that faith is at work is only apparent upon close inspection. Faith is the driving force or element that empowers us to go through the process. When witnessed in action by others, their response generally is one of: "Oh, that's what it is, that's how they made it through." Though they may not understand faith in God, they have certainly heard of it! Be encouraged and demonstrate it, saints! Faith at work is what empowers us to clearly show others how to live and sustain this lifestyle. Faith in action provides sequential, orderly guidance that can not be obtained or understood through natural means or methodologies. Yet, it works beneath the surface, and the results of its presence are visible for all to see. Walk in it so that others can follow the Lord by your example. Be sure to tell them how you overcame so that they know it is possible for them to do the same!

Now, let us talk about that 'good report' we are to start building by working our faith. Note, right there in middle of how faith works and who God is in this passage is guidance to us for how we are to flow in faith and overcome every obstacle we face in order to glorify the Lord. We are to overcome by the examples of the Christian role models and mentors that came before us. The Bible has numerous examples of how they lived and succeeded. Our Father gives us the history of the good report obtained by the men and women of God so that we can see the process of faith they went through in action. Their faith enabled them to know Him and His ways even the more! Their testimonies serve as encouragement to us to go through God's processing and let faith arise within us. Faith, for them, was tried, tested, and proven to be the only way to please God. This also ensured that they would give Him the glory in the Kingdom for their completed assignments. This same process of faith will also propel us into Kingdom history, the same way with the same miraculous results.

Now we know from **Hebrews 11:1-3** that whenever you deal with faith, it has to be spiritual and it is personal. To get further assurance, let's look again at **Hebrews 11:3** jointly with **Hebrews 11:6** and **Romans 1:20**:

> *"³Through faith we understand that the worlds were framed by the word of God, so that things which are seen were not made of things which do appear." ...."⁶But without faith it is impossible to please him: for he that cometh to God must believe that he is, and that he is a rewarder of them that diligently seek him."*

"¹:²⁰For the invisible things of him from the creation of the world are clearly seen, being understood by the things that are made, even his eternal power and Godhead; so that they are without excuse:"

So why is this important to know? Again, first, a critical fact is that faith is between Christ and you! Your faith must rest in God, Himself. We are charged to understand the structure and order of the things of God and His Kingdom. There can be no more excuses for not doing so and not doing so continuously. Warriors of the most high God, we are told here that faith **demands** that we understand the profundity, which is a deep, thorough, mature understanding of God as they relate to us, and who and what's around us! It is a matter of survival.

Secondly, faith almost always deals with things you *can not* see, feel, or touch with any of your natural senses. In other words, you can not comprehend the matter of faith with your natural senses or abilities. That's why one of the best ways to look at this passage is to study it from *the aspect of your now and your next*. "Your now" being the physical state you are currently in. "Your next" being the physical manifestation of your future into time yet to come.

To further understand the awesomeness of God in how faith works, let's look closer at the part in this passage where the Word tells us, *"so that things which are seen were not made of things which do appear"*. Things becoming evident to us now are not the cause or answers to the "things" we know about. Nor are they not causing or creating additional "things" to occur either. All of the "things", whether they are matters, issues, or whole circumstances, were addressed in the beginning by God! Just because we are just now starting to "see" and become aware of these "things" does not mean that they were not there before we became aware of them. Faith allows us to know that the Lord is aware of each intricate detail, and well able to handle them without our intervention. We only need to allow Him to lead us and guide our participation!

Let's go further into breaking this down into more bite size pieces. "Things" already here were not and could not have been made from "things" coming after them. Right? Right! Any existing "things", in fact, are the building blocks and strategies for the "things" coming. Now let's solidify this by looking to our beginning, our Father, the Alpha. His word is the foundation and He is the beginning point for all these "things", past, present and yet to come. The unveiling of, and access to all of this is wrapped inside our faith. Foremost, again, you have to believe that God is! Our grasp of this truth is strengthened in the Word. We are told that He is the Alpha and the Omega, and this truth is emphasized four times in the **Book of Revelation (1:8, 1:11, 21:6, 22:13)** alone. Starting in **Revelation 1:8**:

> " *I am Alpha and Omega, the beginning and the ending, saith the Lord, which is, and which was, and which is to come, the Almighty.*"

As our Father told Job in **Job 38** and **39**, *He divinely formed* and intimately understands all the answers pertaining to the world, the living things in, on, above, and under the world; and the miraculous workings of the same. The depth of our personal revelation and breathe of our accessibility is driven by the maturity levels of our faith. When we get the order straight in our mind and heart, no man, including ourselves, will be able to trip us up over this issue again! He is the Alpha and Omega, our Creator. This is the cornerstone and the origination of our faith.

Additionally, faith allows us to "see and know" in the spirit past, present and future events in a Godly manner. Remember, faith demands that we understand the concerns of God as they relate to us, and who and what's around us! Specifically, who He is, His promises to you, and what He says and is saying pertaining to us. Faith is God's vision for our life, our purpose, our destiny, and our goals. Faith requires our holy boldness to access it in order to cause it to materialize in the natural. *Sustaining, unwavering faith gives us God's permission to access and bring forth the promises that He has for all of u*s.

How do we now wrap this up into workable wisdom regarding faith from this passage? Good question, I'm glad you asked. Here we go: *Given that faith is made up of all the issues and concerns that you have, are in the midst of, and will ever encounter, know that in the beginning of the forming of the world and us, God spoke it all into orderly existence.* This includes from the beginning to the end, with a *"stacked" outcome* in our favor as His children!

So what is the process for building up and working our faith in that truth? We need to understand that the things that we see could not possibly have been created by anything that came after them. Therefore, we are to walk in the revelation that the Creator came before the creations. We must rest in the knowledge that when our Creator did this, we were lovingly on His mind. Because of that fact, all of our needs were also considered and included in His initial plan. Everything is already done, and has been set into motion from the very moment that God established creation by His word. For us to access this divine plan, we have already been given the instructions for how to embrace it in His word.

For the things we do not fully comprehend, this is where faith bridges the gap between the Creator and His creations. Faith allows us to know with definite assurance that God has given us a purpose. If and when we are in alignment with His will, He will make certain that all the "things" seen and not seen, some we may **never** even know about, fall into His established order for the fulfilling of His word and covenant with us. How can I say that? Well it wasn't me. It was God in **Romans 8:28** where we are told:

> *"And we know that all things work together for good to them that love God, to them who are the called according to his purpose."*

Now let's look at the manifestations of the aspects of faith.

What does "faith" do?

FAITH REMOVES MOUNTAINS AND CONTINUOUSLY CATAPULTS US INTO FRUITFULNESS! This is the hidden treasure to seeing what faith does, or better stated, what the manifestations of faith looks like. The key to seeing this manifestation in your life, Warrior, is that you have to keep moving! No matter what! How? Know this: Faith can and will eradicate MOUNTAINous situations and issues. Additionally, as our faith continues to develop incrementally, it will propel us strategically from one point in our lives to the next as we strive to live triumphantly. This will occur as long as we STAY in the battle. How do we stay in the Battle? By striving to live in the state of richness, productivity, and fertility that God preordained for our lives. Now that's quite an ambitious charge. However, by faith, Warriors, we must move in it. So let's learn how this can be done by investigating each part of this mandate.

Foremost, we know that faith is the critical element needed for hearing God and being victorious in the Battle. To help us further understand this, let us first look at getting rid of all hindrances by checking out **Matthew 17:19-21**:

> *"Then came the disciples to Jesus apart, and said, Why could not we cast him out? And Jesus said unto them, Because of your unbelief: for verily I say unto you, If ye have faith as a grain of mustard seed, ye shall say unto this mountain, Remove hence to yonder place; and it shall remove; and nothing shall be impossible unto you. Howbeit this kind goeth not out but by prayer and fasting."*

Here we are told by Jesus that the reason the disciples could not do what He was able to do was because of their unbelief or lack of faith. To do the impossible, which also means the unexplainable, we only need to have faith at the level or size of a tinny, tiny grain of mustard seed. To some of you, the impossible has been, and may still be, hearing God's voice for yourself. If this is still your issue, look at this too as a removable mountain to be demolished in order for you to be fully effective in the battle. Take a minute to visualize the size of a *grain* of a mustard seed compared to a MOUNTAIN! I don't care where you place the mustard seed in, on or near the MOUNTAIN, in all aspects the end results will exceed and surpass all that you could have asked for or even imagined.

Given this fact, once you know what it is God is telling you to do it, get rid of all the contradictions, called **mountains** as mentioned in **Matthew 17:20**, so that you can see all the possibilities. Warrior, note that we are told we cannot only move, but REMOVE these things that blind us from seeing our full potential.

Remove in this case **does not** mean revisiting the same issues over and over again. Remove for us means to cause the situations, issues, relationships, and problems that hinder us from progressing in God to change their location, position or residence. If we look closely at this passage, Jesus has also given us the authority to **tell it where** to go! It's time that we give these things their change of address and eviction notices so that we can fully assess and see the promises of God manifest on a daily basis by faith! Developing and putting our faith to work to manifest the promises of God empowers us to not only relocate every obstruction, but also boldly explore every opportunity, without blockages.

Still struggling with how to remove a particular thing from your life so that the promises of God can manifest according to your faith? Then read on to the very next passage because your answer is right there in the next verse: **Matthew 17:21**!

"Howbeit this kind goeth not out but by prayer and fasting."

Yes, the strategic weapons of prayer and fasting will strengthen your faith to do the incredible. It is so simple, yet equally difficult none the less. *Why* is this necessary? To build up your most holy faith so that God's glory can manifest in your life! You must come to realize that faith is the primary substance of warfare. Your faith becomes even more powerful if you take the time to fast and seek God prior to and during a major battle.

Again maturing faith works as the powerful illumination that others, especially your enemies, can see in your life as one of God's Warriors! So know that the more built up your faith is by the Word, fasting and praying, the better equipped you will be to stay in the battle, natural and spiritual. Still don't know where to start? Put your faith to work by fasting, praying, and then being totally open to receiving your directions from God by faith.

If you feel like your faith is not manifesting the results you are expecting and that you are not moving on what God is telling you to do, check out your level of faith in that particular area. If you are not moving on what God is saying to you, it is almost always pertaining to the area of faith for that situation. How can I make such a statement? What I have found is believing or having **faith** in the things and mysteries of God is very simple. It is so simple in fact that for some, the simplicity of the whole thing is mind blowing! Therefore, we get in the way and it becomes very difficult for us to understand what's really going on. This leads to further questioning and additional investigation on our part to understand. This process of trying to understand the things of God with our natural mind can start to run us in circles. It can work us right into realms of procrastination and doubt; thereby turning the promised end result of a simple situation, or issue, into unbelief. Watch out for this pitfall, Warrior. Once you fully grasp what faith is capable of doing, you are better equipped to stay out of these realms of unbelief. Remember to remove *every* mountain; both visible and those not seen!

Developing and maturing in the areas of faith is no different than any other field that we want to be exceptional in. It takes the same dedicated efforts and concentration to become a skillful Warrior in God as it does in any other area of life. Perfecting our faith in order to clearly hear God is the same as the Olympic trained athlete who is driven to perfection by the passion of their sport. The same must be the case with us as one of God's people. His desire is for us to live a life full of faith, or as stated earlier, in faithfulness. By faith, we must come to know His voice, focus on what He is telling us to do, and then move in obedience without procrastination.

Sometimes we just need to begin speaking the word 'manifest' over the things God has spoken to us both in His Word and to our spirits. Just take a minute to recall some of the promises that you know the Lord has given you. Take one in particular. Do one at time so that you stay focused. Find a passage in the Word that directly relates to that promise. Meditate on that scripture with that promise in your mind and heart. Once you got them both imbedded in your spirit, begin to speak "manifest" over it. As the Lord reveals to you things about that promise or situation, take action and then repeat the process above with the new information that you have. Continue to do this until you see the full manifestation. It will come, you just must stay diligent and persistence. Stay on your post, and keep your watch. It will come to pass.

Now, let's move to the second part of our mandate: fruitfulness. To live in the realm of faith that will continuously manifest divine results, there are major things that the Lord has given us the authority to overcome and be victorious in. However, they do require our faith to access and galvanize these things towards fruitfulness. As mentioned earlier, fruitfulness has three aspects to it: richness, productivity, and fertility. We are to actively strive to implement each one of these aspects into our lives as Warriors. Richness includes those things that add value to our purpose. Productivity includes those things we accomplish that are directly related to our purpose. Lastly, fertility involves an impartation of ourselves that reproduces who we are in the life of someone else. This is done to add value to their live as they strive to accomplish their specific purpose. In all cases, the combination of these aspects drives us to work towards completing the work assigned to us.

Excellence arrives when our faith shows up. We are told about the importance of faith and its corresponding work in **James 2:18 - 20**:

[18] Yea, a man may say, Thou hast faith, and I have works: shew me thy faith without thy works, and I will shew thee my faith by my works. [19]Thou believest that there is one God; thou doest well: the devils also believe, and tremble. [20]But wilt thou know, O vain man, that faith without works is dead?"

Listen, Warrior, don't just do stuff to be doing stuff. That does not add prosperity to your life. Don't work without purpose just for the sake of working. That is not true productivity. Don't lead others without a clear, divine destination in view. That is not the impartation of fertility that God intended. Warrior, that is just not fruitful. Working this way in any one of these aspects is not effective, and will distract you and others every time from your true purpose(s).

This is particularly important as it relates to hearing the voice of the Lord and warfare. We have to be ever so careful to make sure our heart and motives are right before God in the things we do while fulfilling our Kingdom purpose. Also, note that we as the people of God can not become accustom to living in the realms of miracles only. Yes, God is a miracle worker, but this can NOT become your style of living. We are expected to walk in faith as we accomplish the works of the Kingdom. That is to be the norm. Work it, work it, and work it some more! **James 2:18 - 20** commands us to do the impossible in our lives, to achieve the extraordinary in all that we do, and impact the destiny of others along the way! Even the enemy knows our capabilities to do the incredible through God. Wow, once we put our faith to work and then get to WORK, the territories that would be reclaimed for the Kingdom would be innumerable!

In looking at **Matthew 17:19-21** again, along with **James 2:18 - 20,** we must also realize that what we have to put in, in no way equals or is even comparable to the magnitude of what we will get out of it. So let's continue to further study this area to help strengthen our level of faith for hearing God with the Word of God.

There is always more to your circumstances than meets the natural eye. Faith empowers us to know that God has covered us by filling in the gaps, especially on the Battle field. By working our faith we show that we expect the unexpected to manifest. ***But doesn't expecting the unexpected make the unexpected the expected?*** Hmm. Consider that! That's faith. When we are actively living by faith in God we will rarely be caught unprepared or off guard. Therefore, there is no room for unbelief or doubt because our faith brings assurance that everything will be all right. Why? Because by faith we know it just will.

So how are we to increase the flow of faith? Through the learning and development process laid out in His Word. We achieve understanding for the things of God by studying the Bible. As we know, it is our instruction manual for what has been, what is now, and what is to come. It helps us to understand the matters of the past. The Bible helps us with the things that we see and face right now. It leads us towards the circumstances that will impact our future. We know this by faith!

Warrior, you must walk in the knowledge of faith as though your life depends on it. Why? Because your life does depend on it! God, our Father, is the Creator of all things. This includes the things men think they have figured out and the things they, as men, have not yet even considered. Yes, every original thing is authored by God. And yes, His Son, Jesus is who we serve as Christians. What a lineage to be a part of! Therefore, your weaponry, Warrior, is to fill every open area in your heart and mind with the Word of God. You must develop the discipline of bringing every thought and imagination subject to the Word of God. This will empower you to live by faith victoriously! So let's see how it works in more detail.

The Faith Workout - The Faith Partners!

Now it's time to get to work, Warriors. You are more than equipped and empowered with the knowledge that you have been given in this book, and especially in this chapter. There are just a couple of more elements that need to be added to your repertoire in order to "round out" your spiritual weaponry. This last set of instructions will work hand in hand with your faith; thereby creating a partnership that will be unstoppable by the enemy, in heaven and on earth. So let's go!

There are a couple of intermediary actions that are required of us to ensure that faith is activated and forming in our lives at all times. First, remember that you must know without a doubt that God is ABLE! Second, you must believe that the Lord has empowered you and therefore, you can! Third, you cannot act on faith in silence. You must speak up, and say what it is you are expecting to happen. Speaking it out helps to manifest the results in the natural, and brings those things to life! So know that God is more than capable, that <u>you can</u> and <u>say so</u>! Do this in Jesus' name, and there is **nothing** within the will of God that will be unattainable to you!

Quick side bar here: Don't be afraid to ask the Lord the question because you really don't want to know or are afraid that the answer will be different than what you want to hear. This includes that foolishness I hear God's people say sometimes - "I can hear what the Lord is saying for every one else but me.". Does that even make sense in the natural? Can you only hear some people talking and not others? Now it is one thing if they are really not saying anything. But if they are speaking and yes, God is still speaking to us, then you should certainly be able to hear Him, and them. Yes, God will sometimes be silent on certain matters in our lives. But this is usually because He already gave us the answer and is waiting to see what we are going to do next. This example of His silence, however, is an exception and is not the norm. God is always talking to His people! So ask your questions, so that you know what your next move is suppose to be! If you are listening for His voice, you WILL hear Him! Still can't hear Him - then remove that mountain. How? *By Fasting and Prayer*!

Hmmm. It's time to quit playing with the matters of God by making up excuses for missing the mark and for why things are not happening as you now know they should be. Taking this position of denial or lack of commitment could cost you a lot more in the long run! When you find yourself in this kind of situation, you can believe it is the result of a lack of focus, obedience, or even faith at the root of your situation! Always keep in mind that God knows your beginning and your ending. The Lord knows what He has in store for you. Warrior, be aware that the very next instruction or answer that you have been seeking will usually have a rippling effect to other situations you are waiting to be settled. Whew, that's just the beginning of our workout - *are you sweating yet?*

Listen up Warrior, and get your gear. There are certain ongoing things that are critical to the utilization and efficacy of your faith. Specifically, how and when you work your faith, and then, how productive and effective it is in accomplishing its expected results. So how do you make faith work continuously? This is done with the added ingredients of love, empowerment and prayer. Love being the ability to flow in a state of being closely bound in relationship with Jesus through faith. "Empowerment" means being commissioned and having the authority to move freely throughout the Kingdom of God, both in the spirit and the natural. Prayer being the facet of you simply speaking from your heart to the heart of God what it is you want to see manifest in any given situation according to His will. When you fully understand the varying realms of faith, it becomes much easier to accept the impact that it can make in your life. So, by now you should be wondering and eager to know how to apply what you have learned about faith to your daily life.

For us as warriors the three ingredients mentioned above tap directly into how we are to function on the Battlefield. Faith is critical to fighting a good fight for the Kingdom, and in your life. I discuss fighting the good fight in great detail in *"Breaking Through Towards Spiritual Maturity"*. What is critical now for going into the next dimension is how we embrace all of these things of God. So let's tie this together by focusing in on what our warfare attire should be by looking at **1Thessalonians 5:8,** which says:

"But let us, who are of the day, be sober, putting on the breastplate of faith and love; and for an helmet, the hope of salvation."

Hmmm, this is for those of us that are paying attention to the seasons, and are operating in and on time with the movements of the Lord. This is referencing the maturing Warrior. The mature Warrior is one who is marked by temperance and seriousness; not showing any extreme or excessive qualities in emotion or judgment. This is one who is "thoughtful" in their movements. This is one who stops for a moment to consider the consequences of their actions on others and themselves.

As maturing warriors, we are to be in season and strategically thoughtful in every move we make. Remembering to cover our heads with the dream that all are to become a part of the Kingdom of God. That's what we are fighting about, right? The aspiration that not one be lost! This can only be accomplished by love, divine empowerment, and prayer *through faith*! Never forget the "Cause". If you need your memory jarred go back to **Chapter 11**.

Warrior, pay close attention to what we are instructed to wear. The symbolism of the breastplate is that it is visible and the markings on it identify who they belong to, who the Warrior is, and what they are fighting for. We belong to God. We are Warriors in His army. We are fighting for the salvation of others so that the Kingdom of God will continue to be glorified on the earth. Others are be able to identify us as a result of the way they see us display our faith and love for one another as we powerfully move forward in fulfilling our destinies.

Also, particularly to be noted here is that faith is tied to the most powerful weapon in the Kingdom: love. Love is something that is so powerful, yet so tender in its delivery and manifestation. When love shows up to produce what we have confessed by faith, even the worse situation can be brought to its knees and demolished. We are not to do as the world does by taking on their ways, and placing our faith in things that make the world what it is. Warrior, we are to focus, watch continuously, and not become lulled to sleep. When we don't this, we get tossed back and forth by man and the matters of this world.

So, Warrior, what does your breastplate look like to others? Can they tell who's side you are on at any given time? We are charged to continuously build up our faith in the Lord our God, not in ourselves and not in the things of the world! We are to serve by faith with the love that is established in our hearts, especially as we pursue after Him. Even when we don't understand or know the whole story, we are to keep the assuring faith that He does!

Next Warrior, do not forget that your level of spiritual power comes from your level of faith and prayer. Furthermore, this is sustained by the love of the Lord! Let's look at **Jude 1:20-21:**

> *"[20]But ye, beloved, building up yourselves on your most holy faith, praying in the Holy Ghost, [21]Keep yourselves in the love of God, looking for the mercy of our Lord Jesus Christ unto eternal life."*

Finally, know that getting to the "true" reality of God is a lifetime process. Within this process, you never fully arrive but are always in route to your fulfilling your destiny. This is the case as long as you stay within His will through focus and obedience, while being sustained by your faith in Him. Therefore, realize that your individual growth in this area is continuous. As you build your beliefs, you build up your perception and position of where, what, and who God is to you in your life. This leads to varying dimensions of trust in God. These varying dimensions of where your truth for Him is, in any given area of your life ranging from wavering all the way to total submission, are key indicators of where your faith actually is.

This in turn determines where your faith needs to be nurtured, established, strengthened and solidified.

Where ever you are, you still must continuously work your faith in order to build it up! As you go "higher" in God, the tests, trials, and challenges do get harder! So, yesterday's dose of faith is not going to take you through today's issues. And worse case, when you arrive at tomorrow, if you have not been exercising your faith, it will show up in the outcome and how you go through the situation. So let us turn to **Romans 10:6-17**.

> *"*⁶*But the righteousness which is of faith speaketh on this wise, Say not in thine heart, Who shall ascend into heaven?* ⁷*Or, Who shall descend into the deep?* ⁸*But what saith it? The word is nigh thee, even in thy mouth, and in thy heart: that is, the word of faith, which we preach;* ⁹*That if thou shalt confess with thy mouth the Lord Jesus, and shalt believe in thine heart that God hath raised him from the dead, thou shalt be saved.* ¹⁰*For with the heart man believeth unto righteousness; and with the mouth confession is made unto salvation.* ¹¹*For the scripture saith, Whosoever believeth on him shall not be ashamed.* ¹²*For there is no difference between the Jew and the Greek: for the same Lord over all is rich unto all that call upon him.* ¹³*For whosoever shall call upon the name of the Lord shall be saved.* ¹⁴*How then shall they call on him in whom they have not believed? and how shall they believe in him of whom they have not heard? and how shall they hear without a preacher?* ¹⁵*And how shall they preach, except they be sent? as it is written, How beautiful are the feet of them that preach the gospel of peace, and bring glad tidings of good things!* ¹⁶*But they have not all obeyed the gospel. For Isaiah saith, Lord, who hath believed our report?* ¹⁷***So then faith cometh by hearing, and hearing by the word of God.***"*

Hmmm, well this is one of those passages of scripture that you have to work backwards to gain its full understanding. God gives us the end result, which is faith, first in this scripture. Notice that the verse is separated into two parts: first, the end result, and then, how to get to the promised end, which is faith. Yes, we know that the Word of God develops your spiritual hearing. So work it Saint, study the word and work your faith!

Remember that hearing is the action of hear. As stated earlier "hearing" means taken in, understood and absorbed. In this particular reference, it is directly related to what is received through preaching, teaching and witnessing. The "and" in **verse 17** implies "then, or what's to follow" and joins the two parts of the verse together. Also, notice that come has "eth" added to it. The "eth" functions just like "ing" when added to a word, meaning that whatever the subject is, that thing or issue is continuously being done.

So it follows then from what you are constantly hearing of the Word of God, your faith will persistently develop. It will continually be established and strengthened. You need to make sure that you are sitting in a place that allows you to hear the Word of God in order to constantly build your level of faith. This verse tells you what you must do to continuously develop and increase your faith. Let's look at this closer: The **Word of God,** which comes first, must be heard continuously. Remember this is a part of your spiritual **equilibrium** or balance for hearing God. The more you hear the Word, rehearse it, practice it, say it, the more it becomes solidified in your spirit, heart and mind. Your spiritual hearing is directly tied to your spiritual ear, which is your heart. Recall that what is in your heart builds your faith by whatever you are feeding it.

This passage covers the gamete of everyone that can, is and will ever come into the Kingdom of God. All levels from outside the doors, to in the pews, and yes, all the way up to the pulpit. We all have a responsibility within the Kingdom in developing faith within ourselves and within each other. And faith meets and empowers us at every level of growth to do this. How? Through PRAYER!

Additionally, we are told here that a key part of the wisdom of faith is knowing your authority, and that the things and matters of God, belong to God. Our role is to intervene as He leads us. Even with salvation, that area in Him is personal and between Him and the individual. We are only to function as the liaisons between the Creator and His creations. We have a role to play working in establishing faith in ourselves and in others.

Our faith is to be contagious in this area to everyone that we encounter. In **Romans 10:15**, when our Father speaks of 'beautiful feet', He is letting us know that there are two things regarding our walk in the ministry of Jesus Christ. One is that it be pleasing to Him. Two is that when we do flow in this area we bring excitement to the senses of others and stir up emotions within them that pave the way between our Savior and them. This pathway eventually leads them to a divine, life changing encounter. Remember, we are to be contagious!

In looking closer at this passage, the background here is that in **verses 6-15**, Paul describes the many situations and benefits for why the Word of God must be spread to others, how it should be done, why it has to be preached, why it is necessary for it to be taught, and how this process builds faith. The key for this lesson in this passage begins with **verse 16**, this passage goes on to say:

*"But they have not all obeyed the gospel. For Isaiah saith, Lord Who hath believed our **report**?"*

'Report' here refers to the Word of God, which is really our testimony of what we believe. We are charged to give others an account of whom and whose we are from the pulpit to the pew to outside the walls of the church! The Word of God must be proclaimed to others because a lack of knowledge pertaining to the things of God will not only hinder us from achieving our purposes, as ordained by God, but can literally destroy us as stated in **Hosea 4:6:**

"My people are destroyed for lack of knowledge: because thou hast rejected knowledge, I will also reject thee, that thou shalt be no priest to me: seeing thou hast forgotten the law of thy God, I will also forget thy children."

Listen when we are silent in our faith, it impacts generations to come. YES, it is generational. So, the question is asked here, how can we, as the people of God, be obedient to what we do not believe or in other words, have faith in it. Looking to **Romans 10:17** for our answer, we are told what we are to do. We are to look and listen for the Word of God continuously. We are to get to the point that we are automatically seeking God in everything we come in contact with through His Word to see how it applies to our next.

There is one more thing to be note here, let us look at **Romans 10:16** and **17** together.

> *"But they have not all obeyed the gospel. For Isaiah saith, Lord Who hath believed our report? So, then faith cometh by hearing, and hearing by the word of God."*

First notice this is a conversation between God and Isaiah, with Isaiah seeking an answer and God responding! Next, note that the "so", connects these two verses. Your part in this is to develop your faith by studying and hearing the word of God that has been given to you by the ways described in **Romans 10:6-15**. The results of doing this will empower you to be more obedient to the will of God and what He is saying directly to you. Because look, your level of faith is personal, it belongs to you and you only. No one can carry this for you. No one can build it up in you, or for you. You have to work it. You own it and are responsible for your level of Faith. Are you still with me? Good!

Now, I know we have heard 1,001 teachings on faith. You know why? Faith is extremely important as a Kingdom principle. I'm sure you were taught in the area of prayer that we are to cover one another in prayer. If you can't pray anything else for your brother or sister, pray that their faith in God be enlarged. Why? Because we all benefit with each incremental increase of someone else's faith as we all work together in God's Kingdom! How do I know? Let's seal it with the Word. Look at **2 Corinthians 10:15**.

> *"Not boasting of things without our measure, that is, of other men's labor; but having hope, when your faith is increased, that we shall be enlarged by you according to our rule abundantly,".*

We are specifically told here that we are not to take credit for something we did not do or have an impact on. We are instructed to pray right from the start for the harvest of the Kingdom. Once they enter into the Kingdom, we are to STILL CONTINUE to pray for them. We are to pray for their growth and for their destinies to be fulfilled. Yes, we rejoice at the point of salvation, however our work in the faith does not stop there! We are to continue to pray and expect the best to occur in and through their lives. We all benefit from them coming into the family of God! As their faith increases, our power as a whole increases exponentially. This continues to make us even more powerful in achieving the things that must be fulfilled for the Kingdom. We need to know that we need one another to fulfill our Kingdom assignments. Therefore we need to act accordingly. Yes, this is all accomplished through and by faith.

See why faith is SO important? I need you in the Kingdom, divinely focused and obediently striving to fulfill your purpose. Reciprocally, you need me doing the same. If I weren't you would not have this book to read to move you to your next! So what is the Kingdom waiting on you to do? Hmmmm. Warrior, get to work!

In closing this chapter, looking back at **Romans 10:16,17,** along with **2 Corinthians 10:15**, we get this: Your faith is activated through your obedience to what you have heard from the pulpit, in the various biblical teachings, classes you have been attended and other Kingdom saints that you have come in contact with. As you grow in the faith, you become stronger in the Kingdom. Also, equally important, along the way you can bet that others have been and continue to pray for your strength in the areas of faith and spiritual growth. So remember this principal: *"Your knowledge of the Word of God is critical to your level of faith, and so is supporting one another in the Faith!"*

So now that is the intangible stuff surrounding FAITH. Let us now draw nearer to our King with what we have learned so far so that we can stay fit for Battle!

CHAPTER 13

Staying Replenished in the Midst of the Battle: Intimacy with the Lord

As we continue to transition further into dealing with the issue of faith in warfare and tying all the components together, I am now going to ask you a "heart" question. Transitioning from the head knowledge of faith to the spiritual realm involves looking at your limitations in this area and striving to move closer to God. Developing and nurturing your faith will allow you to do this. "Moving closer" means becoming and staying intimate with the Lord.

With the tremendous strives we have made in knowledge so far, now it is time for you to ask yourself a critical question; and answer it honestly. "Do you absolutely believe that the Lord will initiate and begin a conversation with **you** directly?" Absolutely by now, your level of confidence in this area must bring about a resounding "YES!" in your entire being, especially as one of God's Warriors. It really is a matter of the heart! So now, let us look at the importance of pursuing and maintaining intimacy with the Lord, and then identify some tools for overcoming and remaining victorious in the battle.

Overcoming Battle Fatigue

So, as Warriors, do we really get tired and worn out in the Battle? You better believe it! And if you don't find a way to balance it, I didn't say quit, I said BALANCE your life in this area, it could literally cause you to stop functioning! So what's the key to doing that? I am glad you asked!

I was at a conference a number of years ago, and had accepted the call of Intercessor several years prior to that. I had come to a point where ministry and the weigh of it all was beginning to be very tiring and weighty. This was extremely exhausting, in fact and all I wanted was a LONG sabbatical away from it all. However, I knew this wasn't possible because when I did try to take a break earlier the Lord spoke VERY clearly and said, "Daughter, you are on call 24/7!" Being that I had worked for IBM a number of years, I knew exactly what that meant. So I knew I had to find a way to balance it all out.

Well, in this particular Prayer class, I asked the person teaching the class, who is a highly respected Bishop in the realms of Intercession, "How do intercessors deal with and overcome battle fatigue?" Having experienced it first hand I wanted to know what to do and how to train upcoming warriors in order to help them through these times. After a moment of consideration, he finally answered, "You must stay intimate with the Lord.". Hmmm, I thought. I was really expecting something far more elaborate, but then it began to set in and make sense as time past. Something so simply stated yet powerful in its impact: "You must stay intimate with the Lord.". Well said Bishop Murphy, well said! We will look at Intimacy in more detail in the next section, however right now our task is to resolve the challenge of Battle Fatigue.

Now, some may believe that true Intercessors / Prayer Warriors do not experience Battle Fatigue. Don't you fool your self. Oh YES we do! Let me tell you what it is so that you can recognize the symptoms, and fight accordingly.

Let's first look at exactly what Battle Fatigue is. To overcome battle fatigue, you first have to realize that you have it. Battle fatigue means a labor, manual or menial work performed by military personnel in warfare where weariness from labor or exertion sets it. Furthermore, it is the temporary loss of power to respond to ensuing conflict and attacks, along with the tendency to breakdown under repeated stress. All soldiers and warriors experience it at one point in time or another; especially in lengthy, strenuous, tiring battles. Yes, it is a state of mind and a matter of the heart. That is why it is critical to stay even the more in presence of God during these times.

What does this look like in the natural? Let's see. There can be some sleepless nights. Missed calls to prayer time with the Lord. There can be a loss of the desire to pray on behalf of others; or even a loss of the desire to pray on behalf of your self. Or how about a straight out loss of desire to pray period! It can also be seeking others to strengthen you because you know you are called to pray and just don't have the energy or desire to do so. It can also be finding all kinds of other things to do FIRST before or instead of your usually pray time. What used to be joyful is now tedious and mundane in the areas of prayer. Are you getting the picture? Well now, well now, it's OK Warrior, help is here!

So how do you get through it? How do you survive it? Even better, how do you overcome battle fatigue? There's only one answer: By spending time in God's presence. How so? This time is just like taking a brief leave from your circumstances. Have you ever been on a long awaited vacation away from home, work and the daily routine of it all? Recall the rejuvenation you felt after a few days! You could take on the world, right? So, how much more capable is the Lord able to relieve the stresses of ministry and warfare? Warrior, you *cannot leave Him* out of the daily equation!

Listen Warrior, battle fatigue will cause you to give up. Depending on the severity of it, I have called it the 'crash and burn' effect. In this state, your spirit man feels so drained that your physical body would drag too. When you give up, there is a strong desire to go back to doing the things that you feel worked in the past. Also, sometimes you will be in the midst of a battle and not recall what you are fighting about because you have been fighting so long. Listen, trust me when I tell you I was there! I was ready to walk away from ministry all together and return to corporate America, where I *knew* I had been successful in the past.

The saying, "Nobody can do me like Jesus!" is soooo appropriate especially when you get weary from the battle. Absolutely nobody and nothing! There is no replacement for the refreshing waters that our Savior can give you to replenish your weary spirit. But you must pursue Him for it. Show up for prayer and show for roll call on the Wall! We must go boldly to the Throne of Grace when we feel fatigue setting it. How? Let's look at again at **Jude 1:20:**

'20 But ye, beloved, building up yourselves on your most holy faith, praying in the Holy Ghost, 21 Keep yourselves in the love of God, looking for the mercy of our Lord Jesus Christ unto eternal life."

Here is what I did; and yes, this is what you must do when you sense that battle fatigue is trying to overtake you. *You must keep yourself in the love of God*! Love is both an offensive and defensive weapon as discussed in the previous chapter. In this case, you are to use the love of God and your love for Him as a covering, a shield and refuge from the onslaught of the enemy. Irregardless of what you have been doing or not doing in the eyesight of God, you are to repent and return boldly to the throne of Grace. The key is that you must do it on a daily basis; and do it until you feel your strength being restored. At the same time, you have to access the Word of God to pull on the faith that God has deposited within you!

At times you may even fill like you don't want to hear another thing about church or anything else spiritual. But let me tell you Warrior it is a tactic of the enemy. Saturate your atmosphere with the Word of God either in music and/or tapes. Let it play rather you are listen to it intentionally or not!

The answer is not to quit. If you do then the onslaught will intensify, until finally you are completely lulled to sleep and placed in a state of ineffectiveness. You may even be telling yourself that's OK with you. *NO* Warrior, that is really not OK with you and eventually, this could lead to spiritual death. You know too much and have come too far to allow that to happen. When all else fails, just think on the love of God that He has for you and that you once knew so well and have forgotten! Ask Him to bring it to your remembrance. But DO NOT quit like a dishonorably discharged soldier!

Always keep in mind that it's got to be about taking the journey of loving Jesus Christ the more so that He can love you back! It's just that personal and that is how you combat battle fatigue. Now let's draw even closer to Him.

Intimacy with Jesus

There are times when the very foundation of your faith will be shaken as a result of intense encounter(s) on the battlefield. At times, this battle, and the struggle of fighting it, will seem to overwhelm you. It will feel like the battle is driving you to the point of being drained of every ounce of fight in you. At times, it may even seem like you are fighting ALL by yourself, and all you really want to do is rest or quit! In the previous section, we said the key to dealing with and overcoming this type of situation can only be obtained by developing and maintaining intimacy with the Lord. This is a level in your relationship with Him that when nurtured will sustain you through anything you will ever have to face. Let's first look at **Jeremiah 29:11**:

> *"For I know the thoughts that I think toward you, saith the LORD, thoughts of peace, and not of evil, to give you an expected end.*

Our Father has expectations for your life, and a desired end that should be produced as you walk in this life. Yes, we know now that faith is developed and strengthened through intimacy with God. "Intimacy" means something of a personal or private nature, marked by a very close association. It is contact or familiarity with one's deepest nature, and it is marked by warm fellowship developed by a long, ongoing association. Intimacy deals with your innermost parts.

For us as Warriors in the Kingdom, intimacy is a state of being more than close to the Lord. To know the Lord's ways, you must focus on Him. To know His will, you must learn and be obedient to His Word. To know His thoughts, you must have the faith to be in relationship with Him. To truly know His heart, you must be intimate with Him. Faith is that gift that leads us into deeper dimensions in and with the Lord.

Listen closely. Since we are going deep, let's get there! What man calls uncertainty, God calls faith! Most challenges to your faith will come from or be triggered by external forces and situations. However, if they are not resolved quickly, they will inevitably turn into internal battles. Though you may try and resolve them within yourself, the majority of the time these "things", like issues, thoughts, and internal conflicts will lay dormant until they are challenged again. Intimacy with the Lord is the one sure way to obliterate even the most stubborn internal issue.

Much too much time is spent by us trying to resolve these "things" by ourselves, within ourselves. In most cases, when you really get down to the root of the issue, these internal conflicts and battles are really between God and you. They always stem from what you perceive as areas of lack, be it in finances, health, employment, relationships, etc. The root of them comes from where and how you see, feel or believe a particular person, thing, situation, or even God is suppose to be.

To take it a step further, some of us look at the lives of others and say why not me too. We look at how they are prospering, and even in some cases how God has anointed them. But let me caution here because I can guarantee you that you do not want to go through or pay the price they had to pay to get there. Some have lost spouses, children, employment, health, finances, etc. These things took place in their lives to prepare them for what the Lord had in store for *their* unique destinies!

Warrior, you have your own pathway and burdens to carry, designed specifically for your life and testimony! Quit trying to give them away and go through the Battle for yourself! Intimacy with the Lord is the only sure way to access the fullness of what His expectations are for you!

Now if we are really ready to be real with this situation: our real issue, rather we want to admit it or not, is with God and how, in our perception, He is handling the matters of our life. That's real personal, I know, but goes directly to the heart of the matter none the less. Our Father extends to us an open, always available invitation for when we are struggling to understand a particular matter and in **Isaiah 1:18**. He says:

"Come now, and let us reason together, saith the LORD: though your sins be as scarlet, they shall be as white as snow; though they be red like crimson, they shall be as wool."

Hmmm, Warrior, we need to develop the discipline of taking these issues to Him directly not to every body that you come in contact with, but to Him. If He instructs us in **Matthew 18** to talk to our brothers and new converts when we have concerns with them, why could we not do the same with Him, decently and in order? The Lord is the only one that has the "medicine" to heal these internal wounds and conflicts anyway. We need to stop wasting time in this area and resolve these issues with Him as quickly as possible so that the enemy gains **no** foot hold or access through door ways we open with regrets, bitterness, envy, anger, etc., and so that we can continue the pursuit of purpose! Intimacy with the Lord opens the doors of healing and restoration.

Let's look at one last passage as we deal with intimacy with Him. Let's look at how to do this boldly and with joy. We are told that *"Deep calls unto deep..."* in **Psalm 42,** and are given a road map for how to fulfill this directive. Therefore, let's investigate this matter in more detail by dealing directly with **Psalm 42:1-7:**

"¹ As the hart panteth after the water brooks, so panteth my soul after thee, O God. ² My soul thirsteth for God, for the living God: when shall I come and appear before God? ³ My tears have been my meat day and night, while they continually say unto me, Where is thy God? ⁴ When I remember these things, I pour out my soul in me: for I had gone with the multitude, I went with them to the house of God, with the voice of joy and praise, with a multitude that kept holyday. ⁵ Why art thou cast down, O my soul? and why art thou disquieted in me? hope thou in God: for I shall yet praise him for the help of his countenance. ⁶ O my God, my soul is cast down within me: therefore will I remember thee from the land of Jordan, and of the Hermonites, from the hill Mizar. ⁷ Deep calleth unto deep at the noise of thy waterspouts: all thy waves and thy billows are gone over me."

Wow, does that not sound and look like Battle Fatigue and a cry for the Lord to give you relief? Well be encouraged Warrior, because this is a Psalm of instruction to us and relates directly to the intense longing for God that we have that is intended to help us with this issue. As we progress through this passage, grab this revelation: ***True relief can only come from the depths of your spirit being touched by His!***

"Deep" here is defined as extending far inward away from the surface; and it can be difficult to penetrate or comprehend; high in saturation. It is going beyond the conscious. For us, it is tapping into the very heart of God. On the other hand, intimacy is the state of belonging to or characterizing one's deepest nature. With intimacy comes an intense longing to spend time with whatever you have established that passion for. In this instance, intimacy marks you with what ever you are in closely associated. For us as Warriors on the Battlefield, this marking, or passion, has to be directed towards the Lord!

In **Psalm 42:1-7** a situation is being described where a battle fatigue Warrior has found himself. As stated earlier, it is a situation that most of us can relate to and can learn from what we are instructed to do to overcome it. There is a crying out in the spirit by the psalmist to the Lord. He has found that the day to day fight and the surprise attacks are overtaking him. Going further into the place that he is in, the psalmist says that he is among those that believe as he does. In fact, his perspective has not changed on the awesomeness of God, however he doesn't understand why he feels SO off balance and uncomfortable regarding what is happening in his life right now. And NO one around him can help him. Furthermore, he knows that he knows that he knows that God is an ever present help! Even more powerful in this passage is that because of his relationship with the Lord he knows he can freely tell Him what is on his mind and in his heart. This painfully revealing dialogue of testimony can only come from an established level of intimacy with the Lord! And the greatest revelation that the psalmist gives is that the Lord can directly affect his disposition even more so than a true love in the natural. That's a pretty power statement because all we have to do is think back on how we felt and acted when that "true" love entered the room, or when we heard their voice, or even when we just think about them. Just imagine how much more influential in our lives that power of love can be flowing directly from our Lord! Wow!

Also note Warrior, there is a weapon of warfare that we have not talked much about and that is Praise. The psalmist confirms for us that praising God even in the most difficult times actually confuses the enemy. So much so that the enemy retreats so they can figure out what to do next. Warrior, know that when they do, this is the time to draw nearer to God. Do this so that your faith in the assured victory can be reestablished and affirmed. The psalmist tells us at the same time to recall the mightiness of God in previous battle. Both strengthen you to press on. Do this so that you can continue on in power!

Just like the breastplate mentioned in the previous section, because you are marked and smeared with the very essence of the Lord, others should know that you are in close relationship with Him without you even mentioning it. You have to get so passionate about your relationship with the Lord that you become driven to fellowship with Him, to pursue after His presence just as it is the instinctive, natural behavior of an animal to go in search of water. The longer it takes them to find water, the thirstier they get, the more they press on until they find it. They don't stop searching because they know instinctively that they will die without it! We must be equally desperate, never giving up the pursuit of intimacy with our Savior and Father! Even at the most troubling times, you must go deep! You have to know who you are fighting, why you are fighting and that God has got your back. This is about moving and progressing into your future and you must have faith in God for the things to come. Faith allows you to stay intimate with the Lord no matter what the situation is.

God has invested the awesome gift of LIFE embedded with purpose, destiny, and a tremendous wealth of potential into you. Additionally, you have also invested too much into this to go back now. No matter where you are in your life, you are on your way somewhere once you put your hand in the hand of the Lord and yield your heart to the will of His Heart! If you don't complete what you have started, how can you say you did not like it? You will always wonder, what if?

So YES, you must finish and finish well. Many times we want to give up and quit. HEY, you really can't quit because besides you thinking about what you want, there is also another major reason. What is it? *It is the FACT that there are others that are waiting on you to do what God has commissioned you to do so that they can fulfill their interconnected destinies.* Who told you you had a choice anyway? You can not quit, you must live, and you will choose to live the life that the Father has purposed for you! *I decree it as so in Jesus' name that you will fulfill your purpose and you will finish well. In Jesus' name it is so!* So get about the Father's business and go forth Warrior!

Yes, to do this well, you have to be totally surrendered to Him, and completely trust in Him. It all has to do with your individual will forsaking all that you know, want and desire to get to the true answer versus the religious answer and above all to get to God's will! The Lord Jesus summons us to Him. He draws us with living waters that refresh, replenish and satisfy our thirsts and desires for Him. I talk about this in the first book, "*Breaking Through Towards Spiritual Maturity*". We must recognize the call, we must listen for the sound of His summons, His audible voice; and then we must respond. He is the "Deep" and He is calling out to those that desire to be and go deeper in Him. This flows out of intimacy, which is face to face contact with Him. *Child of God, the Lord wants to rain on you, so don't put up an umbrella, GET IN THE RAIN and let Him saturate your spirit!*

Standing on the Promises

Well, now Paris, I am committed to continuously seeking God's face so that that intimacy is not broken and so that I can stay replenished in the battle. But even when I do this, why so much struggle? Why so much turmoil in making a decision for God? Why is what I am doing appear to not be working out in my favor? Wow, you have a lot of good questions.

Let's address them by first acknowledging the fact that we have the promises of God! Second, let's look at **Hebrews 12:1-3** to see how we are to endure:

> *¹ Wherefore seeing we also are compassed about with so great a cloud of witnesses, let us lay aside every weight, and the sin which doth so easily beset us, and let us run with patience the race that is set before us, ²Looking unto Jesus the author and finisher of our faith; who for the joy that was set before him endured the cross, despising the shame, and is set down at the right hand of the throne of God. ³For consider him that endured such contradiction of sinners against himself, lest ye be wearied and faint in your minds.*

Here, we are forewarned and should not be surprised, but expect to experience and endure persecution once we begin to obediently walk in the truth of His agreement with us. Just as the elders have and others before them. We are empowered to do this with assured confidence because we know the promise of God's covenant to keep us. Therefore, we must be able to withstand the onslaught and harassment of both family and foes.

Also, we draw nearer to God in a more intimately personal relationship, at times faith will cause us to break away from long-held religious traditions; thereby bringing another realm of heightened persecution and unfilled expectations and promises by and from man. Knowing all this, we are told to persevere, remain confident and unmovable in our positioning with Him in the Kingdom with the expectation of fulfilling the covenant. This is how we are to live: by this covenant of faith. This stance and lifestyle commitment to faith pleases our Father.

As Christians, to overcome any negative thing, we must learn to seek out a righteous outcome. Remember, to effectively conquer **gaps**, we must begin to think of each one of them that we encounter as Goals Accessing Potential Solutions. Get rid of the "n" left in faint and end the word with "h" help! Work your FAITH and live by the help of the Word. Warrior, work your faith!

A pastor friend of mine and I were in a conversation. I was in some pretty tough times as I waited for the move of the Lord to lead me out of a particular wilderness season. We had talked about a revival and he asked what did I want God to do. At first, I said, "I need a revival". Then it struck me, even after the revival I would still be in the same position. So, I said to him, I just want the Lord to do what He promised He would do. Pastor Ron said to me, what did He promise? Simple enough question right? However for the life of me, I could not remember one of them, besides the very general life sustaining things.

So what was wrong with that? What was wrong with not knowing the specific things that God had ordained for me personally? Well, the Lord makes us promises that are tailor made to our individual situations and purposes. They are supposed to sustain in the hope that what's coming is far better than what we are currently facing and that there is a cause to continue on. The problem was that I had become so weary that I took my focus off the promises of God. We grow faint and weary in long Battles and lose sight of what the Promises are. We lose focus, and when this happens there is a danger of indifference that can set in. Again, as mentioned earlier, the "whatever" or "it is what it is" perspective enters in. Watch out for this trap! Know what God has promised you directly so that the cause for fighting is personal and stays clear to you. Remind yourself by keeping a journal of your conversations with the Lord and revelations of His Word. Read them from time to time, especially in the dry seasons. Keep in mind that *all* of His promises are yea and amen!

Having Patience means that we must learn to wait well. Get rid of the "no"s and negativity that growing faint in the Battle brings and get some help working your faith! Get rid of the naysayers and energy draggers that are around you. Get rid of the "n" left in faint and replace it with a "h"! So that you are looking at faith directly in its face! And then, work your faith and allow it to work you!

Listen Warrior, the key to tying these last three sections together on intimacy with the Lord is the development of the discipline needed to be still to hear what God is saying. How? By:

- Listening for His voice and responding to His call;
- Drawing nigh by seeking Him through out your day;
- Looking and expecting Him to show up;
- Searching for Him with your whole heart;
- By giving praise and testimony of His grace; and finally,
- Looking in the pages of His work, the Bible, to know and understand Him even the more.

So let us look at some more specific tools for doing this continuously!

Tools for Keeping Your Spirit Tuned for Hearing God

Finally for this chapter, let's close with seven tools for keeping your spirit tuned up for hearing God. They are: 'Become a Reflection of His Glory', 'Know That God's Love Will Sustain You', 'Always Be Prepared To Receive', 'Study & Meditation Time', 'Prayer Time', 'Keep A Journal', and 'Give Him Thanks'. So let's wrap this up!

Become a Reflection of His Glory

For continued, unrestricted access to hearing God, we must strive to become a reflection of Him. The more we seek to walk in His ways in obedience, the easier it will be to hear God clearly. Have you ever developed a friendship with someone that just immediately clicked! You could freely share anything with that person and they seemed to understand immediately where you were? That's because you have things in common with one another, a likeness. And this likeness makes it easier to talk and understand one another. The more we have in common with the Lord, the easier it is to talk to Him! **II Corinthians 3:18**, which states:

"But we all, with open face beholding as in a glass the glory of the Lord, are changed into the same image from glory to glory, even as by the Spirit of the Lord."

Also remember to reference **Psalm 27:8** as our key scripture for this book. Both passages tells us to continue to strive for this likeness in Christ!

Know that God's Love will constrain you!

We have to learn as people of God, that regardless of who has done what to us, made us angry or betrayed us, we are still to love them. How? This is because of the love that the Lord has empowered us with. **2 Corinthians 5:14** tell us:

> *"For the love of Christ constraineth us; because we thus judge, that if one died for all, then were all dead:"*

Our response and perspective of them must be governed by the love that Jesus has towards us. This love will keep us from saying and doing things that will need to be corrected at a later time. This love will control our temperaments. This love will arrest us and bring us subject to His will. This love will restrict us from crossing into territories and over boundaries that could do more damage than help. Let the love of God sustain you in all matters!

Always be prepared to Receive

Always be open to hear God's voice. Any place, any time! And watch out for people that may try and restrict or limit your ability to hear from Him. Someone once said God only talks in one word directions. Yes, He speaks that way if that's all you can handle! He is a gentleman. He won't go anywhere uninvited. And every morning I open my eyes, I have found that when I am ready I will say good morning Lord. And not until I do, will He respond back with Good Morning My Child. Or sometimes, I'll just say Lord and He'll answer Yes and that's all I need. He's always with us. Back it up, you say. **Deuteronomy 31:6** tells us He will never leave or forsake and that means He is with us always. So be ye ever ready!

"Be strong and of a good courage, fear not, nor be afraid of them: for the LORD thy God, he it is that doth go with thee; he will not fail thee, nor forsake thee."

For those of us that are more visual, I am going to describe Push/ Pull technique that has help me focus and access what the Lord is saying to me. It is very much like the automatic amen or uncontrollable praise that you feel well up in your very being from the belly up. It is exactly what it says, it is the pushing down and pulling up out of your spirit to hear what the Lord is saying in the spirit. It is like inhaling and exhaling to focus. It is a movement of your thoughts and feelings from your mind to your heart, from the physical to the spiritual. I describe it this way because you are pushing down from your head (or suppressing and silencing) all the hindrances and noise going on your mind and pulling up from your belly or commanding your spirit to arise in order to access the things of our Lord. This is the whole concept of prayer if you really think about it. You literally are making an conscious effort to get to God. To effectively do this, you must focus with your whole heart with the faithful expectation that He is hearing your petitions and will join the "conversation".

Study and Mediation Time

Study and mediate on the Word! And get to know the word for yourself. Take the time to think about anything that is spoken to your spirit. If its not supported in the word, God didn't say it! Let's look at this a little closer! With mediation, but very careful not to let your mind just sit idle! **1 Timothy 5:13** gives a good example of the dangers of being idle!

"And withal they learn to be idle, wandering about from house to house; and not only idle, but tattlers also and busybodies, speaking things which they ought not."

Look idle time leaves you to your own devices and imagination for what to do to fill the time. Where's that lead you? Into gossiping, putting things before our eyes that we shouldn't, listening to things we shouldn't, and fellowshipping with people we probably should not be. This is especially if they enjoy and are allowed to do, and join you in doing, the first three things mentioned! When I say mediation, I mean on the word of God. What are you thinking about or mediating on? **Philippians 4:8** is an excellent outline of what these things should be! Use it as your map when in doubt.

> *"⁸ Finally, brethren, whatsoever things are true, whatsoever things are honest, whatsoever things are just, whatsoever things are pure, whatsoever things are lovely, whatsoever things are of good report; if there be any virtue, and if there be any praise, think on these things."*

Daily Prayer Time

Are you prey for the enemy and his plan to destroy you because you did not pray? Spend Time with Him. How can you know His voice and you haven't spent time talking with Him. I used to say Lord, "Lord please turn up the volume, I can hardly hear you". But I learned that it wasn't that He needed to speak louder, I needed to be quieter. Allow Him to minister back to you. Time spent with Him helps keep you tuned to Him.

Also, you must make yourself available and accessible to the Lord. What do I mean by this? You have to connect with this thing. It has to be personal to you. It has to be important to you. Your relationship with God has to be a priority to you. Also, don't get wrapped up in the "traditional" sense of prayer. Prayer is simply having a conversation with God, at any time, any place.

Keep a journal!

This can be a spiral notebook. Write in it daily, whether it is Scriptures, words, conversations. Start with something small. As you grow stronger, walk with Him with the bigger steps. It will be gradual. Do not under estimate the power of the written word. A journal will also help you keep straight exactly what was said. Don't be surprise that after one minute, the exact words in your mind have already changed. Write it down immediately. Write the vision. As the word says in **Habakkuk 2:2-3:**

> *"²And the LORD answered me, and said, Write the vision, and make it plain upon tables, that he may run that readeth it. ³For the vision is yet for an appointed time, but at the end it shall speak, and not lie: though it tarry, wait for it; because it will surely come, it will not tarry."*

This makes the strategy plain. It gives you a clear path to follow and reference back to. As the Lord fills in the blanks, your purpose in each particular assignment will become clearer. .... until it is time for it to fully manifest and bring forth life. Amen.

Give Thanks!

Faith is the belief and trust in **and** loyalty to God all wrapped up into a beautiful package. Faith is a gift from the Father, just as your hearing, your salvation and speaking in tongues are gifts! **Ephesians 1:16-17** tells us that,

> *"¹⁶ Cease not to give thanks for you, making mention of you in my prayers; ¹⁷ That the God of our Lord Jesus Christ, the Father of glory, may give unto you the spirit of wisdom and revelation in the knowledge of him:"*

You need to know that all the gifts from God must be received by faith in your heart first. This acceptance is not a mind or mental action, it is a matter of the heart. With it being a matter of the heart, its acceptance comes about because of who you are. It solidifies and strengthens your relationship with the Giver. Remember that faith is what is needed to enhance and lift your way of hearing and comprehending from the natural and "head" way to the spiritual and "heart" way of understanding God. Faith does not have to be an external, emotional response. The intensity for what you have faith in is what's important, not the outward display; which again points all aspects of faith back to the heart.

Remember to thank God daily for the use of His gift! For His speaking into your life and that in itself is a blessing. **Ephesians 5:20** says:

"Give thanks always for all things unto God and the Father in the name of our Lord Jesus Christ".

We can do this by examining three levels of performance in the Kingdom of God fueled by our levels of faith. The first is your ability. This is the natural or acquired facility in a specific activity. Capability is the second and it is the physical, mental, financial, and/or legal power to perform a specific activity. The third is Mastery, and it is the right and power to command, decide, rule, or judge a particular activity. *Mastery* is the same as *Dominion*!

We have already been given dominion by our Father. In the **Book of Genesis**, God gave us dominion over all the earth. **Faith** is the main ingredient that stirs and empowers us to stand in our rightful positions of headship. Not so much over one another, that's His job. This dominion is the power to rule over everything else of God. This is the ultimate area of living for every Kingdom Warrior. And this applies to whatever area that God has charged you to possess.

In **Chapter 14** of this book, in connection with comprehending and flowing with the Cause and in our faith, we will develop a better understanding for where the battle can take place and how to protect ourselves. Additionally, we will learn first that we must speak out and speak up when it comes to all matters in our lives and second, the importance of maintaining a God filled, stress free living environment. That is quite an ambitious task, but a very necessary one, so let's go further and look at how we finish well!

Part Five:

"Finishing The Battle Well!"

CHAPTER 14

Recognizing Where the Battle is!

As stated in the previous chapter, in connection with comprehending the Cause, we will continue to develop a better understanding for where the battle can take place and how to protect ourselves in each of these areas. In this chapter, we will look at:

- Where the Battle is?
- Who and what is around you?
- Who is closest to you that can affect your decision making abilities?
- Who has "enough" influence to make you change your mind or course of action? and
- Who and what are you most vulnerable to?

Finally, we will learn that we must speak out and speak up when it comes to all matters in our lives in order to maintain a God filled, stress free living environment. That is quite an ambitious task, but a very necessary one.

Per the Holy Spirit my assignment is to: "Teach you how to war in the Spirit for His name sake." Now that the foundation has been laid, we can move on towards getting a better understanding of some more of the tactics used by the enemy's camp. Remember that now that you have been forewarned, you can properly prepare for the Battle. Never forget that the Lord will forewarn you, provided that you are listening! So let's continue on!

So where's the Battle?

As Christians, we are to expect troubles and pressure in our lives. However, the New Testament encourages us by pointing out that such experiences develop our faith and increase our levels of maturity as stated in **James 1:2-4**:

> *"My brethren, count it all joy when ye fall into divers temptations; Knowing this, that the trying of your faith worketh patience. But let patience have her perfect work, that ye may be perfect and entire, wanting nothing."*

Additionally, you need to keep in mind that what you are going through right now is nothing compared to the way things will be during the time of Tribulation. So let's get comfort doing "main land" security on the home front first!

To do this well, first and foremost, you need to know that it is critical that you allow the Lord to develop and sharpen your ability of knowing both your internal and external surroundings at ALL times. Recall that this is a major component of discernment. Also remember that this weaponry is crucial to any Warrior on the Battlefield, and it can **only** be developed and mastered by continuous use. Yes, as with any skill, you have to use it to understand how it can be perfected. For example, you don't see any professional athletes hit the field until they have properly prepared themselves with hours of practice needed to perfect their skills. Especially if they expect to win! And it should be no different for us as Warriors in the Kingdom.

So let's look closer at these skills for perfecting this gift of discernment. Most critical to this gift is the fact that you must be able to effectively access and answer these three questions pertaining to your personal state at any point in time: where you are *mentally*, *physically,* and *spiritually*. This should be done in each of these areas. The ability to do this quickly, accurately, and with ease will increase as your level of spiritual maturity increases. Do not hesitate to write down what the Lord reveals to you. When you, expect an answer. When you receive your answer, act accordingly!

Now that you have dealt with YOU, then it is time to attack your external surroundings. These areas will be referred to as "domains". Ask the Lord to help you to identify where to begin in order to address your external surroundings, or domains. This can be done by asking and discerning who and what is around you in all three of these areas. As a Warrior, this must become second nature to you.

In focusing in, there are also three critical domains you need to keep close watch on at all times. They are your **House**, your **Courtyard**, and your **World**. Let's look closer at all three briefly and then later we will get into more detail on each.

First, there is your **House**, which includes those people, places and things that are closest to your heart. It is an environment where you feel safe and secure. Next, there is your **Courtyard**, which includes those that are just outside of your House, yet are in your immediate circle of relationships. They are the people, places, and things you associate with on a regular basis. This is an environment where you feel comfort. The last domain is your **World**, which consists of everyone and everything else that you come in contact with. This includes those people, places and things of God *and* those that are definitely not of God. Be mindful that as you mature you will also easily recognize those things that are not of God in any one of these three areas and be able to deal with them accordingly. Your World represents all the conditions and circumstances that affect and influence the levels of growth and development in your life, purpose, and relationships. The most important thing to remember in all three domains is that you must discern what is going on with each one of these areas internally and externally *at any given time,* **and** *in any given place.*

To determine the "climate" of His surroundings, Jesus used this spiritual weaponry of discernment all the time. Paul had to do it too. So why wouldn't you? To do this effectively, you must work at sharpening this aspect of your spirit man. Also, you have to know that distractions can come from ANY where. To help you identify the state you are in, in order to get through the Battle field, here are a few questions that can assist you in this process.

- Have you taken the time to know who can sway you?
- What can make you change your mind?
- What can make you go against what God has told you to do?
- Who can distract you?
- Why are they able to do this?
- Who has given them this kind of authority and power over you?

You need to get accustom to asking yourself these investigative questions. When the answer seems to be hidden or hard to detect, then seek the Lord the more.

Now, let's look at a couple of domain situations that will prayerfully further help you grow in this area that the Lord had to face. While doing this, be sure to take a closer look at your House, then your Courtyard, and finally, your World surrounding you. At the same time, remember that the enemy can be in any one, or all of these three areas. None of them are 'immune" to the enemy's attacks, tricks or presence. So never let your spiritual guard of discernment down. This means even when you feel that since you are under attack in one area, the others must all be OK and therefore they don't require your attention. Do **NOT** let your guard down in any of your domains. The Battle can be raging in any one or ALL three domains. To help us better understand these three, let's continue on and gain insight into what Jesus faced in each of His domains.

Your House

Let's start by considering the House of Jesus by looking at **Matthew 26:36-38:**

> *"Then cometh Jesus with them unto a place called Gethsemane, and saith unto the disciples, Sit ye here, while I go and pray yonder. And he took with him Peter and the two sons of Zebedee, and began to be sorrowful and very heavy."*

As we see here, Peter, John and James were in Jesus' House, his inner circle of supporters. Yes, they were definitely in His House. Additionally, I am sure you can identify people in your House that represent the significance of these disciples to you. Remember, your House includes those people, places and things that are closest to your heart.

John was the disciple that laid his head on the chest of Jesus. How close he must have been to Jesus for Jesus to allow John to actually hear His heart beat! You can't get any closer. Jesus definitely must have felt safe and secure with them, to allow them to see His vulnerability and ask them to cover Him as He prayed. Yes, your House is where you let your guard down. It is where you can be you in order to deal with who you **really** are. It is a place where you feel safe and secure, and very few people and things are given access to this area of your life.

Let me reiterate here that *very few* should be given access to your House! Why do I stress this? Notice what happens here: they fell asleep when Jesus needed them on point the most! Regardless of how innocent the offense, all three of them, that were in His inner circle, fell asleep! "Asleep" means to be insensitive to what is going on physically. Those closest to you are not always going to understand what is happening to you, especially when God is doing a major work with and through you. So they too at times will be insensitive and completely unaware of the urgency of the matters in your House.

Additionally, you may even have those in your House that you know you can not trust fully, but must stay connected to. Peter is a good example of this in **John 13:37-38:**

> *"³⁷Peter said unto him, Lord, why cannot I follow thee now? I will lay down my life for thy sake. ³⁸ Jesus answered him, Wilt thou lay down thy life for my sake? Verily, verily, I say unto thee, The cock shall not crow, till thou hast denied me thrice."*

Peter walked, lived, ate, and fellowshipped with Jesus. In fact, as stated in **Matthew 14:29**, Peter is the disciple that walked on water to get to Jesus!

"And he said, Come. And when Peter was come down out of the ship, he walked on the water, to go to Jesus."

You would think that Peter should have known and reverenced Jesus fully as the Messiah. But yet, just as Jesus foretold Peter of his forth coming denial of Him, Peter stood steadfast in his own belief that he would never betray Jesus. As complex as I am sure Jesus was, they still should have known him better. Just as you will find that there are some in your House that will not be able to stand the entire time, or all the time with, and for, you.

This is why a forgiving heart is important in our relationships with one another. No one is perfect or totally infallible in personal relationships. People are still people, even you. So be sure to maintain open, honest and immediate communications with those in your House so that you can resolve each situation and issue as they arise with the members of your House. If your House is in order, no one can stand against you.

Your Courtyard

Now let's look closer at the immediate surroundings around your House. The outside world can't come against you as long as those close to you are there for you right? Hmmm, really? **Matthew 26:14-15** tell us:

"Then one of the twelve, called Judas Iscariot, went unto the chief priest, And said unto them, What will ye give me, and I will deliver him unto you? And they covenanted with him for thirty pieces of silver. And from that time he sought opportunity to betray him."

Yes, Judas may not have been in the House, but he certainly had access to Jesus' Courtyard. So at what price will someone in your Courtyard betray you? The pieces of silver Judas took for Jesus was equal to the cost of a broken, useless slave. A good slave back then was worth twice what Judas accepted for the betrayal of his "friend". Thirty pieces of silver, according to **Exodus 21:32**, was the price paid to the master whose slave had been gored by an ox. This insult would ultimately be charged to the Messiah himself by someone in His Courtyard. This act of treason is also considered a supreme insult to our Father!

Look, Warrior, it's going to happen to you. If it happened to Jesus, why would you be exempt? Someone in your Courtyard, someone very close to you will inevidentably betray you. The key area of growth not to miss here is that when it does happen, how will you handle it? Let's look at **Luke 17:**

> *"Then said he unto the disciples, It is impossible but that offenses will come: but woe unto him, through whom they come! "*

Two key things here to note are that first Jesus did feel bad about the way Judas treated Him. But He knew it was for God's purpose, a part of His overall plan, and a key in His destiny. King David even speaks to betrayal in **Psalm 41:9**:

> *"Yea, mine own familiar friend, in whom I trusted, which did eat of my bread, hath lifted up his heel against me."*

Here David was expressing the sad reality of being betrayed by a friend. This someone was actually in his Courtyard. Yes, there are Judases in your life whose whole purpose for this time is to push you towards fulfilling your purpose. Though the experience will be painful and extremely unexpected, it will work out for your good in the end, and during the process God will perfect you. Let's look at **John 17:12** for further confirmation:

> *"While I was with them in the world, I kept them in thy name: those that thou gavest me I have kept, and none of them is lost, but the son of perdition (destruction); that the scripture might be fulfilled."*

The Lord knew His divine purpose was to redeem us back to our Father. It was foretold in the scripture, especially in this passage.

Additionally, Jesus knew fully who Judas was and the purpose of his assignment. He knew that our Father's divine plan included this act of betrayal by Judas. God has given us this same capability to know. Again, it is Spiritual Discernment! As we learn the ways of our Father, we too can anticipate the Lord's strategies for us, the schemes of the enemy, and as a result flow in our full purposes.

Also, don't miss the key area of growth to be noted here as you pursue after your purpose. It shows up in your demonstration of what you do with the information once God has released it to you. Will you handle it your way or God's way? The choice is yours. But if you show yourself untrustworthy to God with what He has given you and you continually misuse the information, the Source will eventually cease to flow!

On the flip side, there were also consequences for Judas. They can be seen in **Matthew 26:24:**

> *"The Son of man goeth as it is written of him: but woe unto that man by whom the Son of man is betrayed! it had been good for that man if he had not been born."*

In most cases, those that betray you in your Courtyard, will know that you know what they are about to do. However, they will still be compelled to fulfill their assignments of betrayal. Be aware that most of the time those in your Courtyard are more concerned with themselves, their own thoughts and beliefs. They will swiftly give you over to the enemy to suit their needs, desires, and for whatever else they perceive to be true about you.

Even the "decision-making" enemy, the ones in authority, will be baffled at times as to why people turned on you! This was the case with Pilate when the Jews of that time turned on our Messiah. When Pilate asked for the accusation against Jesus, the people admitted that there was none deserving of death according to Roman law. At this point, Pilate realized that Jesus has been delivered to him on account of their jealousy. The people had no ideal how precious and costly Jesus and his blood really were then, and still is now! Just as others will not always realize how precious you are to God, or what He has in store for you to do! Nope, they really didn't realize the power of our Lord's Blood. Oh, if they had only really known Who was in the Courtyard! Wow! So, Warrior, be on the alert because some will look at you the very same way as they did Jesus as you progress higher in the Kingdom! Stay on guard in your Courtyard!

Your World

This last domain is broader than the other two. It consists of things seen and unseen, known and unknown. Your World involves everything that you come in contact with, or that comes in contact with you, on a day to day basis. This included people, places, media, and things. The many influences on the circumstances in your life are tremendous when you are dealing with your World. These outside influences are not as easily controlled as the entities in your Courtyard or even in your House. If you are not careful, these influences can put you in bondage quicker than the speed of light, and leave you guessing on what happen! They can throw fire bombs into your Courtyard that cause your House to be under siege. They will come against you and yours leaving points of impact that can be devastating and life changing!

Let's take a look at **Matthew 27:1-4b:**

"¹When the morning was come, all the chief priests and elders of the people took counsel against Jesus to put him to death: ²And when they had bound him, they led him away, and delivered him to Pontius Pilate the governor. ³Then Judas, which had betrayed him, when he saw that he was condemned, repented himself, and brought again the thirty pieces of silver to the chief priests and elders. ⁴Saying, I have sinned in that I have betrayed the innocent blood. And they said, What is that to us?"

First, notice that they did three things to Jesus: they constrained Him; they took Him to a place where they felt they were in control of the situation; and then they handed Him over their enemy, who was in this case, an indifferent person of authority. Indifference is a dangerous thing, especially when it is someone that is holding your life and future in their hands. Or so they thought!

Secondly, the key to remember here, and in any battle or attack that you face, is that revenge belongs to God. This is a very sensitive, yet critical area in warfare. Not following this directive of God can lead to many open doors in your natural and spiritual walk, starting with unforgiveness! Though we may want to "settle" the score, vengeance belongs to the Lord, as **Deuteronomy 32:35-36** says:

"To me belongeth vengeance, and recompense; their foot shall slide in due time: for the day of their calamity is at hand, and the things that shall come upon them make haste. For the LORD shall judge his people, and repent himself for his servants, when he seeth that their power is gone, and there is none shut up, or left."

Additionally, Apostle Paul confirms this in **Romans 12:19** by telling us:

"Dearly beloved, avenge not yourselves, but rather give place unto wrath: for it is written, VENGEANCE IS MINE; I WILL REPAY, saith the Lord."

Again, remember, this Battle is not about you. Though you are a target, you are not the intended Bull's Eye! It is about God's Kingdom and His glory. This includes how the battle is fought, how it is won, and everything in the middle required to be victorious. The "woe unto to him" is directed at those that allow themselves to be used by the enemy! The backlash of their actions belongs to God! Only He can rightfully judge what their repayment will be; only He can repay the misdeed in full; and He is the only One that can handle their reactions and responses on ALL levels!

Finally, notice that Matthew makes the distinction between the roles of the priests and Judas and, realizes that all are equally guilty for what took place. Therefore, each one will be held accountable, individually! The same will be the case with those that betray you. Yes, I know the closer they are to you, the deeper the "cut". I need to add this word of wisdom here too: stop letting people and situations cut you! Stop putting yourself in the line of fire, again and again and again. Some of the drama and things that you go through with people in your life can be avoided all together if you learn how to "duck"! In other words, just say "no"!

With that in mind always remember to be aware of who is around. You can not just stop talking to people. Yes, you do have to interact with them to fully accomplish your God given purpose in life. If you have people issues, allow God to deliver you from them so that you can get on with your life! These people have been placed around you for a reason. Know that you have the power and authority to know the "whos" and the "whys". Utilize it Soldier!

Remember that even though you may really want to go after the ones that betray you, misuse you, lie on you, and deceive you, you are *not* to go after them physically. As further support, I love the way my Pastor explained it to us in a Monday night Bible Class. The reason we are not to do it our way is because *only God* can fully and successfully give "repayment" and at the same time, handle the retaliation of the enemy from it! Although you may not see it, know how it happened, or even know what happened, you can believe that God will deal with your Judas and other enemies on your behalf. The interesting thing to me is that even the ones that are used by God to move us towards fulfilling our purposes will still be dealt with for their wrong doings by God, like Pharaoh and Judas.

Finally, Warrior, you better know there has been some form of retaliation by the enemy aimed directly at you as you strive to live upright before the Lord. Some attacks never even hit your awareness radar because God more than shielded you! Yes, He can handle it, you can not! So what can you do? Talk to the Father about it and hear what His desire is for you in each situation in the Battle in your domains. You can go after them in prayer, then release the matter fully over to Him to handle. Finally, be sure to hear what the Lord wants you to do pertaining to understanding and recognizing how to protect your domains. So, how do you fully protect the territories that God has given you charge over? Read on!

CHAPTER 15

Recovering ALL in the Battle!

And you shall recover all!

Fighting the good fight of faith as described by the Apostle Paul in the **Books of Timothy** is not an easy or minuscule matter. In fact, it is very strenuous, tiring and at times, laborious. But the foreknowledge that we are victorious is sufficient to push us as the Warriors of the Lord Jesus onward. Our Father promises us that we already have the victory in this Battle. We only need to embrace this truth, and possess and inhabit the land. Land being a general term meaning ALL our stuff in all of our domains! Remember God's promise to King David in **1 Samuel 30:8**:

> "And David enquired at the LORD, saying, Shall I pursue after this troop? shall I overtake them? And he answered him, Pursue: for thou shalt surely overtake them, and without fail recover all."

This applies to us too! So let's get clarity on what God is saying to us here. Per Webster, 'recover' means both to save from loss and restore back to a 'normal' position. What's 'normal'? 'Normal' is to conform to a type, standard or regular pattern. Being normal in the Kingdom of God means we are striving towards being transformed into His image. *Obedience is the key*. To conform means to bring into harmony or be in agreement with prevailing standards.

'Conform' also means to be of the same shape or be identical. Yes, this is a renewing of the mind and being transforming into His image. Basically, for the Warriors of the Lord, 'conform' simply means to be obedient to His Will!

What's all that mean? Well, let's put it all together. For us as His children, the type is His Image. For us as His Warriors, the standard is His Word. For us as His children, the regular pattern is our day to day walk in Him. The established standard is the Word of God, and the regular patterns are the ways of God. So, becoming "normal" requires that we constantly check to make sure that our Spiritual Equilibrium is in alignment and that we are walking in His ways as we are being transformed into His vessel as described back in **Chapter 1**. One last definition is the word 'ALL'. 'All' simply means ALL, everything is included! Once this position of being "normal" is gradually established, then it is very easy to follow the directives of God and achieve the victorious results that King David experienced.

Now that we are talking the same language, let's see what else is going on. There is a very distinct pattern here that we too can follow when we need to get directions and strategy for the Battle. First, King David asked, and he was specific about what he wanted to do and the outcome he expected. And God answered him the same way, specific with the expected end. But note to that King David had to act on the promise and directive of our Father once he received his answer. So let's bring this to your immediate domain address!

Protecting Your Domain

In referencing the keys from the previous chapter, note that there were three apparent areas of exposure used by people and situations close to Jesus. All really should have been a part of Jesus' support system. Instead they were a part of the system set up to destroy Him. So they thought. The same will hold true with you as you walk and live this Battle! In staying victorious in all three of your domains, there are two critical strategies that you must incorporate in your weaponry today! First, you have to speak up and out about what's going on around you! Secondly you have to keep your environment clean! Doing these two things on a continuous basis will allow you to take, and maintain control over your domains and thereby, be victorious in each and every situations! Let's look closer at each one of these strategies.

So how come you are not saying anything?

Many times I have had the saints of God ask me what to do or come to me upset about a particular situation saying they don't know what's going on, or that they are facing a major situation. I'll ask "What did God say?" or "Did you ask God?". More often than not, the response is either complete silence with a quick look away, or a response that says, "I don't know what God is saying about it because I didn't ask Him yet?" What on earth are you waiting for? Who would know *better*? I have come to the conclusion that some of us like to be upset about the situation. Yes, we like the drama of being uncomfortable and uncertain about the next move. Right? We must, if we haven't asked our Creator, and the Controller of our destinies, what's really going on. Listen up Soldier, calm down, humble yourself, open your mouth and ASK HIM!

One of the things we, as Christians, do not do is ASK our Father what's going on BEFORE we react! Do we think He's too busy *or* is the real problem that we are too busy? Why not check in with the Source? A question that takes less than a minute to ask and could help you to avoid hours, days and sometimes even years of issues caused by going the wrong way or off course. You got to *ASK*! It is as simple as, "Lord I need clarity. I need to know what's really going on here, should I go, should I stay? Lord, what is your will for this matter and how may I serve and glorify you in it? "

This doesn't only apply to Battle strategies, this also applies to your daily walk and your destiny. You have not because you asked not! In the most critical situations, your very inheritance in the Kingdom can hinge on a simple answer from the Lord. An answer that is only attainable once you open your mouth. Look at **Psalm 2:8**:

> *"I will declare the decree: the LORD hath said unto me, Thou art my Son; this day have I begotten thee. Ask of me, and I shall*

give thee the heathen for thine inheritance, and the uttermost parts of the earth for thy possession."

Furthermore, the **Book of John** tells us six times to ask in His name and He shall give it. "He shall give it" means He will answer your request! Take a look:

John 14:13: *"And whatsoever ye shall ask in my name, that will I do, that the Father may be glorified in the Son."*

John 14:14: *"If ye shall ask any thing in my name, I will do it."*

John 15:16: *"Ye have not chosen me, but I have chosen you, and ordained you, that ye should go and bring forth fruit, and that your fruit should remain: that whatsoever ye shall ask of the Father in my name, he may give it you."*

John 16:23: *"And in that day ye shall ask me nothing. Verily, verily, I say unto you, Whatsoever ye shall ask the Father in my name, he will give it you."*

John 16:24: *"Hitherto have ye asked nothing in my name: ask, and ye shall receive, that your joy may be full."*

Warrior, get these passages deep in your spirit. They are important keys to the overall Kingdom strategy for everything that we may do. How important this strategy must be for us to grasp! Especially since the Word brings it to us through the disciple Jesus specifically said He loved. Chosen vessel, I am here to confirm to you that as an heir and Warrior of the Kingdom you *are* in the number of those that He loves! So why would He leave you in the dark pertaining to the concerns and situations in your life that will ultimately glorify Him? He didn't just think of the importance of seeking Him first for your answers off the cuff. Nor is it a trivial instruction of the necessity for *you* to make your requests known with a specific purpose in mind. Both of these are divine directives with power and authority available to His people. Therefore, you need to develop the discipline of accessing your Battle strategy directly, and immediately from Him. So, let's see the power of this directive in action by looking at the second strategy.

How do you keep your House/Domain Clean?

Warrior, you have been positioned to possess the land and claim your territory! To possess the land means you have the legal right of use, a divine level of authority, and full realization of the benefits of the dominion. It also means you are responsible for the maintenance and upkeep of your domain. To claim your territory means that you must take control of each one of the domains assigned to you. Remember that your domain consist of the various areas that you have authority in and influence over. Once you learn to walk in the authority that God has placed in you, Warrior, you will not hesitate to demand those things that God says are rightfully yours right out of the hands of the enemy! Be it by influence or by seizure. This is exactly what "possessing the land and claiming your territory" is all about. Standing firmly in who God says you are in the Kingdom!

To do both of these effectively, you must keep your House clean. Why? This must be done because this is your innermost sanctuary. How? Pray, pray, pray! There should not be a room in your house that has not been prayed in freely! What do I mean by 'prayed in freely'? I mean that you are not challenged in the room by unknown forces, you are not afraid of going into the room because it feels "weird", nor do you dread the thought of praying in the room because you sense something is not right! Take control of every room in your domain! Possess it and claim it in the name of Jesus, and know that the blood of Jesus covers you! Sometimes the enemy needs to be reminded of that FACT! So remember to open your mouth and say it is so.

The Prayer Sweep

So now let's look at the strategic aspect of standing in authority in your domain. How do you pray for cleansing in your house? This is **an important strategy**, so pay close attention, Warrior! I know by now I should not need to say this - but I will any how. Please, please, please Child of the Most High God, do not play with this! This is a very serious matter **and** you better be prayed up, especially the first time you cleanse your house! Why? Because no telling what you might run into in the spirit, and even in the natural! In the natural, look for the interruptions and distractions to come, like the phone ringing, the kids fighting and crying - you get the picture. OK, I feel better now that I forewarned you. Last thing, always remember first and foremost to pray and seek the Lord before you start. Now let's get busy cleaning your House!

One of the keys to this process is to go room by room. Ask for God's covering and protection in each and every room. Ask that by His Spirit every window, every entrance way, every floor, every door, every ceiling, every crack, every corner be cover with His blood in each room that you enter. Why every place in the room and not just the doorway as some of us have been taught previously? We must remember that we are dealing with spirits. Rather you acknowledge their existence or not, they are around you. Since they are spiritual beings, physical barriers do not hinder their entrance. But the spiritual covering of our Father does!

Ask the Lord to reveal to you anything and everything that is in your house that is not of Him. Ask Him to reveal and expose every open doorway that must be shut! Now a "doorway" in the context of spiritual warfare refers to any access point that you have open to the supernatural. Access points can be good or bad. They can include things like your involvement with drug use, profanity, unforgiveness, lying, stealing, fear or even doubt. Access points can also consist of acts that you have participated in like varying forms of divination such as palm reading and astrology, games like the Ouija board and tarot cards, and sexual acts. They can be very simple, innocent actions or very complicated, blatantly horrendous ones.

The Lord's blood cleanses and protects you from them all. If you want to be free of them in you and your surroundings, repent and return to Him. They can also be actual things that you have brought into your home, knowingly and unknowingly, that carry spiritual significance, like statues, dolls, movies, some furnishings and clothing, etc. All gifts are not as innocent as they appear. They can be entrance ways to spiritual things not of God.

As you pray, no matter how strange it sounds, you bind "it" by name (yes verbally say it) in the name of Jesus, then cast it into the lake of fire in Jesus name (yes, say it out loud!). Again, yes, you speak it out, as simple and direct as this: *"In the name of Jesus, I bind the spirit of "it" by name and cast "it" by name in to the lake of fire in the name of Jesus."* Critical to note here is the importance and authority of the name of Jesus! Remember Warrior, It's not you, it's Jesus. Don't get it confused! It doesn't necessarily have to be at a loud, intense level, but speak it out as you are lead by the Holy Spirit. As you listen for the voice of Lord, speak out what you hear in the spirit vocally.

Also, remember, you don't rebuke anything. Don't forget the example of the angel Michael in **Jude 9.** The proper way to remove spirits that have taken up residence in your home and life, is to say, *"the Lord Jesus rebuke you, leave now"*. This is a spiritual matter, so NEVER deal with it in the flesh, especially within your own might!

Let's look at some practical examples. For example, if it is revealed to your spirit that the spirit of lying is in your house, you bind this spirit in Jesus name, cast it out and loose the Spirit of Truth. As stated in **John 16:13** we have the power and authority to know what is going on on the Battle field. All you have to do is ask. Take a look:

> *"Howbeit when he, the Spirit of truth, is come, he will guide you into all truth: for he shall not speak of himself; but what-soever he shall hear, that shall he speak: and he will shew you things to come."*

We were never meant to be caught off guard or unaware, especially with the indwelling of the Holy Spirit. The Lord will speak directly to your heart in the midst of warfare to let you know exactly what weaponry to use and speak!

Another example: if the spirits of jealous and envy are revealed to be in your home, you bind them both by speaking out loud, "I bind the spirits of jealousy and envy in the name of Jesus and cast you out of this place in Jesus name and I loose the Spirit of Love." If you know a specific scripture to say by all means say it! God's Word gives us power. Jesus' name gives us the Authority! Remember that spirits can not read your mind, therefore you must speak it out. Once you bind "it" by name, and cast it out, PLEASE do not forget to get your instructions from the Lord on what to <u>loose</u> in the atmosphere, so that something else unwanted does not come in to fill the "vacancy". We will cover the "why" in more detail in the next section. For now, know that there can be no place in your life that He is not the Ruler.

After the first time your clean "sweep" your house, sanctify it unto the Lord. A scripture to carry from room to room during prayer and to speak among your family members is **Joshua 24:15**:

> *"And if it seem evil unto you to serve the LORD, choose you this day whom ye will serve; whether the gods which your fathers served that were on the other side of the flood, or the gods of the Amorites, in whose land ye dwell: but as for me and my house, we will serve the LORD."*

One more time, when doing a prayer sweeping, start from the top, upper most room and work you way down, room by room. As you go from room to room, you may realize that some rooms are easier to pray in than others. Ask the Lord to reveal to you why and what it is. When you have prayed in the last room, you may feel lead to open your main door of entrance. If so, do so and say, "Go out, in Jesus name, get out, you are not welcome here and you can not stay." After that is done, be sure to ask the Lord to post warring angels around the perimeter of the property, east, south, west, and north. Strange behavior, I know, but necessary action. Remember, this is a spiritual battle.

I can't say this enough, but this is a Battle, and you MUST be prayed up when you do this. And always remember God has not given us a spirit of fear. So if that is what you sense, then call on the Lord immediately so that you can regain the control and sense of confidence that you need to persevere. Pray in the rooms of your house, apartment, and even your work space. Now don't get all wild and crazy with it at work, but take authority over the territory you are in so that you are able to do the job to the best of your abilities. This must be done on a regular basis. Why? Let's look at the obvious, people and things are constantly in and out of your House.

The first time will be the hardest, and yes, you will be tired afterwards. But don't skip a single place or space because once you start you will be removing these spirits from their hiding places and they will be looking for other places to go. Don't stop, until you have covered every space in the house. If you do, all you have managed to do is move these spirits to another location in your home. That's not what you want to do. You want to completely evict them from your residence! If it is not your home, then cover every place that you rest in.

Do not hesitate to speak PEACE every time you enter your front door and any room in your home. Why? This should be done because your home must become your place of refuge, your place of restoration, and the place where you are able to rest. Reclaim and then proclaim that your home belongs to God just as Joshua did in **Joshua 24:15:**

"And if it seem evil unto you to serve the LORD, choose you this day whom ye will serve; whether the gods which your fathers served that were on the other side of the flood, or the gods of the Amorites, in whose land ye dwell: but as for me and my house, we will serve the LORD."

You will more than likely sleep like you have not in some time and as you get more mature in this area, you will be able to easily tell when it is time to do it again. Some tell-tell signs are all of a sudden everyone is arguing in the house, or you are angry all the time for no obvious reason, or you are sad all the time, or worried constantly. If this is occurring, you know it is time for a Prayer Sweep! Once you have done this completely, then allow the Lord to help you resolve the matters that are at the root of the issues causing unrest in your home. Remember Warrior, you have the authority to declare peace in the atmosphere, especially in your home!

Does it really take all that?

Yes, you better believe and know that it really does take all that, and then some! There are consequences to not being vigilant

in keeping your domains clean and free of things that should not
be there as you strive to live victoriously. Why? There are three
powerful passages that answer the "WHY". We will cover this in the
next section in more detail. For now know that there can be no place
in your life that He is not the ruler over, especially if you are going
to be victorious on all battle fronts.

Let's begin by looking in the domain of your House by checking
out **Mark 3:25-30**:

> *"²⁵And if a house be divided against itself, that house cannot
> stand. ²⁶And if Satan rise up against himself, and be divided,
> he cannot stand, but hath an end. ²⁷No man can enter into
> a strong man's house, and spoil his goods, except he will
> first bind the strong man; and then he will spoil his house.
> ²⁸Verily I say unto you, All sins shall be forgiven unto the sons
> of men, and blasphemies wherewith soever they shall blas-
> pheme: ²⁹But he that shall blaspheme against the Holy Ghost
> hath never forgiveness, but is in danger of eternal damna-
> tion: ³⁰Because they said, He hath an unclean spirit."*

This is personal. It goes right to the heart of the matter.
'Strongman' is one who leads or controls by force of will and character or by military methods. 'Blaspheme' means to speak of or
address with irreverence or disrespect. 'Blasphemy' is the act of
insulting or showing contempt or lack of reverence for God. It is the
act of claiming the attributes of a deity, which consists of the rank
or essential nature of God, who is a heavenly, supreme being. Wow,
this is a dangerous disposition to take. You deny His existence and
you don't stand a chance not now and definitely not later! Which
brings us right back to the very basics of Who is really the Master
of your life? Pay attention Warrior, because once you know who the
Holy Spirit is, you are accountable for what you know! No reneging
on your side of the deal!

Now, let's look at another passage where this precaution is given,
Luke 11:21-26:

"²¹When a strong man armed keepeth his palace, his goods are in peace: ²² But when a stronger than he shall come upon him, and overcome him, he taketh from him all his armour wherein he trusted, and divideth his spoils. ²³ He that is not with me is against me: and he that gathereth not with me scattereth. ²⁴ When the unclean spirit is gone out of a man, he walketh through dry places, seeking rest; and finding none, he saith, I will return unto my house whence I came out. ²⁵ And when he cometh, he findeth it swept and garnished. ²⁶ Then goeth he, and taketh to him seven other spirits more wicked than himself; and they enter in, and dwell there: and the last state of that man is worse than the first."

This passage takes the fight out of your House and into your Courtyard! It is necessary, not only to be rid of these evil spirits in your House, but to also be indwell (filled with His Spirit) by good (think on these things). The alternative is disastrous! Jesus warns us in this passage that we can not be indifferent or neutral between Him and Satan. It just won't do. You must make a choice! Pay attention to the tricks and wiles and things he's been able to use against you. Another interesting position in this passage is that our Lord does not represent Satan to the disciples as a weakling or figure of minor consequence. Remember I said earlier, do not ever underestimate Satan - you are not nearly as smart as he is and he's been in his job a lot longer than you have been in yours!

Finally, the World around you is surrounded with all kinds of places, people and things that are not of God. You are charged with knowing what they are and consequences of even entertaining them. So, let's look at **Matthew 12:43-45:**

"⁴³When the unclean spirit is gone out of a man, he walketh through dry places, seeking rest, and findeth none. ⁴⁴Then he saith, I will return into my house from whence I came out; and when he is come, he findeth it empty, swept, and garnished. ⁴⁵Then goeth he, and taketh with himself seven other spirits more wicked than himself, and they enter in and

dwell there: and the last state of that man is worse than the first. Even so shall it be also unto this wicked generation."

Here we are instructed from a broader perspective of dealing with the demonic forces that we will face. The Lord is looking at the nation as a whole, yes the World around you. Yes, you can keep it swept clean, but you must continuously be alert and consistently fill it with the things of God. Only by inviting Christ to be the ruler of your World, will you know the full blessings of the Lord. Not doing this will bring them back seven times worse than it was before. They get thirsty too and need a place to "rest". What once did not catch your attention will not be of slight, but increasing interest. Hmmm, how can I say that? I can say that because we are progressing rapidly in knowledge, technology, accessibility, and abundance in both the good and bad. It's right there in the passage. Each generation progresses beyond their predecessors.

Note in all three situations that you can believe that the enemy will be back and Warrior, you better be prepared! The enemy's strategy will always be the same in that he will return with stronger reinforcements. These reinforcements will include bigger, badder, bolder demons and spirits to help the ousted one regain its territory. Their desires for its original dwellings are so intense that this foul spirit will even risk giving up its original position of power as the strongman to another demonic spirit. It doesn't care, just as long as he has a place to rest too.

Also, two more words of wisdom here. First, don't get adventurous and go out trying this in places you do not have the authority to do so, like someone else's house. Power and authority are not the same! Yes, God has given us the power to tread on serpents and cast out demons. However, we must also have the authority to evict these unwanted spirits, which is the legal right to operate within a particular jurisdiction or territory, in order to utilize that power. Therefore, unless you have been given the authority to do this, you will definitely pay some consequences for going on the battlefield without the proper coverage. It's like going into a place with no windows or lights that you have never been in, and having everyone look at you like, "what are you doing here?" Worse yet, you don't even know you are lost yet!

Trust me, I did that once earlier on, and I was so sick in a matter of hours that I could not breathe, I was freezing and what ever was in that house wanted me out! Several other things, including an usually gentle dog becoming extremely aggressive, took place until finally my husband made the decision to move us from the home where we visiting to a hotel for the rest of the time we were in that city. Yes, I learned it through hands on experience and I couldn't dial our head Intercessor or my Pastor's phone number quick enough!

Further confirmation that it was very real and not a coincidence was that I was fine and without symptoms the next morning! I had to call my Bishop to find out why I could not pray and decree God's will anywhere I wanted to without consequence. Oh, what a lesson to learn about authority. Yes, there are places that the enemy has authority over and in and therefore, we must become skillful prayer warriors and follow the instructions of His Spirit when we enter onto the Battle field. Don't learn this lesson the way I did, the attack was so swift, that I literally could not get my balance to discern what was going on! Believe me; it will not happen again to me like that! Now I know, and ask the Lord when I am in "strange" places to lead me in prayer.

The second word of wisdom to remember is that if other Christians are acting out around you or you yourself are not feeling like "you": realize that not everything is caused by demons. However, the point to note is that when it is an evil influence that is operating, we as God's people must recognize it as such and deal with it according to His Word. I do not believe that Christians can be demon possessed. However, they can be attacked in their minds, wills, emotions and body. They can be troubled, pressed, harassed, depressed, obsessed, oppressed, in bondage, and bruised in their physical beings, House, Courtyard, and/or World. This can occur in any one at a time, or even several at a time, or all at once.

However, be encouraged because there is nothing going on in your life that God is not aware of! No matter what it is! And He is the Way Maker! So open your mouth and say something **TO HIM about it! Silence is one of the enemy's strongest weapons against** us. Speak up, speak out, and be consistently vigilant! It's time you truly recognize that there is a Cause; this is a Battle, you ARE in it, you ARE already victorious and you WILL RECOVER ALL!

CHAPTER 16

Hearing God in Battle - The Summary

Hearing God involves seeking His presence to get directions regarding all aspects of your Christian walk. The key to walking victoriously in this life, of course after you have accepted our Lord Jesus Christ as your Savior, is the revelation that everything you will ever face is already won. You just need to learn, master and apply the links of focus, obedience and Kingdom level faith to your life!

In this manual we have covered many of the major tools and strategies available to you through the Holy Spirit because of your relationship with King Jesus. We determined that this Christian life-style involves a Battle and you are in it. We then investigated some critical tools for discovering how to move through the War in order to progress the Kingdom. Following that, we began to examine how to align ourselves with the unique and personal call of God. In doing this, we were able to ascertain that many times it will seem like the enemy is relentless in their pursuit of us. Therefore, we learned ways to stay fit for the battle. Finally, we took a look at strategies for completing our Kingdom assignments successfully, to the glory of our Father!

One of the most awesome revelations revealed regarding the love of our Savior is that there are many ways that He speaks to instruct and lead us. These ways include during our studying time, by inspiration or impressions on our heart and in our spirit, via divinely given dreams and visions, and of course, through our life experiences. Even more amazing is that during any one of these ways, He can, and will, interrupt us by *speaking* directly to us. And **yes**, there will be times as you grow to recognize His voice, that it will be audible!

However, be sure to maintain balance Warrior! Never forget that a critical part of your spiritual hearing is your Spiritual Equilibrium. The Word of God, which brings a state of intellectual and emotional balance, and the Spirit of God, who helps you maintain harmony between your day to day life and your spiritual walk are always available to you. Use them! Remember to listen to and for God with your whole heart, and allow the peace of God to rule your heart and mind when making decisions. Above all else Warrior, always be thankful for what He is doing and saying.

To further prepare and equip you, we also covered some strategies for identifying and eliminating those things that are not of God and that can interfere with and cause confusion in your hearing. Use them also! The only way you will perfect your hearing gift and these skills is with practice. If you find that you have made a mistake, repent for missing the mark, get back up and try again. Life is going to throw you some curves; but you have been given the gifts of salvation, grace and forgiveness. So remember that through true repentance any and every situation can be rectified. Every situation!

In this Battle, stay aware of the fact that because this is spiritual warfare, you should always fight in the Spirit realm **before** you physically show up for combat. Since this is a spiritual battle that manifests in the supernatural realm first, do not attempt to fight it with your natural abilities without your spiritual armor and instructions first. The Word says that the Holy Spirit will reveal these things to you. So do not go through the battle spiritually blind folded. Receive your victory in the spirit, **first**.

Then, remember not to doubt what you hear, BUT focus and discern who's speaking! Warrior, there are a few more confirming concepts that you need to know. First, as you begin to operate in this Kingdom knowledge, your spiritual changes and growth are going to be phenomenal! Next, know that this is only the beginning to you hearing God clearer and moving in the spirit with more power and authority. Then, know that you are now able to speak His will more accurately in your life, the life of others, and into the earth to make an impact for His Glory. Finally, yes, know that you have been empowered with the knowledge to walk even closer with our Savior. Why is God doing this? Our Father is doing this because He desires to pull you beyond where you are, and closer to Him. He desires that you too have that Eli and Samuel experience described in **1 Samuel 3**.

Listen, Warrior no man knows the time. However, we are called to be alert and fully cognitive of the seasons and their transition. We must be armed and ready to go as the Lord commands. As **Ecclesiastes 3** states there is a time and season for everything. Warrior, you need to know that this is your season, right now, as you are finishing this book, and this is the right time. Be it a time of preparation, a time of growth, or a time of restoration *this is your season!* And the only way you will be certain of the hour is to tap into and listen to the Source. For as it is stated in **Mark 13:32 - 36:**

> *"But of that day and that hour knoweth no man, no, not the angels which are in heaven, neither the Son, but the Father. Take ye heed, watch and pray: for ye know not when the time is. For the Son of man is as a man taking a far journey, who left his house, and gave authority to his servants, and to every man his work, and commanded the porter to watch. Watch ye therefore: for ye know not when the master of the house cometh, at even, or at midnight, or at the cock crowing, or in the morning: Lest coming suddenly he find you sleeping."*

So stop wasting time and don't miss your seasons to accomplish what God has placed in your hands. Position yourself for what God has for you. Walk in the newness you have received. Lastly remember, staying connected to Him requires continuous, ongoing intimacy! My prayer for you is **Psalm 121:8,** which says:

> *"The LORD shall preserve thy going out and thy coming in from this time forth, and even, for ever more."*

Warrior of the Most High God, I pray you were blessed by this book and that the Spirit of God seal the works that He has begun in you. Be blessed in the Lord and may the peace of God reign in your life. Amen.

Remember:

"The Battle is not over until it's over, and God has the final say!"

Printed in the United States
115233LV00005B/28-99/A